SOME EXTENSIONAL TERM MODELS FOR COMBINATORY LOGICS AND λ-CALCULI

PhD thesis

Defended June 16, 1971

A 2020 republication with

motivation
the making of
2020 hindsight

HENK BARENDREGT

Series on Term Rewriting and Logic*: Volume 1*
First Published: December, 2020 $v1.0$
Second imprint: January, 2021 $v1.1$
Third imprint: March, 2021 $v1.2$
Forth imprint: April, 2021 $v2.0$

Preface

This book is a republication of my PhD dissertation from 1971, at Utrecht University under supervision of Dirk van Dalen and Georg Kreisel with several natural additions. Included are the following Parts.

Part I. **The thesis itself.** The thesis is about the (type-free) λ-calculus and the related theory combinatory logic, often including the principle of extensionality. These theories started in the 20's and 30's, with work of Schönfinkel and Curry on combinatory logic and of Church, Rosser and Kleene on λ-calculus, and gave the theory of computable functions a strong boost. The foundation of computability was strengthened by Turing's alternative description via what are now called Turing Machines and his demonstration that the computational models of λ-calculus and Turing Machines select the same class of computable functions. In this way the Church-Turing Thesis did arise, claiming that the 'correct' definition of intuitive and at the same time mechanical computability was found by either λ-calculus or Turing Machines.

Nevertheless λ-calculus and combinatory logic were generally not yet recognized in the mathematical or computer science communities as being fruitful, because of the lack of a clear meaning of self-application. Kleene expressed some disappointment on the reception of his results in λ-calculus and translated several of them into the theory of computable functions. In the early 70's it was still the case that λ-calculus was frowned upon. This in spite of the then recent work of Dana Scott, late 1969, who constructed mathematical models of this theory, giving a clear interpretation of the binding effect of the operator 'λx', similar to how a quantifier is interpreted in predicate logic.

Work on the thesis started with a motivation to study the type-free theories, notably in the extensional case. In Chapter 1 a self-contained introduction is given containing as main results the following: (i) the representation of the computable functions using λ-terms; (ii) the full equivalence between λ-calculus and combinatory logic in the extensional case; (iii) the consistency of the theories involved via the syntactical proof of the Church-Rosser theorem. Chapter 2 contains as main results (i) the strengthening of the extensionality principle by the *ω-rule*; (ii) it is shown that the theory remains consistent after adding this rule; (iii) the partial validity of the ω-rule in the extensional case. In Chapter 3 the notion of *solvable* term is introduced. It is shown that (i) undefinedness of partial computable functions can be represented by unsolvability; (ii) if $\mathsf{F}\mathsf{Z} = \mathsf{I}$ for an unsolvable term Z, then $\mathsf{F}\mathsf{X} = \mathsf{I}$ for all terms X (the *Genericity Lemma*); (iii) it is consistent to equate all unsolvable terms, resulting in λ-theory $\mathcal{H}$. A first Appendix lists all auxiliary versions of the λ-calculus and combinatory logic used to prove the above results. A second Appendix presents a simplified proof of the Church-Rosser theorem for the λ-calculus, due to Martin-Löf, based on an argument by Tait for the same result in combinatory logic.

The thesis includes translations of compulsory parts in Dutch: a summary, my 1971 CV, and a set of Propositions to be explained now. A PhD thesis in the Netherlands back in the 1970s was supposed to contain a list of 'Stellingen', i.e. theses, not on the subject matter of the dissertation. The rumor goes that professors not having read the thesis still could ask questions during the defense, but this out-dated obligation disappeared in later years. There were eight propositions in Dutch. These have been translated into English, included in this republication, and some are commented on: Proposition VIII, about windmills turning their wings counterclockwise and Proposition VII, about the power of posthypnotic suggestions.

Part II: **Motivation & Failure**. My plan was to make a model of combinatory logic (with extensionality to cover also the λ-calculus) using computability theory. The plan did not work. The model turned out to be trivial, as terms without a normal form were equated in the model, Barendregt (1971a), improved in Barendregt (1975) and included here. Several attempts to save the model failed, but gave rise to the main topics in the thesis: (un)solvable terms and a strengthening of extensionality, the ω-rule.

Part III: **2020 Hindsight**. This Part starts with a description of several results in the theory known early 1969 and can be read as an introduction to the subject. Then the main notions and their properties of the thesis, developed during 1969-1971 are described. After that a sketch is given how some of the notions naturally resulted in useful ideas for the book Barendregt (1981). After that it is sketched how the theory did develop in later years, with a bias towards topics I do like at the moment.

Part IV: **The making of a PhD**. Here the story of the making of my PhD with the interaction between the teacher (my principal supervisor Kreisel) and the student (myself) is told. It is a reprint of Barendregt (1996) written for the 70-th birthday of Georg Kreisel. It describes the *couleur locale* of circumstances during my working on this PhD thesis and beyond.

Acknowledgments

To Gilles Dowek, Herman Geuvers, Jan Kuper, Assia Mahboubi, Giulio Manzonetto, Göran Sundholm, Sebastiaan Terwijn, Jozef Urban, and Freek Wiedijk I am grateful for various forms of assistance preparing the text. To Jan Willem Klop and Jörg Endrullis, respectively scientific son and grandson, I am indebted for the idea of republishing the dissertation with KDP and I thank them for the non-trivial support to realize this!

Henk Barendregt

December 11, 2020
Faculty of Science, Radboud University
Nijmegen, The Netherlands

Part I

The thesis itself

SOME EXTENSIONAL TERM MODELS FOR COMBINATORY LOGICS AND λ - CALCULI

PROEFSCHRIFT

ter verkrijging van de graad van doctor in de Wiskunde en Natuurwetenschappen aan de Rijksuniversiteit te Utrecht, op gezag van de Rector Magnificus Prof. Dr. F.van der Blij, volgens besluit van de Senaat in het openbaar te verdedigen op woensdag 16 juni 1971 des namiddags te 4.15 uur

door

HENDRIK PIETER BARENDREGT
geboren op 18 december 1947 te Amsterdam

promotor: PROF. DR. G. KREISEL
(Stanford University, California)

dit proefschrift kwam tot stand mede
onder leiding van de lector
DR. D. VAN DALEN

*) Met verbeteringen 2006 aangegeven met potlood. (With corrections 2006 in pencil.)

FOR YOU

Acknowledgements.

I feel indebted to professor Kreisel and Dr. van Dalen for their stimulation and criticism while preparing this thesis.

I thank Beulah MacNab for correcting the English text, Mrs. Breughel for careful typing and Mr. van Zoest for drawing the figures.

Contents

Introduction

This thesis consists of two parts which are, physically, separated into the present 'proefschrift' and a supplementary part II published in Barendregt [1971].

The subjects studied are formal properties of extensions of combinatory logic and of the λ-calculus, and (formal) relations between them. But neither the choice of problems nor even of the techniques introduced in the proofs can be properly understood without a description of the notions which we intend to study. Such a description will be given in this introduction. The summaries of the text which follow the introduction not only quote the main formal results but interpret them in terms of the aims described in the introduction. Strictly speaking, we do not only summarize results actually stated in the text, but include background material and, sometimes, alternative proofs.

Rules: the intended interpretations. Whatever other interesting models the formal theories considered here may have, in particular the projective limits recently introduced by Scott [1970], the original intention of the founders of our subject was to study rules; or, in other words, to study the old-fashioned notion of 'function' in the sense of definition. In contrast to Dirichlet's notion (of graph, that is the set of pairs of argument and associated value) the older notion referred also to the process of stepping from argument to value, a process coded by a definition. Generally we think of such definitions as given by words in ordinary English, applied to arguments also expressed by words (in English); or, more specifically, we may think of the definitions as programmes for machines, applied to, that is operating on, such programmes. In both cases we have to do with a <u>type free</u> structure, permitting self application, a feature which is often held to be 'responsible' for the contradictions in the first formulations of set theory (by Frege). Similarly the first formulation of the λ-calculus turned out to be inconsistent (paradox of Kleene-Rosser [1935]). In contrast the first formulation of combinatory logic was consistent (but not some of its later extensions as shown by the paradox of Curry [1942]).

Evidently, the type free character as such is not problematic. We have not only the examples informally described in the preceding paragraph, but also many familiar and natural structures in elementary algebra where an object acts both as argument and as function. Specifically, in the theory of semigroups an element a determines the function with the action

$$x \to ax$$

(and in group theory an 'element' determines its co'set').
It seems plausible that the contradictions are connected with the aim of providing <u>foundations for the whole of mathematics</u>.
Before we distinguish between different meanings of such general concepts as 'set' or 'rule' employed in different areas of mathematics, it is tempting to put down axioms and rules, some of which are valid for one meaning, some for another. In this way contradictions are liable to arise.

Be that as it may, here we do not propose to use combinatory logic or the λ-calculus as a foundation for the whole of mathematics; but rather in the study of those parts of the subject which <u>actually present themselves as being about rules</u>. A paradigm of such parts is <u>numerical arithmetic</u> which is 'about' rules in the literal sense that

$$5 + 7 = 2 + 10$$

asserts:
The LHS and RHS <u>reduce</u> to the same <u>numeral</u>, that is to the same <u>normal</u> (or <u>canonical</u>) form when the computation <u>rules</u> for addition are applied.

From this point of view, perhaps the single most important feature of a <u>language</u> (for a theory of rules) is that <u>each term should code its own reduction procedure</u>; not necessarily a deterministic one, but a class of 'equivalent' ones. Thus implicit in an interpretation or 'model' of the language is an <u>immediate reduction relation</u> or 'multiplication table'. In fact, in CL or the λ-calculus the intended reduction procedure is <u>only</u> implicit, that is we may assign a specific procedure to each term metamathematically, but the intended <u>immediate</u> reduction relation cannot be expressed in the purely equational languages of CL or the λ-calculus. Moreover, throughout this thesis (usually in connection with certain 'conservative extension results') we introduce additional symbols for reduction relations and axioms which make more explicit the intended meaning of the formalism. By the way our use of such additional 'structure' is parallel to the use in set theory of <u>ordinals</u> and their <u>order</u>, and of the relation between sets x and ordinals α (α is the rank of x); the only difference is that in the case of set theory, at least in the presence of the axiom of foundation, the extensions considered are not merely conservative but <u>definitional</u> (familiar from

Tarski, Mostowski, Robinson [1953]).

Term Models. In the light of the preceding paragraph, one fundamental role of terms is clear: they are the objects on which we, literally, operate and they are the objects which code the operations. Another role, to be distinguished from that of terms-as-elements-of-the-intended-reduction-relation, is the use of terms in a formal theory of this relation, as is clear from the assertion about numerical arithmetic mentioned earlier on. The difference is particularly striking for terms of the formal theory which contain variables, when we think of the reduction relation as being a relation between closed terms (also called: interior of the term models considered below).

The reason for speaking of term models, which suggests model theory, is this. Whatever our specific intended interpretations may be, our formal theory can also be interpreted in traditional model theoretic style. In fact, some of the more general results are consequences of such superficial syntactic features as these: When regarded as theories on 'standard' formalization,

CL is a purely equational system and, a fortiori, axiomatized by universal formulae,

and so is the λ-calculus (if for each term λxt we associate a function symbol f_t with n arguments, if λxt contains n free variables and the axiom $f_t a = [x/a]t^*$, where t^* results from t by replacing the λ-expressions in t by the associated function symbols).

By what has just been said we do not think of these 'applications of model theory as profound but rather as separating general (some would say 'trivial') properties from the specific properties of our intended interpretation. Adapting a phrase from Bourbaki, model theory provides here the 'hygiene' of proof theory (used for establishing the more specific properties).

A typical example of such uses of elementary model theory occurs in the analysis of <u>extensionality.</u> This property (of a term model cannot be expressed equationally, but needs the logically complicated form,

$$(\forall x\ E_1) \to E_2$$

for suitable equations E_1 and E_2. Hence it cannot be expressed directly in CL. However, <u>as far as equational consequences of</u> (this axiom of) <u>extensionality are concerned</u>, <u>they can also be generated by the purely equational rule of extensionality</u>. Thus, in contrast to the defects of equational theories, mentioned above, for expressing the intended reduction relation, these theories are adequate for formulating and solving problems of extensionality, in consequence of the following quite general 'model theoretic' result. (For arbitrary quantifier-free A_1 and A_2, in place of equations E_1 and E_2, Shepherdson [1965] finds a more delicate rule to replace axioms $\forall x\ A_1 \to A_2$.)

Let S be any set of atomic formulae of a predicate logic, closed under logical deduction (that is substitution of a term of the language for variables), and under the rule: derive $P_0^{(i)}$ for $P_1^{(i)},\ldots,P_{k_i}^{(i)}$ $(i \in I)$ where the P's are all atomic.
Then the term model of the theory (in which P is interpreted as $S \vdash P$), satisfies the axioms corresponding to the rules:

$\forall\vec{x}(P_1 \wedge \ldots \wedge P_k) \rightarrow P_0^{(i)}$.

Proof. Suppose that $\forall\vec{x}(P_1 \wedge \ldots \wedge P_k)$ is satisfied in the term model, then $P_1(\vec{t}),\ldots,P_k(\vec{t})$ hold for all terms $\vec{t}$, hence in particular for $\vec{t} = \vec{x}$. Thus $P_1,\ldots,P_k$ all hold in that model, hence $P_1,\ldots,P_k$ are provable in S. Hence by the rule P_0 is provable in S and therefore satisfied in the model.

Thus, in particular, if $k = 1$, P_1 is the equation $Mx = M'x$ and P_0 is $M = M'$, the result mentioned above follows.

Such hygienic uses of model theory are to be distinguished from model theoretic <u>constructions</u> formulated by use of sophisticated notions studied in mathematical practice and (hence) well-understood; for example the use of ultraproducts. Here we may, so to speak, look at the constructions and read off properties of these models which are not at all evident from the axioms. Particularly when consistency, that is the existence of suitable models, is involved, it is not at all necessary that the constructions provide <u>all</u> models of the theory considered: it is more important that we have 'enough' models (for some specific purpose) and that they be manageable. Similarly Scott's lattice theoretic models are useful despite the fact established in §3.2 <u>that not all extensional models of CL are among them</u>.

But it is of interest to observe that the particular model left out from Scott's collection of models, is very natural from a computational view. In this model the so called fixed-points which all act in the same computational way are identified.

To conclude this discussion of the role of model theory in our study of CL and the λ-calculus, we may perhaps compare it with the use of non-standard models of arithmetic (as developed at the present time). We establish consistency results by analyzing computation procedures and then restate them as properties of suitable term models. Similarly, one establishes consistency results for formal arithmetic by proof theory or recursion theory (Gödel's incompleteness results) and may then apply the completeness theorem for predicate logic to infer the existence of some non-standard model of arithmetic with required properties. Probably it is fair to say that the known non-standard models are not of intrinsic interest. In contrast, our formulations for term models are directly relevant to what we are talking about since, as we have said already, we study operations on terms and operations coded by terms.

Finally a comment on versions of the λ-calculus or CL with types (cf. Sanchis [1967]). Here the situation is much simpler. In terms of models, the theory with types can be immediately interpreted in familiar mathematical terms. One model consists of the collections of all set-theoretic functions of finite type (over an infinite domain). For the more interesting models HRO and in extensional version HEO see Troelstra [1971].
In terms of computation, it is shown in Sanchis [1967] that in the theories with types all terms have a normal form, contrary to the situation in the type free theory.

This normalizability of all terms of the typed λ-calculus has also an interesting 'negative' consequence for definability problems, specifically of <u>recursion operators</u> (for any given types). In the type free calculus we have an R with the property that, for (variable) M,N and each numerical $\underline{n}$

(*) $$RMN\underline{0} = N$$

$$RMN\underline{n+1} = M(RMN\underline{n})\underline{n}$$

In contrast, there is a specific type τ such that <u>no</u> term of the typed λ-calculus satisfies (*) for M,N of relevant types. (A refinement is possible showing that (*) do not hold for certain closed M,N.)

The proof uses the following facts.

1. The normalizability of the terms in the typed λ-calculus can be established by the principles of first order arithmetic. Consequently there is a provably total <u>valuation function</u> v, assigning to each (Gödel number of a) term, the (Gödel number of) its normal form.

2. By 1. all number theoretic functions which are (locally) definable are primitive recursive in v because if the term F defines f, then the Gödel number of the term $F\underline{n}$ is $\phi(n)$ for a primitive recursive function ϕ, and from $v(\phi(n))$ it is possible to recover f(n) primitive recursively.

Corollary. Not all functions provably recursive in first order arithmetic are represented in the typed λ-calculus.

3. Let f_0 be a provably total function, with Gödel number e_0, which is not primitive recursive in v. Such an f_0 can be defined by the use of recursion operators. For, f_0 being

provably total we have

$\vdash \forall x\, \exists y\; T(\underline{e}_0, x, y)$ in intuitionistic arithmetic.

Hence by the dialectica interpretation of Gödel [1958] there exists a term t in the typed λ-calculus with R such that $T(\underline{e}_0, \underline{n}, \underline{\tau(n)})$ is valid for all $n \in \omega$.

Hence f is represented by $\lambda n.u(t(n))$ where u represents the U of Kleene's normal form.

Now we discuss in more detail the subjects treated in the text.

Consistency. The first formulation of the λ-calculus being inconsistent, a revised formulation (the λI-calculus) was proved consistent by Church and Rosser [1936]. More informatively their theorem establishes the uniqueness of the normal forms and the fact that the normal form of a normalizable term M can be found simply by reducing M. This reduction can be made deterministic, by the standardization theorem, cf. Curry, Feys [1958] Ch 4E. However, the fine-structure (i.e. whether it is from the human point of view the shortest possible reduction) of the standard reduction is not discussed.

Finally, cf. remark 1.2.18, there is now a simple proof of the Church-Rosser theorem by Martin-Löf [1971]. This will be given in appendix II.

The relation between the λ-calculus and CL. Several possibilities of mapping λ-terms into CL (see 1.4.6) have been discussed (cf. Curry, Feys [1958] Ch 6A). But, without extensionality, they do not preserve the set of provable equations. They do, if extensionality is included but not the provable reductions nor the normal forms. On the other hand the translations do preserve application and therefore by 3.2.20½ the <u>solvability</u> of closed terms. The importance of this is seen below. In particular, in the extensional case consistency results can be transferred. In this way the ω-consistency of the λ-calculus follows from the corresponding result for CL.

<u>λ-definability</u>. We begin with the λ-calculus since, traditionally, λ-definability and not combinatory definability is treated. A number theoretic partial function f is said to be λ-definable if there is a term F such that $\lambda \vdash F\underline{n} = \underline{m} \iff f(n) = m$ and $F\underline{n}$ has no normal form if f(n) is undefined. (Here $\underline{n}$ is the nth numeral). We changed this definition, requiring not only $\lambda \vdash F\underline{n} = m \iff f(n) = m$, but also that $F\underline{n}$ be unsolvable if f(n) is undefined. In this case we say that F strongly defines f.

The concept of strong λ-definability has several advantages.
(i) If f_1, f_2 are defined by terms F_1, F_2, then it is <u>not</u> true that $f_1 \circ f_2$ is defined by $\lambda x.F_1(F_2x)$. For example let f_1 be the constant zero function and let f_2 be everywhere undefined. Then $f_1 \circ f_2$ is totally undefined but $\lambda x\, F_1(F_2x) = \lambda x\, \underline{0}$ represents the constant zero function.
Hence it is not immediate that the λ-definable functions are closed under composition.
Use of strong definability is made by representing the composition $f_1 \cdot f_2$ by $F = \lambda x.(F_2xI\; F_1(F_2x))$. If $f_2(n)$ is undefined $F_2\underline{n}$ is unsolvable and hence $F\underline{n}$ is unsolvable, and if $f_2(n)$ is defined $F_2\underline{n}I$ is essentially the same as I.

ii) Traditionally the λ-definability of the partial recursive functions was proved by use of Kleene's normal form theorem. The representation thus obtained is not intensional with respect to definitional equality. Using strong λ-definability we give a representation of the partial recursive functions preserving their definition trees. This is not to be regarded as a mere technical improvement but simply central to the objects which are here intended. In this context, see Kearns [1969] who uses an extension of CL to give a faithful representation of the computations of a Turing machine.

iii) Application to undecidability results, see below.

In contrast to the representation of say the primitive recursive functions in the predicate calculus, their representation in the λ-calculus is not global, that is, their defining recursion equations are not derivable for the representing terms with a free variable, but only for each numerical instance.

For example in the extensional case (this is not essential) the term F with Fxy = xy represents exponentiation since $\lambda + \text{ext} \vdash \underline{n}\underline{m} = \underline{m^n}$. Hence the function 1^x is represented by G with $Gx = x\underline{1}$. Now we have for all numerals $\lambda + \text{ext} \vdash G\underline{n} = \underline{1}$, but not $\lambda + \text{ext} \vdash Gx = \underline{1}$ since $\lambda \vdash G(K\underline{0}) = K\underline{0}\underline{1} = \underline{0}$.

(It should be admitted that F is not the standard representation of exponentiation as this will be done in §1.3, but similar examples can be given there.) It is unlikely that there exists a global representation of the primitive recursive functions at all, since in contrast to the representation in predicate calculus, all models of the λ-calculus must contain 'non-standard' elements (such as the element denoted by K).

Undecidability results. As was mentioned above, the translation going from the λ-calculus to CL preserves solvability of closed terms. Thus undecidability results about the λ-calculus as in §1.3 transfer to CL, without any need for a parallel development of CL-definability.

We note that the role of unsolvable closed terms in the λK-calculus is similar to the role of those closed terms in the λI-calculus which have no normal form. In particular

i) In the λK-calculus it is consistent to equate all unsolvable terms (see §3.2) and in the λI-calculus it is consistent to equate all terms without a normal form (see part II).

ii) For some purposes unsolvable terms can replace familiar arguments involving negation. See for example 3.2.19 where it is proved that Con, the set of equations consistent with the λ-calculus is complete Π^0_1.

An example of an undecidability result which does not need strong representability is 1.3.17 for which we give here an alternative proof (cf. Smullyan [1961]).

Let A,B be disjoint r.e. sets, recursively inseparable.

Define $f(x) = \begin{cases} 0 & \text{if } x \in A \\ 1 & \text{if } x \in B \\ \uparrow & \text{else} \end{cases}$

then f is partial recursive. Let f be defined by the term F. If T were a recursive consistent extension of the λ-calculus, then $C = \{n \mid T \vdash F\underline{n} = \underline{0}\}$ would be a recursive separation of A and B.

<u>A minimal extensional term model</u>. In Chapter II we define a model of CL which is minimal in two respects. Firstly its domain consists of the <u>closed</u> terms only, which are, as was stated in the introduction, principal object of our study. Secondly the model is minimal with respect to the equality relation, that is to the set of terms that are equated. It is clear, that the model is generated by the ω-rule described in §2.1. Formally the theory enriched with the ω-rule is a strengthening of the rule of extensionality: to infer $M = M'$ we do not require a derivation of $Mx = M'x$ with variable x, but only derivations of $MZ = M'Z$ for all closed terms Z (with no uniformity on these derivations). Two questions, so to speak, at opposite poles are

a) Is the theory consistent?

b) Is the theory conservative over the λ-calculus + ext?

Ad a) In §2.2, 2.3 it is shown by transfinite induction, that the extension of CL (or the λ-calculus) by the ω-rule is consistent.

Ad b) In §2.5 it is established for equations $M = M'$ where M and M' are not <u>universal generators</u> that the ω-rule is conservative. We prove this by showing the existence of <u>variable like closed terms</u> Ξ such that $M\Xi = M'\Xi \Rightarrow M = M'$.

This result includes the known special case (a consequence of the theorem of Böhm [1968], cf. §2.1) of equations between normal terms since they are not universal generators.

In this connection it is to be understood that our use of closed terms which are not in normal form is not haphazard: as we see it, different meanings, that is programmes, are to be given to certain (different) terms which have no normal form; for example if $M \equiv \lambda x.x\underline{0}\Omega$ and $N \equiv \lambda x.x\underline{1}\Omega$, where Ω does not have a normal form, then M,N have no normal form but $MK = \underline{0}$ and $NK = \underline{1}$.

Unsolvable terms. These terms were already mentioned in 'λ-definability' above, in connection with the definability of functions, where they were needed to provide particularly heriditarily undefined values. From the computational point of view this means that such terms do not do much. In accordance with this we now consider the possibility of putting them equal and establish (3.2.16) that this can be done consistently, even in the presence of extensionality (added in print: or the ω-rule). It is the term model of this theory that is not among Scott's collection of models mentioned above. We note that in general the addition of extensionality not only adds new theorems (cf. the remark following 1.1.16) but can be problematic. In particular in 3.2.24 we provide a consistent extension of CL which becomes inconsistent when extensionality is added.

Recursion theoretic structures for the λK- and the λI-calculus. By a recursion theoretic structure we mean here a combinatory structure where the domain consists of $\omega \cup \{*\}$ and the application operator is interpreted as Kleene brackets, i.e. $n \cdot m = \{n\}(m) = U(\mu z\ T(n,m,z))$. $*$ has to be treated as the undefined element, it serves to make the application operator total, with the additional property that $\{n\}(*) = (*)$ (cf. the theory of Wagner and Strong (Strong [1968])).
This kind of construction can of course be made more general. In-stead of Kleene's brackets which come from his particular

equation calculus for computing recursive functions from recursion equations, an other equational calculus (and other numberings of equations) may be considered. In this way one discovers exactly which properties of numberings and equation calculi are relevant to our subject.

Perhaps the most essential difference between the λI-calculus and the λK-calculus is that the former is 'more' systematic or deterministic, not allowing short-cuts. All programmes that are 'represented' in a term of the λI-calculus have to be performed, while in the λK-calculus some subprogrammes can be skipped. For example we reduce KMN to M without looking at the value of N. (This may be compared to a 'stupid' evaluation of $0.(2^{15} + 3^6)$ in numerical arithmetic where we evaluate $2^{15} + 3^6$ and a short cut using the reduction $0.x \to 0$; actually the λI-calculus itself does 'stupid' numerical computations.)

Because of this systematic feature of the λI-calculus we can find a recursion theoretic model for it or better for its combinatory equivalent, described in Rosser [1936], here called CL_I. It is like CL but with primitive constants I,J and the axioms IM = M and JMNLP = MN(MPL). For suitable numbers i,j the structure $® = \langle \omega \cup \{*\}, i, j, \cdot \rangle$ is a model for CL_I. In part II of our thesis thesis we will prove that

(1) M has no CL_I normal form $\Longleftrightarrow$ $\square_R(M) = *$.

The proof uses a formalization of the description of the recursive functions as is in Kleene [1959].

This implies that it is consistent with CL_I to equate all terms without a normal form.

The recursion theoretic structure obtained by use of Kleene's particular equation calculus is not a model for CL. Though there are numbers $i,k,s \in \omega$ which satisfy $i \cdot x = x$, $k \cdot x \cdot y = x$ and $s \cdot x \cdot y \cdot z = x \cdot z \cdot (y \cdot z)$ for all $x,y,z \in \omega$ no k satisfies $k \cdot x \cdot y = x$ for $y = *$.

However the structure ®' = $\langle \omega \cup \{*\}, i, k, s, \cdot \rangle$ realizes the language of CL, but is not a model of it, and satisfies an analogue to (1) namely

(2) M has no CL-normal form $\Longleftrightarrow \sqcap_{R'}(M) = *$.

Considering finally the canonical mapping: $M \to M^{WS}$ of the language CL into the language of Wagner and Strong, we find a term M in Part II such that

M has no CL (and hence no CL_I) normal form but $M^{WS} = *$ is not a theorem of the theory of Wagner-Strong.

Since however properties (1) and (2) hold for our intended objects of study, we should wish to <u>extend</u> the theory of Wagner-Strong; specifically to extend their language. Since the proofs of (1) and (2) for ® and ®' required an analysis of computations, the extended language should refer to the latter, in particular to <u>length</u> of computations (as pointed out to us by C.Gordon).

CHAPTER I

Preliminaries

§1.1. The λ-calculus.

The λ-calculus is a theory studied thoroughly in the thirties (by Church, Kleene, Rosser and others). It has been designed to describe a class of functions V, where the domain of all functions is V itself. Therefore the objects we consider are at the same time function and at the same time argument. (A similar situation we have in most set theories: there the objects are at the same time set and at the same time element.) Hence we have the feature that a function can be applied to itself. In the usual conception of a function in mathematics, for example in Zermelo Fraenkel set theory, this is impossible (because of the axiom of foundation).

The λ-calculus defines (or better represents) a class of (partial) functions (λ-definable functions) which turns out to be the class of (partial) recursive functions. In fact the equivalence between the Turing computable functions and the μ-recursive functions was proved via the λ-definable functions:
Kleene [1936] proved: the μ-recursive functions are exactly the λ-definable functions.
Turing [1937] proved: the computable functions are exactly the λ-definable functions.
In this sense the λ-calculus played a central role in the early investigations of the theory of the recursive functions.

The consistency of the λ-calculus was proved by Church and

Rosser [1936]. Because some theories related to the λ-calculus turned out to be inconsistent (paradox of Kleene-Rosser [1935], paradox of Curry [1942]), we see that this consistency proof is not a luxury. In contrast to most mathematical theories, and like set theory, the λ-calculus was initiated before any models were known. In group theory for example many concrete groups were known long before formal group theory was developed. Not until the end of 1969 however, were the first models in ordinary mathematical terms for the λ-calculus constructed (Scott [1970]).

In the λ-calculus we have the fundamental operation of application. The application of a function f to a will be written as fa.

Apart from this application we have an abstraction operator λ The intuitive meaning of λx ... is the function which assigns ... to x. Its use is illustrated by the following formula (not a formula of the λ-calculus by the way)

$$(\lambda x \cdot x^2+2x+1)3 = 16.$$

Now we give a formal description of the λ-calculus.

1.1.1 <u>Definition</u>

We define the following language L_K:

Alphabet: a,b,c,... variables

λ,(,) improper symbols

= equality

Terms: Terms are inductively defined by

1) a variable is a term

2) if M,N are terms, then (MN) is a term

3) if M is a term, then (λxM) is a term (x is an arbitrary variable).

Formulas: if M,N are terms then $M = N$ is a formula.

1.1.2 <u>Definition</u>

An occurrence of a variable x in a term is called <u>bound</u> if this x is "in the scope of x". Otherwise we call this occurrence of x <u>free</u>.

$BV(M)$ $(FV(M))$ is the set of all variables in M that occur in M as a bound (free) variable.

BV and FV can be defined inductively as follows:

$$BV(x) = \emptyset$$
$$BV(MN) = BV(M) \cup BV(N)$$
$$BV(\lambda xM) = BV(M) \cup \{x\}$$

$$FV(x) = \{x\}$$
$$FV(MN) = FV(M) \cup FV(N)$$
$$FV(\lambda xM) = FV(M) - \{x\}.$$

A variable can occur free and bound in the same term (e.g. $((\lambda x(xy))x)$).

Note that, as is common, we use for equality in the object-language and in the metalanguage the same symbol "=". When we need to distinguish between them we write (as Curry does) "≡" for equality in the metalanguage. This is mainly the case when we mean syntactic identity.

1.1.3 <u>Notation</u>

i) $M_1M_2 \ldots M_n$ stands for $((\ldots(M_1M_2)\ldots)M_n)$ (association to the left).

ii) $\lambda x_1x_2\ldots x_n \cdot M$ stands for $(\lambda x_1(\lambda x_2 \ldots(\lambda x_n M)\ldots))$

iii) $[x/N]M$ stands for the result of substituting N in those places of x in M which are free:

$[x/N]x = N$

$[x/N]y = y$

$[x/N](M_1M_2) = ([x/N]M_1)([x/N]M_2)$

$[x/N](\lambda xM) = \lambda xM$

$[x/N](\lambda yM) = \lambda y([x/N]M)$.

In the above $x \neq y$.

1.1.4 <u>Definition</u>

The λ-calculus is the theory in L_K defined by the following axioms and rules:

I 1. $\lambda xM = \lambda y[x/y]M$ if $y \notin FV(M) \cup BV(M)$

2. $(\lambda xM)N = [x/N]M$ if $BV(M) \cap FV(N) = \emptyset$.

II 1. $M = M$

2. $\dfrac{M = N}{N = M}$

3. $\dfrac{M = N,\ N = L}{M = L}$

4. $\dfrac{M = M'}{ZM = ZM'}$ $\dfrac{M = M'}{MZ = M'Z}$ $\dfrac{M = M'}{\lambda xM = \lambda xM'}$

In the above M, M', N, L, Z denote arbitrary terms and x,y denote arbitrary variables.

We say that ...2 is a direct consequence of ...1 if $\dfrac{\ldots 1}{\ldots 2}$.

1.1.5 Remarks

1. Axiom I 1. allows us the change of bound variables (like $\int_0^1 x^2dx = \int_0^1 y^2dy$).

If M = N is provable using only axiom I 1. (and the rules of II) then we say that M is an α-variant of N (notation $M \equiv_\alpha N$). If $M \equiv_\alpha N$ then only the bound variables are renamed. Note that $M \equiv_\alpha N$ is a statement of the metalanguage.

Axiom I 2. expresses the essential feature of the λ operator.

The Axiom and rules of II express that = is an equality.

2. If we would drop the restriction in I 1. we would get (λa·ab) = (λb·bb) which is in conflict with our intuitive interpretation of λ.

If we would drop the restriction in I 2. we would get

a) (λa(λb·ba))b = λb·bb

b) (λa(λc·ca))b = λc·cb

which is also undesirable. In (a) there is a difference between the "local" variable b and the "global" variable b. The restriction in I 2. is just to prevent confusion of variables.

3. If we would restrict the definition of terms as follows:

3') If M is a term and if x ∈ FV(M), then λxM is a term,

then we get a restricted form of the λ-calculus, the so called λI-calculus. Our form of the λ-calculus is called the λK-calculus because we can define a term K = λab·a, with the property KMN = M, which is impossible in the λI-calculus. In the absence of K many theorems are a bit harder to prove; see Church [1941] who treats the λI-calculus.

4. Axioms I 1. and I 2. are called α-resp. β-reduction.

5. $\lambda \vdash M = N$ means that $M = N$ is a provable formula of the λ-calculus.

1.1.6 Examples

Define $I = \lambda a \cdot a$

$K = \lambda ab \cdot a$

$S = \lambda abc \cdot ac(bc)$

Then $\lambda \vdash IM = M$

$\lambda \vdash KMN = M$

$\lambda \vdash SMNL = ML\ (NL)$

A nice exercise is the following.

1.1.7 Theorem (fixed point theorem)

For every term M there exists a term Ω such that $\lambda \vdash M\Omega = \Omega$.

Proof.

Define $\omega = (\lambda x\ \ M(xx))$ with $x \notin FV(M)$

$\Omega = \omega\omega$

Then $\lambda \vdash \Omega = (\lambda x\ \ M(xx))\omega = M(\omega\omega) = M\Omega$. ⊠

This fixed point theorem, so simple to prove, is strongly related to the fixed point theorem in recursion theory (recursion theorem). In 1.1.7 we have proved more than we formulated. The fixed point can be found in a uniform way.

1.1.8 Corollary

There exists a term FP such that for every term M we have

$\lambda \vdash M(FPM) = FPM$

Proof.

Define $FP = \lambda a \cdot \{(\lambda b \cdot a(bb))(\lambda a \cdot b(aa))\}$ ⊠

The Russellparadox and Gödel's self referring sentence can be considered as applications of FP. Therefore in Curry Feys [1958] such a term FP is called a paradoxical combinator.

1.1.9 Corollary

There exists a term M such that $\lambda \vdash Mx = M$. Such a term is called a fixed point.

Proof.

Define $M = FP\ K$ (where K is defined as in 1.1.6).

Then $\lambda \vdash Mx = KMx = M$. ⊠

1.1.10 Definition (See also 1.2.6.)

1) A term M is in normal form if it has no part of the form $(\lambda xP)Q$.
2) A term M has a normal form if there exists a term M' which is in normal form such that $\lambda \vdash M = M'$. In this case we say that M' is a normal form of M.

In the next § we state a theorem (1.2.9) which has as consequence:

1.1.11 Theorem

If M has a normal form, then this normal form is unique up to α-reduction (i.e. change of bound variables).

Examples.

1. $(\lambda a \cdot a)(\lambda b \cdot bb)$ is not in normal form but has the normal form $\lambda b \cdot bb$.
2. $c(\lambda a \cdot a)(\lambda b \cdot bb)$ is in normal form.

In § 1.2 we will give examples of terms that do not have normal forms.

In the λ-calculus we can represent the natural numbers:

1.1.12 Definition

$\underline{0} = \lambda ab\cdot b$

$\underline{1} = \lambda ab\cdot ab$

$\underline{2} = \lambda ab\cdot a(ab)$

$\underline{3} = \lambda ab\cdot a(a(ab))$

etc.

Hence $\underline{n} = \lambda ab\cdot \underbrace{a(\ldots(ab)\ldots)}_{n \text{ times}} = \lambda ab\cdot a^n b$

Note that $\underline{n}$ is in normal form and has the property:

1.1.13

$$\lambda \vdash \underline{n}fx = f^n x.$$

1.1.14 Definition

Let $f: \omega^n \to \omega$ be a partial function.

f is called λ-definable iff there exists a term F such that

$\lambda \vdash F\underline{k}_1\ldots\underline{k}_n = \underline{m}$ if $f(k_1,\ldots,k_n) = m$

$F\underline{k}_1\ldots\underline{k}_n$ has no normal form if $f(k_1,\ldots,k_n)$ is undefined.

In this case we say that F defines f.

If F defines f, but we no longer know f, can we recover f from F? The following gives an affirmative answer.

1.1.15 Theorem

If F defines f then

$$\lambda \vdash F\underline{k}_1\ldots\underline{k}_n = \underline{m} \Leftrightarrow f(k_1,\ldots,k_n) = m .$$

Proof.

$\Leftarrow$ By definition.

⇒ Suppose $\lambda \vdash F\underline{k}_1 \ldots \underline{k}_n = \underline{m}$

Then $F\underline{k}_1 \ldots \underline{k}_n$ has a normal form

so $f(k_1, \ldots, k_n)$ is defined, say

$f(k_1, \ldots, k_n) = m'$.

Hence $\lambda \vdash F\underline{k}_1 \ldots \underline{k}_n = \underline{m}'$.

By 1.1.11 it follows that $\underline{m} \equiv_\alpha \underline{m}'$.

Hence $m = m'$ and therefore $f(k_1, \ldots, k_n) = m$. ⊠

Now we consider the following rule of extensionality:

1.1.16

$$\text{ext} \quad \frac{Mx = Nx \qquad x \notin FV(MN)}{M = N}$$

ext is not provable in the λ-calculus:

Let $M = \lambda a{\cdot}ba$

$N = b$.

Then $\lambda \vdash Ma = Na$, but not $\lambda \vdash M = N$ because M and N are dictinct normal forms. So we may take ext as an extra axiom for the λ-calculus.

$\lambda + \text{ext} \vdash M = N$ means that $M = N$ is a provable formula of the λ-calculus + extensionality.

1.1.17 Theorem

$\lambda + \text{ext} \vdash (\lambda x(Mx)) = M \qquad \text{if} \quad x \notin FV(M)$

(In the literature, this is called η-reduction.)

Proof.

$(\lambda x(Mx))x = Mx, \quad x \notin FV(M)$.

Hence by extensionality

$(\lambda x(Mx)) = M$. ⊠

Note that extensionality follows in turn from 1.1.17:

1.1.18 <u>Theorem</u>

If we assume 1.1.17 as an extra axiom for the λ-calculus, then we can prove extensionality.

Proof.

Let $Mx = Nx \quad x \notin FV(MN)$.

Then $\lambda x(Mx) = \lambda x(Nx)$ by rule II.4.

Hence $M = N$ by 1.1.17. ⊠

1.1.19 <u>Remark</u>

Often in the literature the λ-calculus we described is called the λ-β-calculus. (Because its essential axiom is I.2.: β-reduction.) The λ-calculus with 1.1.17 as an extra axiom is called the λ-$\beta\eta$-calculus. When it is needed to stress that we are working with the λK-calculus, we speak about the λK-β-calculus and the λK-$\beta\eta$-calculus.
Of course we have also the λI-β-calculus and the λI-$\beta\eta$-calculus.

§1.2. The Church-Rosser theorem. The consistency of the λ-calculus.

Since we do not have a negation in the λ-calculus we cannot define the concept of a contradiction. Therefore we define the consistency as follows.

1.2.1 <u>Definition</u>

The λ-calculus is <u>consistent</u> if we cannot prove $a = b$.
(If $a = b$ were provable every formula would be provable.)

As was remarked in the introduction some theories related to the λ-calculus turned out to be inconsistent. Fortunately the λ-

calculus itself is consistent as was proved by Church and Rosser [1936].

We will now give an idea of how this was done. Let us go back to the informal discussion in the beginning of §1.

We had the expression $(\lambda x \cdot x^2+2x+1)3$. After computing we replace this expression by 16. No one would replace 16 by the more complicated $(\lambda x \cdot x^2+2x+1)3$. Hence we can assign a certain asymmetry to the relation = .

This will be expressed by

$$(\lambda x \cdot x^2+2x+1)3 \geqslant 16.$$

$\geqslant$ is called reduction.

Note that reduction is a stronger relation than equality. I.e. if M reduces to N then M is equal to N. Now we will describe an extension of the λ-calculus in which we formalize this reduction relation.

1.2.2 <u>Definition</u>

We define the following language L'_K .

The alphabet of L'_K consists of that of L_K together with the symbol "$\geqslant$".

The terms of L'_K are the same as those of L_K.

The formulas of L'_K are defined as follows:

If M,N are terms of L'_K then $M = N$ and $M \geqslant N$ are formulas.

1.2.3 <u>Definition</u>

In the language L'_K we define an extension of the λ-calculus by the following axioms and rules (see appendix):

I 1. $\lambda xM \geqslant \lambda y[x/y]M$ if $y \notin FV(M)$ (α-reduction)

2. $(\lambda xM)N \geqslant [x/N]M$ if $BV(M) \cap FV(N) = \emptyset$ (β-reduction)

II Same as in 1.1.4. (These state that "=" is an equality.)

III 1. $M \geqslant M$

2. $\dfrac{M \geqslant N,\ N \geqslant L}{M \geqslant L}$

3. $\dfrac{M \geqslant M'}{ZM \geqslant ZM'}$, $\dfrac{M \geqslant M'}{MZ \geqslant M'Z}$, $\dfrac{M \geqslant M'}{\lambda xM \geqslant \lambda xM'}$

4. $\dfrac{M \geqslant N}{M = N}$

Again in the above M, M', N, L, Z denote arbitrary terms and x,y arbitrary variables.

If we want to include extensionality we add the axiom

1.2.4

I 3. $\lambda x(Mx) \geqslant M$ if $x \notin FV(M)$ (η-reduction)

It is easy to see that this extended λ-calculus (with or without extensionality) is in fact a conservative extension of the λ-calculus (with or without extensionality) considered in §1.1. For this reason we also write for the extended λ-calculus $\lambda \vdash M = N$ and $\lambda + \text{ext} \vdash M = N$.

Henceforth, if we refer to the λ-calculus, we mean the extended λ-calculus.

Note that if we have $\lambda + \text{ext} \vdash M \geqslant N$, η-reduction may be used.

With the help of $\geqslant$ we can express an important property of normal forms:

1.2.5 Lemma

If M is in normal form and $\lambda \vdash M \geqslant N$ then $M \equiv_\alpha N$.

Proof.

By induction to the length of proof of $\lambda \vdash M \geqslant N$. ⊠

Remark. It is not true that if $\forall N[\lambda \vdash M \geqslant N \Rightarrow M \equiv_{\alpha} N]$, then M is in normal form.

Consider for example $(\lambda a \cdot aa)(\lambda a \cdot aa)$.

1.2.6 Definition

If we consider the λ-$\beta\eta$-calculus we can define

A term is in η-normal form if it has no part of the form $\lambda x(Px)$.

The concept of normal form as defined in 1.1.8 is then called β-normal form.

A term is in $\beta\eta$-normal form if it is both in β- and in η-normal form.

A term M has a $\beta\eta$-normal form if there exists a term M' which is in $\beta\eta$-normal form such that $\lambda + ext \vdash M = M'$.

If we just speak of normal form, we mean β-normal form.

Analogous to 1.2.5 we have

1.2.7 Lemma

If M is in $\beta\eta$-normal form and if $\lambda + ext \vdash M \geqslant N$ then $M \equiv_{\alpha} N$.

1.2.8 Lemma

If M has a β-normal form, then M has a $\beta\eta$-normal form.

Proof.

Let M' be a β-normal form of M. Then $\lambda \vdash M = M'$, hence a fortiori $\lambda + ext \vdash M = M'$.

By applying I.3 (η-reduction) a finite number of times to M', we obtain a M" which is in η-normal form and $\lambda + ext \vdash M = M''$.

Because η-reductions do not introduce subterms of the form

$(\lambda xP)Q$, M'' will be in $\beta\eta$-normal form, hence it is a $\beta\eta$-normal form of M. ⊠

In Curry Hindley Seldin [1917] Ch.11 E, lemma 13.1 it is proved that the converse of 1.2.8 also holds.

Now we state without proof:

1.2.9 Theorem (Church-Rosser theorem [1936])

If $\lambda \vdash M = N$ then there exists a term Z such that $\lambda \vdash M \geqslant Z$ and $\lambda \vdash N \geqslant Z$.

See Mitschke [1970] for an elegant proof.

Mitschke's proof is still rather long, but much simpler than the original one. In §1.5 we will use Mitschke's ideas to prove a Church-Rosser theorem for combinatory logic.

1.2.10 Corollary

If M,N are terms both in normal form and $M \not\equiv_\alpha N$, then $\lambda \nvdash M = N$.

Proof.

Suppose $\lambda \vdash M = N$, then by 1.2.8 there exists a Z such that

$\lambda \vdash M \geqslant Z$, $\lambda \vdash N \geqslant Z$.

M,N are in normal form, hence by 1.2.5 $M \equiv_\alpha Z$ and $N \equiv_\alpha Z$.

But then $M \equiv_\alpha N$ contradiction. ⊠

From this 1.1.11 readily follows:

1.1.11 Theorem

If M has a normal form, then this normal form is unique up to α-reduction.

Proof.

If $\lambda \vdash M = N_1$, $\lambda \vdash M = N_2$ with N_1, N_2 in normal form, then $\lambda \vdash N_1 = N_2$. Hence by 1.2.10, $N_1 \equiv_\alpha N_2$. ⊠

1.2.11 Corollary

The λ-calculus is consistent.

Proof.

Because the terms a,b are in normal form and $a \not\equiv_\alpha b$ we have $\lambda \nvdash a = b$ by 1.2.10. ⊠

Also the question of the consistency of the λ-calculus with extensionality arises. In Curry Feys [1958] Ch.4D an extension of the Church-Rosser theorem is proved for the λ-calculus with η-reduction. We state this here without proof.

1.2.12 Theorem

If $\lambda + \text{ext} \vdash M = N$, then there exists a term Z such that $\lambda + \text{ext} \vdash M \geqslant Z$ and $\lambda + \text{ext} \vdash N \geqslant Z$.

Analogous to corollaries 1.2.10, 1.1.11 and 1.2.11 we have:

1.2.13 Corollary

If M,N are terms, both in βη-normal form and $M \not\equiv_\alpha N$, then $\lambda + \text{ext} \nvdash M = N$.

1.2.14 Corollary

If M has a βη-normal form, then this βη-normal form is unique up to α-reduction.

1.2.15 Corollary

The λ-calculus with extensionality is consistent.

In chapter II we will prove a theorem stronger than 1.2.15.

Now we state a corollary of the Church-Rosser theorem with the help of which we can show that some terms have no normal form:

1.2.16 <u>Corollary</u>

If M has the normal form N, then $\lambda \vdash M \geqslant N$.

Proof.

If $\lambda \vdash M = N$ and N is in normal form, then by 1.2.8 there exists a Z such that $\lambda \vdash M \geqslant Z$ and $\lambda \vdash N \geqslant Z$, hence by 1.2.5. $N \equiv_\alpha Z$.

So we have $\lambda \vdash M \geqslant N$. ⊠

1.2.17 Examples of terms without normal form.

From 1.2.16 follows that the term $\omega_2\omega_2$ with $\omega_2 = \lambda a \cdot aa$ has no normal form, because $\omega_2\omega_2$ reduces only to itself and it is not in normal form. When we reduce $\omega_3\omega_3$ with $\omega_3 = \lambda a \cdot aaa$, then the result will grow larger and larger. Along this line we will prove in chapter II, the following extreme result:

There exists a term M such that $\forall N \exists M' \; \lambda \vdash M \geqslant M'$ and N is subterm of M'. Such a term is called a universal generator.

1.2.18 Remarks [1)]

1. Apart from the proofs already mentioned two abstract forms of the Church-Rosser

---

1) (Added in proof.) Recently a very simple proof of the Church-Rosser theorem is given by Martin-Löf [1971]. See appendix II.

theorem were proved in Newman [1942] and Curry [1952] which were supposed to imply the original theorem as a corollary. However, as was pointed out by Schroer (see Rosser [1956]) and Newman [1952], it turned out that these general theorems did <u>not</u> have as corollary the original theorem.

Two adequate abstract forms of the Church-Rosser theorem were proved by Schroer [1965] and Hindley [1969].

Mitschke [1970] gave a new proof of the Church-Rosser theorem, which is conceptually simpler than the original one. In §1.5 we will use Mitschke's ideas to give a proof of the Church-Rosser theorem for combinatory logic.

Finally there is another proof of the Church-Rosser theorem by Rosen [1971] . He proves also an abstract form of the Church-Rosser property, which is applicable to the λ-calculus. But this application needs a construction similar to that of Mitschke [1970] and this makes the proof rather long. On the other hand, Rosen's general theorem is also applicable to other fields (like the McCarthy calculus of recursive definitions). See also Curry, Feys [1958] Ch 4 S and Kleene [1962] for historical remarks.

2. Before the Church-Rosser theorem was proved the consistency of combinatory logic was shown already by Curry [1930]. It was shown in Rosser [1935] that this implies the consistencyy of the λ-calculus.

   In part II of our thesis a very simple consistency proof for combinatory logic, due to Scott, is given.

§1.3. The λ-definability of the partial recursive functions. Undecidability results.

The (partial) functions f considered in this § are all number theoretic (i.e. $f: \omega^n \to \omega$).

1.3.1 Definition

We define some standard functions:

1) $U_i^n(x_1,\ldots,x_n) = x_i$ are the projection functions.

2) $S^+(x) = x+1$ is the successor function.

3) $Z(x) = 0$ is the zero function.

1.3.2 Definition

The partial recursive functions can be defined as the smallest class $\mathcal{R}$ of partial functions such that

1) $U_i^n \in \mathcal{R}$

2) $S^+ \in \mathcal{R}$

3) $Z \in \mathcal{R}$

4) If $g, h_1, \ldots, h_m \in \mathcal{R}$ and f is defined by
$f(x_1,\ldots,x_n) = g(h_1(x_1,\ldots,x_n),\ldots,h_m(x_1,\ldots,x_n))$
then $f \in \mathcal{R}$ ($\mathcal{R}$ is closed under substitution).

5) If $g,h \in \mathcal{R}$, g and h are total and f is defined by
$f(0,\vec{x}) = g(\vec{x})$ (where $\vec{x} = x_1,\ldots,x_n$)
$f(k+1,\vec{x}) = h(f(k,\vec{x}),k,\vec{x})$
then $f \in \mathcal{R}$ ($\mathcal{R}$ is closed under recursion).

6) If $g \in \mathcal{R}$, g is total and f is defined by
$f(\vec{x}) = \mu y[g(\vec{x},y) = 0]$
(i.e. the least y such that $g(\vec{x},y) = 0$; if there does not

exist such a y, then $\mu y[g(\vec{x},y) = 0]$ is undefined)

then $f \in \mathcal{R}$ ($\mathcal{R}$ is closed under minimalisation).

The primitive recursive functions are defined by 1) - 5) only. We write $f(\vec{x})\downarrow$ if $f(\vec{x})$ is defined and $f(\vec{x})\uparrow$ if $f(\vec{x})$ is undefined.

In order to show that the partial recursive functions are λ-definable, we will have to show a slightly stronger fact.

1.3.3 <u>Definition</u>

Let f be a partial function which is λ-definable by a term F. We say that F <u>strongly defines</u> f iff

$f(k_1,\ldots,k_n)\uparrow \Rightarrow \forall Z_1\ldots Z_s \quad F\underline{k}_1\ldots\underline{k}_n Z_1\ldots Z_s$ has no normal form.

In this case f is called <u>strongly λ-definable</u>.

Note 1. Our concept of strongly λ-definable should not be confused with that of Curry Hindley and Seldin [1971] Ch 13 A. Our notion of λ-definability corresponds to their strong definability.

2. If a total function is λ-definable it is automatically strongly λ-definable.

Now we will prove that the partial recursive functions are all strongly λ-definable. In order to do this we have to show that:

1) U_i^n, Z, S^+ are strongly λ-definable.

2) The strongly λ-definable functions are closed under substitution, recursion and minimalisation.

1.3.4 <u>Lemma</u>

The functions U_i^n, S^+, Z are λ-definable. (Hence they are strongly λ-definable.)

Proof.

1) U_i^n is defined by $\underline{U}_i^n = \lambda a_1,\ldots,a_n \cdot a_i$:

$$\lambda \vdash \underline{U}_i^n\ \underline{k}_1\ldots\underline{k}_n = (\lambda a_1\ldots a_n\cdot a_i)\underline{k}_1\ldots\underline{k}_n =$$
$$= (\lambda a_2\ldots a_n\cdot a_i)\underline{k}_2\ldots\underline{k}_n =$$
$$= \ldots$$
$$= (\lambda a_{i+1}\ldots a_n\cdot \underline{k}_i)\underline{k}_{i+1}\ldots\underline{k}_n =$$
$$= \ldots = \underline{k}_i$$

2) Z is defined by $\underline{Z} = \lambda a\ \underline{0}$:

$$\lambda \vdash \underline{Z}\ \underline{k} = \underline{0}.$$

3) S^+ is defined by $\underline{S}^+ = \ abc\cdot b(abc)$:

$$\lambda \vdash \underline{S}^+\ \underline{n} = \lambda bc\cdot b(\underline{n}bc) = \lambda bc\cdot b(b^n c)$$
$$= \lambda bc\cdot b^{n+1}c = \underline{n+1}.$$

⊠

1.3.5 Lemma

The strongly λ-definable functions are closed under substitution (i.e. if $g,h_1,\ldots,h_n$ are λ-definable and $f(\vec{x}) = g(h_1(\vec{x}),\ldots$ $\ldots,h_m(\vec{x}))$ (where $\vec{x} = x_1,\ldots,x_n$), then f is λ-definable).

Proof.

Let $g,h_1,\ldots,h_m$ be strongly λ-defined by $G,H_1,\ldots,H_m$ respectively. Then f is defined by

$$F = \lambda a_1\ldots a_n\cdot(H_1a_1\ldots a_nI)\ \ldots\ (H_ma_1\ldots a_nI)G(H_1a_1\ldots a_n)\ldots$$
$$\ldots(H_ma_1\ldots a_n)$$

For suppose that $f(k_1,\ldots,k_n) = k$.

Then $\forall i\ \exists n_i\quad h_i(k_1,\ldots,k_n) = n_i$, therefore $\lambda \vdash H_i\underline{k}_1,\ldots,\underline{k}_n = \underline{m}_i$.

Furthermore $g(n_1,\ldots,n_m) = k$. Thus

$$\lambda \vdash F\underline{k}_1\ldots\underline{k}_n = (H_1\underline{k}_1\ldots\underline{k}_nI)\ldots(H_m\underline{k}_1\ldots\underline{k}_nI)G(H_1\underline{k}_1\ldots\underline{k}_n)\ldots$$
$$\ldots(H_m\underline{k}_1\ldots\underline{k}_n)$$
$$= (\underline{n}_1I)\ \ldots(\underline{n}_mI)G\ \underline{n}_1\ldots\underline{n}_m$$

$= I^{n_1} \ldots I^{n_m} \underline{k}$

$= \underline{k}$

Suppose $f(k_1, \ldots, k_n)\uparrow$. Then there are two cases:

1. $\forall i \, \exists n_i \quad h_i(k_1, \ldots, k_n) = n_i$.

   Then $g(n_1, \ldots, n_m)\uparrow$ and

   $\lambda \vdash F\underline{k}_1 \ldots \underline{k}_n = G\underline{n}_1 \ldots \underline{n}_m$

   Hence $\forall Z_1 \ldots Z_s \quad F\underline{k}_1 \ldots \underline{k}_n \; Z_1 \ldots Z_s$ has no normal form, because G strongly defines g.

2. $h_i(k_1, \ldots, k_n)\uparrow$ for some i.

   Then $\forall Z_1 \ldots Z_s \quad (H_i\underline{k}_1 \ldots \underline{k}_n) Z_1 \ldots Z_s$ has no normal form.

   Hence $\forall Z_1 \ldots Z_s \quad F\underline{k}_1 \ldots \underline{k}_n \; Z_1 \ldots Z_s$ has no normal form.

   (For this case it was needed to introduce the notion of strong definability.) ☒

In the λ-calculus it is possible to define ordered pairs.

1.3.6 Definitions

$[M,N] = \lambda z \cdot zMN$, where $z \notin FV(MN)$

$K = \lambda ab \cdot a, \qquad \tau_1 = \lambda a \cdot aK$

$K' = \lambda ab \cdot b, \qquad \tau_2 = \lambda a \cdot aK'$

Then we have

$\lambda \vdash KMN = M$ hence $\lambda \vdash [M,N]K = M$, thus $\lambda \vdash \tau_1[M,N] = M$ and

$\lambda \vdash K'MN = N$ hence $\lambda \vdash [M,N]K' = N$, thus $\lambda \vdash \tau_2[M,N] = N$.

Hence $[M,N]$ is an ordered pair function with projections τ_1, τ_2.

Note that $M = [\tau_1 M, \tau_2 M]$ is not provable.

1.3.7 Theorem (Bernays)

The strongly λ-definable functions are closed under recursion.

Proof.

Because in 1.3.2. 5) only total functions are considered we do not need to bother about strong definability.

Let f be defined by

$f(0) = n_0$

$f(n+1) = g(f(n),n)$

and suppose g is λ-defined by G.

(For the sake of simplicity we treat the case that f has no additional parameters. The proof in the general case is analogous).

We will prove that f is λ-definable.

Consider $M = \lambda a[\underline{S}^+(\tau_1 a), G(\tau_2 a)(\tau_1 a)]$. Then M has the property

$\lambda \vdash M[\underline{n},\underline{f(n)}] = [\underline{S}^+\underline{n}, G\ \underline{f(n)}\ \underline{n}] = [\underline{n+1},\underline{f(n+1)}]$.

Now we have $\lambda \vdash [\underline{0},\underline{f(0)}] = [\underline{0},\underline{n}_0]$

$\lambda \vdash [1,\underline{f(1)}] = M[\underline{0},\underline{n}_0]$

$\lambda \vdash [\underline{2},\underline{f(2)}] = M[\underline{1},\underline{f(1)}] = M^2[\underline{0},\underline{n}_0]$

....

$\lambda \vdash [\underline{n},\underline{f(n)}] = M^n[\underline{0},\underline{n}_0] = \underline{n}\ M[\underline{0},\underline{n}_0]$

Hence

$\lambda \vdash \underline{f(n)} = \tau_2[\underline{n},\underline{f(n)}] = \tau_2(\underline{n}\ M[\underline{0},\underline{n}_0])$.

Therefore f can be λ-defined by

$F = \lambda a \cdot \tau_2(a\ M[\underline{0},\underline{n}_0])$. ⊠

By 1.3.4, 1.3.5 and 1.3.7 we can already state:

1.3.8 All primitive recursive functions are λ-definable.

1.3.9 Theorem

The strongly λ-definable functions are closed under minimalisation.

(This theorem was first proved for the λI-calculus in Kleene [1934]. We give here a simplification for the λK-calculus due to Turing [1937a]).

Proof.

Let $f(x) = \mu y[g(x,y) = 0]$ where g is a total λ-definable function. (Again for simplicity we suppose that f has only one argument.) We will prove that f is strongly λ-definable.

Let $g'(x,y) = sg(g(x,y))$ where $sg(0) = 0$ and $sg(n+1) = 1$. From 1.3.8 and 1.3.5 it follows that g' is λ-definable, say by G'. Hence

$$G'\underline{k}\ \underline{n} \equiv \begin{cases} \underline{0} & \text{if } g(k,n) = 0 \\ \underline{1} & \text{if } g(k,n) \neq 0. \end{cases}$$

By the fixed point theorem there exists a term M such that

$$\lambda \vdash M = \lambda ab \cdot G'ab(\lambda c\ Ma(\underline{S}^{+}c))b$$

(Define $N = \lambda m\ ab \cdot G'ab(\lambda c \cdot ma(\underline{S}^{+}c))b$ and take $M = FPN$.)

Define $F = \lambda a\ Ma\ \underline{0}$.

Then F strongly defines f:

$$\begin{aligned} \lambda \vdash F\underline{k} = M\underline{k}\ \underline{0} &= G'\underline{k}\ \underline{0}(\lambda c \cdot M\underline{k}(\underline{S}^{+}c))\underline{0} = \underline{0} && \text{if } g(k,0) = 0 \\ &= (\lambda c \cdot M\underline{k}(\underline{S}^{+}c))\underline{0} && \text{if } g(k,0) \neq 0 \\ = M\underline{k}\ \underline{1} &= G'\underline{k}\ \underline{1}(\lambda c \cdot M\underline{k}(\underline{S}^{+}c))\underline{1} = \underline{1} && \text{if } g(k,1) = 0 \\ &= (\lambda c \cdot M\underline{k}(\underline{S}^{+}c))\underline{1} && \text{if } g(k,1) \neq 0 \\ = M\underline{k}\ \underline{2} &= \\ &\text{etc.} \end{aligned}$$

If $f(k)\uparrow$ then $\forall y\ g'(k,y) = 1$, hence $\forall Z_1 \ldots Z_s\ F\underline{k}\ Z_1 \ldots Z_s$ has no normal form, as is readily seen. ⊠

From 1.3.4, 1.3.5, 1.3.7 and 1.3.9 we get:

1.3.10 <u>Theorem</u>

All partial recursive functions are λ-definable.

Remark. The converse of 1.3.10: All λ-definable functions are partial recursive, is intuitively clear from Church thesis. For a proof see Kleene [1936].

We now state some corollaries to 1.3.10 which concern undecidability.

Let $\ulcorner\ \urcorner$ denote the Gödel number of a term or formula in some Gödelisation. For the definition of some notions in recursion theory the reader is referred to Rogers [1967] Ch 7.

With the following we answer a question of Mostowski.

1.3.11 Theorem

The set $\{\ulcorner M = N \urcorner \mid \lambda \vdash M = N\}$ is 1-complete and hence creative.

Proof.

Let X be an arbitrary r.e. set.

Define $f(x) = \begin{cases} 0 & \text{if } x \in X \\ \uparrow & \text{else} \end{cases}$

Then f is partial recursive. Let f be defined by F.

Then

$$k \in X \Leftrightarrow f(k) = 0 \Leftrightarrow \lambda \vdash F\underline{k} = \underline{0}$$

Hence $X \leqslant_1 \{\ulcorner M = N \urcorner \mid \lambda \vdash M = N\}$ via the function $h(k) = \ulcorner F\underline{k} = \underline{0} \urcorner$.

1.3.12 Corollary

The λ-calculus is undecidable.

Grzegorczyk [1970] has proved even that the λ-calculus is essentially undecidable (see 1.3.17).

1.3.13 Lemma (Kleene [1936])

There exists a term E such that

$$\forall M[FV(M) = \emptyset \Rightarrow \exists n \quad \lambda \vdash E\underline{n} = M]$$

See for a proof Kleene[1936] theorem(24), pg.351 or Church[1941] theorem 14 III, pp.47-48.

1.3.14 Lemma

For any terms M_0, M_1 there exists a term M such that

$\lambda \vdash M\ \underline{0} = M_0$

$\lambda \vdash M\ \underline{1} = M_1$.

Proof.

Define $M = \lambda a \cdot a(KM_1)M_0$ (where K is defined as in 1.3.6).

Then $\lambda \vdash M\ \underline{0} = \underline{0}\ (KM_1)M_0 = M_0$

$\lambda \vdash M\ \underline{1} = \underline{1}\ (KM_1)M_0 = KM_1M_0 = M_1$. ⊠

1.3.15 Theorem (Scott [1963])

Let A be a set of terms such that

1) A is not trivial (i.e. $M_0 \in A$ and $M_1 \notin A$ for some M_0, M_1).

2) If $M \in A$ and $\lambda \vdash M = M'$, then $M' \in A$.

Then $\ulcorner A \urcorner = \{\ulcorner M \urcorner \mid M \in A\}$ is not recursive.

(Compare this theorem to the theorem of Rice [1953]).

Proof.

Suppose $\ulcorner A \urcorner$ is recursive and let $M_0 \in A$ and $M_1 \notin A$. By 1.3.14 there exists a term M such that $\lambda \vdash M\ \underline{0} = M_0$ and $\lambda \vdash M\ \underline{1} = M_1$.

Define $B = \{n \mid M(E\underline{n}\underline{n}) \notin A\}$, with E as in 1.3.13.

Then B is recursive, hence there exists a term $\underline{c}_B$ such that

$\lambda \vdash \underline{c}_B\underline{n} = \underline{0}$ if $n \in B$ and

$\lambda \vdash \underline{c}_B\underline{n} = \underline{1}$ if $n \notin B$.

We can assume that $FV(\underline{c}_B) = \emptyset$.

Let n_0 be such that $\lambda \vdash E\underline{n}_0 = \underline{c}_B$.

Then

$$n_0 \in B \Rightarrow \lambda \vdash E\underline{n}_0\underline{n}_0 = \underline{0} \Rightarrow \lambda \vdash M(E\underline{n}_0\underline{n}_0) = M_0 \Rightarrow$$

$$\Rightarrow M(E\underline{n}_0\underline{n}_0) \in A \Rightarrow n_0 \notin B$$

$$n_0 \notin B \Rightarrow \lambda \vdash E\underline{n}_0\underline{n}_0 = \underline{1} \Rightarrow \lambda \vdash M(E\underline{n}_0\underline{n}_0) = M_1 \Rightarrow$$

$$\Rightarrow M(E\underline{n}_0\underline{n}_0) \notin A \Rightarrow n_0 \in B.$$

This is a contradiction. ⊠

1.3.16 <u>Corollary</u> (Church [1936])

The set $\{\ulcorner M \urcorner \mid M$ has a normal form$\}$ is not recursive.

Proof.

Take $A = \{M \mid M$ has a normal form$\}$ in 1.3.15. ⊠

1.3.17 <u>Corollary</u> (Grzegorczyk [1970])

The λ-calculus is essentially undecidable (i.e. has no decidable consistent extension).

Proof.

Suppose T is a decidable consistent extension of the λ-calculus (i.e. the set of theorems of T is recursive).

Define $A = \{M \mid T \vdash M = \underline{0}\}$. Then $\ulcorner A \urcorner$ is recursive because T is. But A satisfies 1) and 2) of 1.3.15. Hence, $\ulcorner A \urcorner$ is not recursive. Contradiction. ⊠

Remark. 1.3.12, 1.3.15 and 1.3.17 were proved independently.

§1.4. Combinatory logic.

Combinatory logic is a theory closely related to the λ-calculus. Considerable parts of it were developed by Curry. See Curry Feys [1958] and Curry Hindley Seldin [1971] for an extensive treatment of the subject.

Combinatory logic is intended to be a foundation for mathematical logic. Therefore it includes "illative" notions corresponding to concepts ~~like~~ such as equality, quantification etcetera. However, we will be concerned only with the combinatorial part of combinatory logic or as Curry calls it: "pure combinatory logic". For illative combinatory logic the reader is referred to the above standard texts.

1.4.1 Definition

We define the following language L_H:

Alphabet:	a,b,c,...	variables
	I,K,S	constants
	(,)	improper symbols
	=	equality
	$\geqslant$	reduction

Terms: Terms are inductively defined by

1) any variable or constant is a term

2) if M,N are terms, then (MN) is a term.

Formulas: if M,N are terms, then $M = N$ and $M \geqslant N$ are formulas.

Again $M_1M_2\ldots M_n$ stands for $((..(M_1M_2)\ldots)M_n)$.

To be explicit terms of CL are called sometimes CL-terms, terms of the λ-calculus are called then λ-terms.

1.4.2 Definition

Combinatory logic (CL) is the theory defined in L_H by the following axioms and rules (see appendix).

I 1. $IM \geqslant M$

2. $KMN \geqslant M$

3. $SMNL \geqslant ML(NL)$

II Same as in 1.2.3.

III 1. Same as in 1.2.3

2. Same as in 1.2.3.

3. $\dfrac{MM \geqslant M'}{ZM \geqslant ZM'}$, $\dfrac{M \geqslant M'}{MZ \geqslant M'Z}$

4. Same as in 1.2.3.

In the above M, M', N, L, Z denote arbitrary terms.

Notation. We write $x \in M$ if x occurs in the term M.

As in §1.1. we can adjoin to CL extensionality.

1.4.3

$$\text{ext} \quad \frac{Mx = Nx \ , \ x \notin MN}{M = N}$$

CL (+ ext) $\vdash$ ... means that ... is provable in CL (+ ext).

For example

1.4.4

$$CL + ext \vdash S(S(KS)K)(KI) = I$$

Curry proved in his thesis that, from a finite number of such theorems as 1.4.4, extensionality is provable. These axioms are called the combinatory axioms. See Curry, Feys [1958] Ch 6 C.

We will show that the λ-calculus and combinatory logic are interpretable in each other.

1.4.5 <u>Theorem</u>

There exists a mapping ϕ: CL → λ (i.e. from the set of terms of L_H into the set of terms of L_K) such that

1. CL (+ ext) $\vdash M = N \Rightarrow \lambda$ (+ ext) $\vdash \phi(M) = \phi(N)$
2. CL $\vdash M \geqslant N \Rightarrow \lambda \vdash \phi(M) \geqslant \phi(N)$

Proof.

Define $\phi(x) = x$ for any variable x.

$\phi(I) = I \quad (\equiv \lambda a \cdot a)$

$\phi(K) = K \quad (\equiv \lambda ab \cdot a)$

$\phi(S) = S \quad (\equiv \lambda abc \cdot ac(bc))$

$\phi(MN) = \phi(M)\phi(N)$

Then it is clear that ϕ has the required properties.

Remark. The converse of 1. and 2. do not hold. For example:

$\lambda \vdash \phi(SKK) = \phi(I)$ but CL $\nvdash SKK = I$

as follows from the Church-Rosser theorem for CL (see §1.5.).

In order to obtain a reverse interpretation, we need first a simulation of the λ-operator in CL.

1.4.6 Definition

For any term M of L_H and any variable x we define inductively a term λ^*xM.

$\lambda^*x\ x = I$

$\lambda^*x\ M = KM$ if $x \notin M$

$\lambda^*x\ (MN) = S(\lambda^*x\ M)(\lambda^*x\ N)$

Remarks.

1. This method of defining λ-terms with I, K and S comes from Schönfinkel [1924], although it is not generally formulated there.

2. It is possible to formulate CL with K and S alone. In that case we define

   $\lambda^*x\ X = SKK$

   because $CL \vdash SKK\ x = x$

1.4.7 Lemma

λ^* has the following properties:

1) x does not occur in $\lambda^*x\ M$

2) $\lambda^*x\ M = \lambda^*y[x/y]M$ if $y \notin M$

3) $CL \vdash (\lambda^*x\ M)N = [x/N]M$

4) $\lambda^*x[y/N]M = [y/N]\lambda^*x\ M$ if $x \neq y$ and $x \notin N$.

Proof.

The proof uses induction on the complexity of M and is in all the four cases similar.

As an example we prove 4).

$M = x$ Then $\lambda^*x[y/N]M = \lambda^*x\ x = I$

and $[y/N]\lambda^*x\ M = [y/N]I = I$.

$x \notin M$ Then $\lambda^*x[y/N]M = K[y/N]M = [y/N]KM$

and $[y/N]\lambda^*x\ M = [y/N]KM$.

$M = M_1M_2$ and $x \in M$.

Then $\lambda^*x[y/N]M = \lambda^*x[y/N]M_1M_2$

$= \lambda^*x([y/N]M_1[y/N]M_2)$

$= S(\lambda^*x[y/N]M_1)(\lambda^*x[y/N]M_2)$

$= S([y/N]\lambda^*x\ M_1)([y/N]\lambda^*x\ M_2)$ by the induction hypothesis

$= [y/N]\ S(\lambda^*x\ M_1)(\lambda^*x\ M_2)$

$= [y/N]\lambda^*x\ M$ ⊠

1.4.8 Lemma

$$\frac{M = N}{\lambda^* x\ M = \lambda^* x\ N}$$ is a derived rule for CL + ext

Proof.

Let CL + ext $\vdash$ M = N

Then CL + ext $\vdash$ $(\lambda^*x\ M)x = M = N = (\lambda^*x\ N)x$

Hence by ext

CL + ext $\vdash \lambda^*x\ M = \lambda^*x\ N$ ⊠

1.4.9 Theorem

There exists a mapping ψ: $\lambda \to$ CL such that

λ + ext $\vdash M = N \Rightarrow$ CL + ext $\vdash \psi(M) = \psi(N)$

Proof.

Define ψ inductively:

$\psi(x) \quad = x$ for any variable x

$\psi(MN) \quad = \psi(M)\psi(N)$

$\psi(\lambda x\ M) = \lambda^*x\ \psi(M)$.

Sublemma

$\psi([x/N]M) \equiv [x/\psi(N)]\ \psi(M)$ if $BV(M) \cap FV(N) = \emptyset$.

Proof.

Induction on the structure of M. (Use: $x \in FV(M) \Leftrightarrow x \in \psi(M)$ and 1.4.7.4).) Now suppose λ + ext $\vdash M = N$. We will show by induction on the length l of the proof of M = N that

(1) CL + ext $\vdash \psi(M) = \psi(N)$.

l = 0 M = N is axiom of the λ-calculus.

case 1. $M \equiv N$, then $\psi(M) \equiv \psi(N)$,

hence CL $\vdash \psi(M) = \psi(N)$.

case 2. $M \equiv \lambda x\ P$ and $N \equiv \lambda y[x/y]P$, with $y \notin FV(P)$.

Then $\psi(M) \equiv \lambda^* x\ \psi(P)$ and

$\psi(N) \equiv \lambda^* y[x/y]\psi(P)$ by the sublemma.

Hence by 1.4.7.2) $CL \vdash \psi(M) = \psi(N)$.

case 3. $M \equiv (\lambda x\ P)Q$ and $N \equiv [x/Q]P$, with

$BV(P) \cap FV(Q) = \emptyset$.

Then $CL \vdash \psi(M) = (\lambda^* x\ \psi(P))\psi(Q) = [x/\psi(Q)]\psi(P)$

by 1.4.7. 3)

and $CL \vdash \psi(N) = \psi([x/Q]P) = [x/\psi(Q)]\psi(P)$ by the sublemma, hence $CL \vdash \psi(M) = \psi(N)$.

<u>$l = k$</u> and the theorem holds for $l' < k$.

$M = N$ is the consequence of a rule of inference. Because of 1.4.8 the rules of inference for the λ-calculus + ext and CL + ext are the same, hence (1) follows immediately by the induction hypothesis.

<u>Remarks</u>

1. It is not true that

   $\lambda \vdash M = N \Rightarrow CL \vdash \psi(M) = \psi(N)$.

   For example $\lambda \vdash \lambda a((\lambda b \cdot b)a) = \lambda a \cdot a$.

   But $CL \nvdash S(KI)I = I$ as follows from §1.5.

2. Also we do not have $\lambda \vdash M \geqslant N \Rightarrow CL \vdash \psi(M) \geqslant \psi(N)$.

   Because of this peculiarity, a special theory of <u>strong</u> reducibility (notation: $\succ$) for CL is developed.

   Then we have $\lambda \vdash M \geqslant N \Rightarrow \psi(M) \succ \psi(N)$ in CL.

   (See Curry Feys [1958] Ch 6 F.)

   In order to distinguish it from $\succ$, $\geqslant$ is called <u>weak</u> reduction.

1.4.10 Theorem

1) $\lambda \vdash \phi(\psi(M)) \geqslant M$

2) $CL + ext \vdash \psi(\phi(M)) = M$

Proof.

1) Induction on the structure of M.

Prove first $\lambda \vdash \phi(\lambda^* x\ M) \geqslant \lambda x\ \phi(M)$ for M a term of CL.

2) Induction on the structure of M.

The essential step is to show that

$CL + ext \vdash S = \lambda^* xyz \cdot xz(yz)$ and

$CL + ext \vdash K = \lambda^* xy \cdot x$. ⊠

Remark. It is not true that $CL \vdash \psi(\phi(M)) = M$.

Take for example $M \equiv K$.

Then $CL \nvdash S(KK)I = K$ as follows from §1.5.

1.4.11 Corollary

The λ-calculus + ext and CL + ext are equivalent:

1) $CL + ext \vdash \psi(\phi(M)) = M$

2) $\lambda + ext \vdash \phi(\psi(M)) = M$

3) $CL + ext \vdash M = N \Longleftrightarrow \lambda + ext \vdash \phi(M) = \phi(N)$

4) $\lambda + ext \vdash M = N \Longleftrightarrow CL + ext \vdash \psi(M) = \psi(N)$

Proof.

1) and 2) follow directly from 1.4.10.

3) $CL + ext \vdash M = N \Rightarrow \lambda + ext \vdash \phi(M) = \phi(N)$ by 1.4.5

$\Rightarrow CL + ext \vdash \psi(\phi(M)) = \psi(\phi(N))$ by 1.4.9

$\Rightarrow CL + ext \vdash M = N$ by 1).

4) Similar proof as 3). ⊠

Because of this equivalence the names for the λ-calculus and combinatory logic are sometimes interchanged.
Scott [1970] in fact constructs a model for combinatory logic + extensionality.

1.4.12 Definition

1) A term M of CL is in normal form if it has no part of the form IM, KMN or SMNL.
2) A term M has a normal form if there exists a term M' in normal form such that CL ⊢ M = M'.

Remark. The terms in normal form can be defined inductively as follows:

1) I, K and S are in normal form
2) If M is in normal form, then KM and SM are in normal form
3) If M and N are in normal form then SMN is in normal form.

Similarly to 1.2.5 we have

1.4.13 Theorem

If M is in normal form and if CL ⊢ M ⩾ N, then M ≡ N.

As in §1.1. we can represent the natural numbers in CL. Then we can define similar to definition 1.1.14 the concept of CL-definability. Analogous to §1.3. it is possible to prove that the partial CL-definable functions are exactly the partial recursive functions. See Curry Hindley Seldin [1971] Ch 13 for details.

§1.5. The Church-Rosser property for combinatory logic à la Mitschke.

In this § we will use the ideas of Mitschke [1970] to give a proof of the Church-Rosser property for combinatory logic (with weak reduction).

In Hindley [197?] this will be proved as an application of an abstract Church-Rosser theorem proved in Hindley [1969].

(Added in print. We have realized too late that for the combinatory equivalent of the λI-calculus the Church-Rosser property was already proved in Rosser [1935] T 12, p.144. This proof carries over immediately to CL (cf.Curry,Hindley,Seldin [1971]). Compare Rossers proof with that of Martin-Löf in appendix II.)

The theorem we are about to prove is:

1.5.1 Theorem (Church-Rosser property for CL)

If CL $\vdash$ M = N, then there exists a term Z such that CL $\vdash$ M $\geqslant$ Z and CL $\vdash$ N $\geqslant$ Z.

In order to show this we have to define several auxiliary languages and theories.

1.5.2 Definition

CL' is an extension of CL where the alphabet of CL' has the additional symbol "$\geqslant_1$" (one step reduction); the language of CL' has the same terms as CL; CL' has as extra formulas M $\geqslant_1$ N (for arbitrary terms M and N).

CL' has the following axioms and rules (see appendix):

I 1. IM $\geqslant_1$ M

2. KMN $\geqslant_1$ M

3. SMNL $\geqslant_1$ ML(NL)

II Same as in 1.4.2.

III Same as in 1.4.2.

IV 1. $M \geqslant_1 M$

2. $\dfrac{M \geqslant_1 M'}{ZM \geqslant_1 ZM'}$, $\dfrac{M \geqslant_1 M'}{MZ \geqslant_1 M'Z}$

3. $\dfrac{M \geqslant_1 M'}{M \geqslant M'}$

Again M, M', N, L, Z denote arbitrary terms.

1.5.3 <u>Lemma</u>

CL' is a conservative extension of CL. Hence in order to prove 1.5.1 it is sufficient to prove the Church-Rosser property for CL'.

Proof.

First show that $CL' \vdash M \geqslant_1 N \Rightarrow CL \vdash M \geqslant N$.

Then the rest follows easily. ☒

Now we will introduce a theory CL* which plays the same role as λ* in Mitschke [1970].

1.5.4 <u>Definition</u>

We define the following language L_H*.

Alphabet: The alphabet of CL' together with the extra symbol ",".

Terms: Terms are inductively defined by

1) Any variable or constant is a term.

2) If M and N are terms, then (MN) is a term.

3) If M, N and L are terms, then S(M,N,L) is a term.

Formulas: If M and N are terms, then

$M \geqslant_1 N$, $M \geqslant N$ and $M = N$ are formulas.

1.5.5 <u>Definition</u>

CL^* is the theory with the language $L_H{}^*$ defined by the following axioma and rules (see appendix)

I 1. $IM \geqslant_1 M$

2. $KMN \geqslant_1 M$

3. $SMNL \geqslant_1 \hat{S}(M,N,L)$

II Same as in 1.4.2 II

III Same as in 1.4.2 III

IV 1., 2., 3. Same as in 1.5.2 IV

4. $\dfrac{M \geqslant_1 M'}{S(M,N,L) \geqslant_1 S(M',N,L)}$, $\dfrac{N \geqslant_1 N'}{S(M,N,L) \geqslant_1 S(M,N',L)}$

$\dfrac{L \geqslant_1 L'}{S(M,N,L) \geqslant_1 S(M,N,L')}$

M, M', N, N', L, L' and Z denoting arbitrary terms.

The essential axiom of this theory is I 3. It freezes the action of S.

Our method of proving 1.5.1 is the following:
First, we (almost) prove the Church-Rosser property for CL^*; then with the help of an homomorphism argument, we obtain the corresponding result for CL', and hence, by 1.5.3 for CL.

1.5.6 <u>Lemma</u>

$CL^* \vdash M \geqslant_1 N \iff$ there exists a term L with exactly one occurrence of a variable x and terms N,N' such that $M \equiv [x/N]L$, $M' \equiv [x/N']L$ and $N \geqslant_1 N'$ is an axiom of CL^*.

Proof.

⇒ Induction on the length of proof of $M \geqslant_1 M'$.

⇐ Induction on the structure of L. ☒

1.5.7 Lemma

If $CL^* \vdash M_1 \geqslant_1 M_2$ and $CL^* \vdash M_1 \geqslant_1 M_3$, then there exists a term M_4, such that

$CL^* \vdash M_2 \geqslant_1 M_4$ and $CL^* \vdash M_3 \geqslant_1 M_4$ (see fig.1)

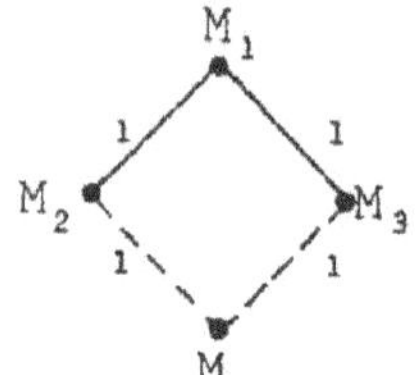

Figure 1

Proof.

First we consider the possibility that $M_1 \geqslant_1 M_2$ is an axiom.

(By repeated use of 1.5.6 we obtain the subcases.)

case 1. $M_1 \equiv IM$, $M_2 \equiv M$

subcase 1.1. $M_3 \equiv M_1$ or $M_3 \equiv M_2$. Take $M_4 \equiv M_2$.

subcase 1.2. $M_3 \equiv IM'$ and $CL^* \vdash M \geqslant_1 M'$. Take $M_4 \equiv M'$.

case 2. $M_1 \equiv KMN$, $M_2 \equiv M$

subcase 2.1. $M_3 \equiv M_1$ or $M_3 \equiv M_2$. Take $M_4 \equiv M_2$.

subcase 2.2. $M_3 \equiv KM'N$ and $CL^* \vdash M \geqslant_1 M'$. Take $M_4 \equiv M'$.

subcase 2.3. $M_3 \equiv KMN'$ and $CL^* \vdash N \geqslant_1 N'$. Take $M_4 \equiv M$.

case 3. $M_1 \equiv SMNL$, $M_2 \equiv S(M,N,L)$

subcase 3.1. $M_3 \equiv M_1$ or $M_3 \equiv M_2$. Take $M_4 \equiv M_2$.

subcase 3.2. $M_3 \equiv SM'NL$ and $CL^* \vdash M \geqslant_1 M'$.

Take $M_4 \equiv S(M',N,L)$

subcases 3.3,3.4 $M_3 \equiv SMN'L$ or $M_3 \equiv SMNL'$
Similar to subcase 3.2.

case 4. $M_1 \equiv M_2$. Take $M_4 \equiv M_3$.

Now we have proved that the lemma for $M_1 \geqslant_1 M_2$ is an axiom. Since $CL^* \vdash M_1 \geqslant_1 M_2$ it follows from 1.5.6 that $M_1 \equiv ...M...$, $M_2 \equiv ...$ $...M'...$ and $M \geqslant_1 M'$ is an axiom of CL^*.

case 1. $M_3 \equiv M_1$ or $M_3 \equiv M_2$. Take $M_4 \equiv M_2$.

case 2. $M_1 \equiv ...N...$, $M_3 \equiv ...N'...$ and $N \geqslant_1 N'$ is an axiom of CL^*.

subcase 2.1. M and N are disjoint subterms of M_1.

Then $M_1 \equiv ...M ...N ...$,

$M_2 \equiv ...M'...N ...$ and

$M_3 \equiv ...M...N'...$.

Take $M_4 \equiv ...M'...N'...$.

subcase 2.2. N is a subterm of M.

Then $M \geqslant_1 M'$ is an axiom, and

$CL^* \vdash M \geqslant_1 M''$

by the reduction $CL^* \vdash N \geqslant_1 N'$.

Hence there exists a term M''' such that

$CL^* \vdash M' \geqslant_1 M'''$ and

$CL^* \vdash M'' \geqslant_1 M'''$.

Take $M_4 \equiv ...M'''...$.

subcase 2.3. M is a subterm of N.

Analogous to subcase 2.2. ⊠

1.5.8 Lemma

If $CL^* \vdash M_1 \geqslant M_2$ and $CL^* \vdash M_1 \geqslant M_3$ then there exists a term M_4 such that

(∗) $CL^* \vdash M_2 \geqslant M_4$ and $CL^* \vdash M_3 \geqslant M_4$.

Proof.

Note that $CL^* \vdash M_1 \geqslant M_2 \iff \exists N_1...N_k$ $CL^* \vdash M_1 \equiv N_1 \geqslant_1 N_2 \geqslant_1 ...$ $... \geqslant_1 N_k \equiv M_2$.

The same holds for $CL^* \vdash M_1 \geqslant M_3$.

Then repeated use of 1.5.7 yields (*). (See fig. 2.)

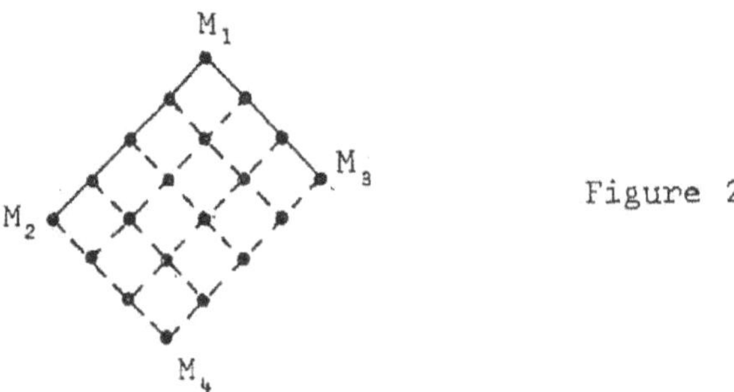

Figure 2.

⊠

Remark. 1.5.7 does not hold for CL', but only

$CL' \vdash M_1 \geqslant_1 M_2$ and $CL' \vdash M_1 \geqslant_1 M_3 \Rightarrow$

$CL' \vdash M_2 \geqslant M_4$ and $CL' \vdash M_3 \geqslant M_4$ for some term M_4.

Therefore an analogue of 1.5.8 for CL' is much harder to prove. From 1.5.8 we can easily derive the Church-Rosser property for CL*. However we do not need to do so.

1.5.9 Definition

We define inductively a mapping Θ: CL* → CL' (in fact from the set of terms of CL* into the set of terms of CL'):

$$\Theta(c) = c \quad \text{if } c \text{ is a variable or constant}$$

$$\Theta(MN) = \Theta(M)\Theta(N)$$

$$\Theta(S,M,N,L)) = \Theta(M)\Theta(L)(\Theta(N)\Theta(L))$$

It is clear that if M is a term of CL', then $\Theta(M) = M$.

1.5.10 Lemma

1) $CL^* \vdash M \geqslant_1 N \Rightarrow CL' \vdash \Theta(M) \geqslant \Theta(N)$

2) $CL^* \vdash M \geqslant N \Rightarrow CL' \vdash \Theta(M) \geqslant \Theta(N)$

3) $CL^* \vdash M = N \Rightarrow CL' \vdash \Theta(M) = \Theta(N)$

Proof.

In all cases the result follows by induction on the length of proof in CL*. ⊠

1.5.11 Lemma

If CL' ⊢ $M_1 \geqslant_1 M_2$ then there exists a term M_2^* of CL* such that CL* ⊢ $M_1 \geqslant_1 M_2^*$ and $\Theta(M_2^*) \equiv M_2$ (see fig. 3).

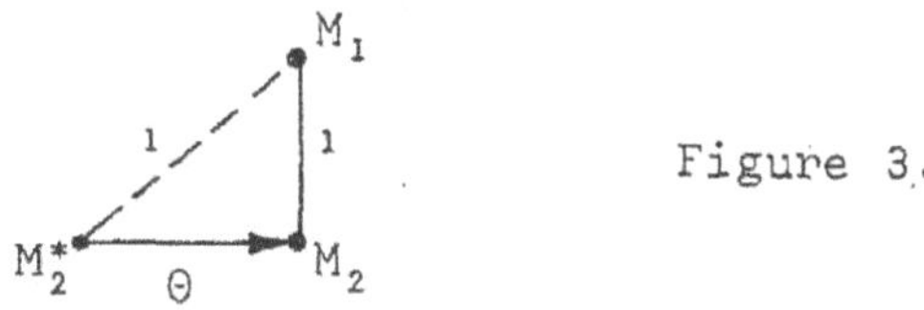

Figure 3.

Proof.

Induction on the length of proof of $M_1 \geqslant_1 M_2$. Suppose first that $M_1 \geqslant_1 M_2$ is an axiom of CL'.

case 1,2. $M_1 \equiv IM$ or $M_1 \equiv KMN$. Take $M_2^* \equiv M$.

case 3. $M_1 \equiv SMNL$, $M_2 \equiv ML(NL)$. Take $M_2^* \equiv S(M,N,L)$.

case 4. $M_1 \equiv M_2$. Take $M_2^* \equiv M_2$.

Suppose now that $M_1 \geqslant_1 M_2$ is $ZM_1' \geqslant_1 ZM_2'$ and is a direct consequence of $M_1' \geqslant_1 M_2'$.

By the induction hypothesis there exists a term $M_2'^*$ such that CL* ⊢ $M_1' \geqslant M_2'^*$ and $\Theta(M_2'^*) \equiv M_2'$. Then take $M_2^* \equiv ZM_2'^*$.

The case that $M_1 \geqslant_1 M_2$ is $M_1'Z \geqslant_1 M_2'Z$ is treated analogously. ⊠

1.5.12 Definition

We write $M \geqslant^* N$ for

$\exists M^*, N^*$ CL* ⊢ $M^* \geqslant N^*$ and $\Theta(M^*) \equiv M$, $\Theta(N^*) \equiv N$.

1.5.13 Main Lemma

Suppose $M \geqslant^* N$.

Then there exists a term N_1^* such that

CL* ⊢ $M \geqslant N_1^*$ and $\Theta(N_1^*) \equiv N$ (see fig. 4.)

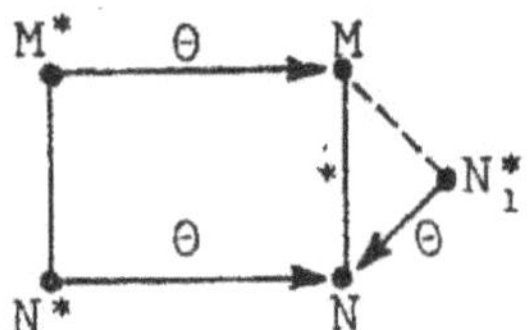

Figure 4

We will postpone the proof of the main lemma until 1.5.18.

1.5.14 <u>Lemma</u>

If $CL' \vdash M_1 \geqslant_1 M_2$ and $CL' \vdash M_1 \geqslant M_3$ then there exists a term M_4 such that

$CL' \vdash M_2 \geqslant M_4$ and $M_3 \geqslant^* M_4$, and hence by 1.5.10 2)

$CL' \vdash M_3 \geqslant M_4$.

Proof.

$CL' \vdash M_1 \geqslant M_3 \Leftrightarrow \exists N_1 \ldots N_k \quad CL' \vdash M_1 \equiv N_1 \geqslant_1 N_2 \geqslant_1 \ldots \geqslant_1 N_k \equiv M_3$.

We prove the lemma by induction on k.

If $k = 1$ then $M_1 \equiv M_3$ and we can take $M_4 \equiv M_2$, then $M_3 \geqslant^* M_4$ follows from 1.5.11.

Suppose now that $\exists N_1 \ldots N_{k+1} \quad CL' \vdash M_1 \equiv N_1 \geqslant_1 \ldots \geqslant_1 N_{k+1} \equiv M_3$.

By the induction hypothesis, there exists a term N_k' such that $CL' \vdash M_2 \geqslant N_k'$ and $N_k \geqslant^* N_k'$.

By 1.5.13 there exists a $N_k'^*$ such that

$CL^* \vdash N_k \geqslant N_k'^*$ and $\Theta(N_k'^*) = N_k'$ (see fig. 5).

By 1.5.11 there exists a N_{k+1}^* such that

$CL^* \vdash N_k \geqslant N_{k+1}^*$ and $\Theta(N_{k+1}^*) = N_{k+1}$ (see fig. 5).

Now it follows from 1.5.8 that there exists a $N_{k+1}'^*$ such that

$CL^* \vdash N_k'^* \geqslant N_{k+1}'^*$ and $CL^* \vdash N_{k+1}^* \geqslant N_{k+1}'^*$.

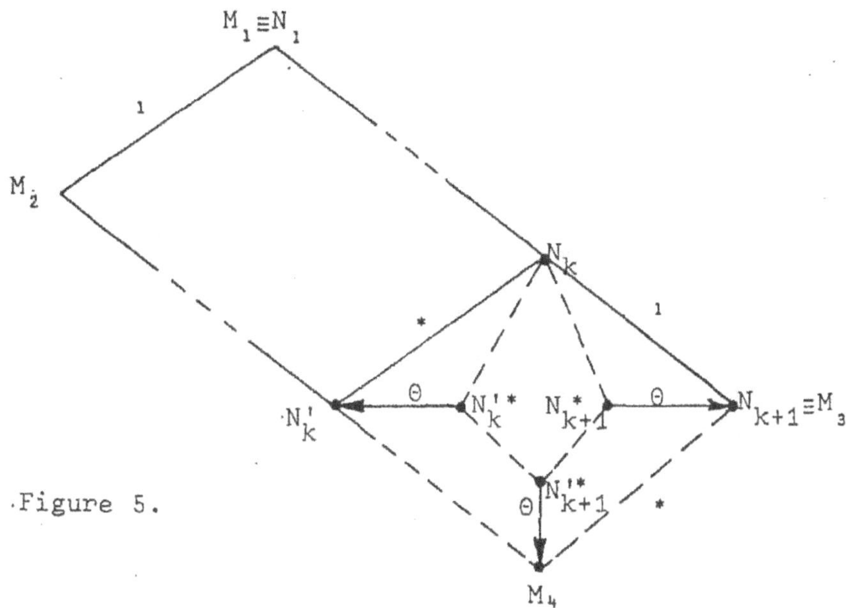

Figure 5.

Take $M_4 \equiv \Theta(N'^*_{k+1})$, then $CL' \vdash N'_k \geqslant M_4$, by 1.5.10 2), and hence $CL' \vdash M_2 \geqslant M_4$ and $M_3 \geqslant^* M_4$. ⊠

1.5.15 Lemma

If $CL' \vdash M_1 \geqslant M_2$ and $CL' \vdash M_1 \geqslant M_3$ then there exists a M_4 such that $CL' \vdash M_2 \geqslant M_4$ and $CL' \vdash M_3 \geqslant M_4$.

Proof.

$CL' \vdash M_1 \geqslant M_2 \iff \exists N_1 \ldots N_k \quad CL' \vdash M_1 \equiv N_1 \geqslant_1 \ldots \geqslant_1 N_k \equiv M_2$.

The result follows easily from 1.5.14, using induction to k. ⊠

1.5.16 Theorem (Church-Rosser property for CL')

If $CL' \vdash M = N$, then there exists a term Z such that $CL' \vdash M \geqslant Z$ and $CL' \vdash N \geqslant Z$.

Proof.

Induction on the length of proof of $M = N$.

case 1. $M \equiv N$. Take $Z \equiv M$.

case 2. $M = N$ is a direct consequence of $N = M$. By the induction hypothesis there exists a Z such that $CL' \vdash N \geqslant Z$ and $CL' \vdash M \geqslant Z$.

case 3. $M = N$ is a direct consequence of $M = L$ and $L = N$. By the induction hypothesis there exists terms Z_1, Z_2 such that $CL' \vdash M \geqslant Z_1$, $CL' \vdash L \geqslant Z$, $CL' \vdash L \geqslant Z_2$ and $CL' \vdash N \geqslant Z_2$ (see fig. 6).

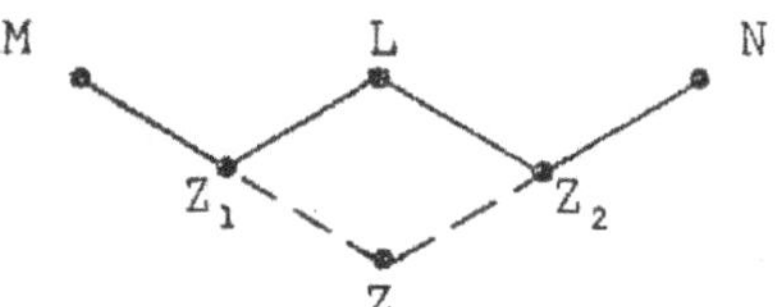

Figure 6.

By 1.5.15 there exists a Z such that $CL' \vdash Z_1 \geqslant Z$ and $CL' \vdash Z_2 \geqslant Z$, hence $CL' \vdash M \geqslant Z$ and $CL' \vdash N \geqslant Z$.

case 4. $M = N$ is $Z_1M' = Z_1N'$ (or $M'Z_1 = N'Z_1$) and is a direct consequence of $M' = N'$.
By the induction hypothesis there exists a term Z' such that $CL' \vdash M' \geqslant Z'$ and $CL' \vdash N' \geqslant Z'$.
Take $Z \equiv Z_1Z'$ (resp. $\equiv Z'Z_1$)

case 5. $M = N$ is a direct consequence of $M \geqslant N$. Take $Z \equiv N$. ⊠

1.5.17 <u>Corollary</u>

The Church-Rosser property for CL (see 1.5.1) holds.

Proof.

This follows from 1.5.16 by 1.5.3. ⊠

In the remainder of this section we will prove the main lemma. In order to do this, we introduce a new theory <u>CL*</u>.

1.5.18 Definition

We define the following language $\underline{L}_H^*$.

Alphabet: The alphabet for L_H^* , with as extra symbol "_".

Terms are inductively defined by

1), 2), 3) same clauses as in definition 1.5.4.

4) If S(M,N,L) is a term, then $\underline{S(M,N,L)}$ is a term.

Formulas are defined in the same way as in 1.5.4.

1.5.19 Definition (see appendix)

$\underline{CL}^*$ is a theory in $\underline{L}_H^*$ defined by the same axioms and rules as CL^* except that

I 3 is replaced by

I 3'. $SMNL \geqslant_1 \underline{S(M,N,L)}$

and there are the additional rules:

IV 5 . $$\frac{M \geqslant_1 M'}{\underline{S(M,N,L)} \geqslant_1 \underline{S(M',N,L)}} , \quad \frac{N \geqslant_1 N'}{\underline{S(M,N,L)} \geqslant_1 \underline{S(M,N',L)}}$$

$$\frac{L \geqslant_1 L'}{\underline{S(M,N,L)} \geqslant_1 \underline{S(M,N,L')}}$$

1.5.20 Definition

We define inductively two mappings $\underline{\Theta}$ and $|\ldots|$: $\underline{CL}^* \to CL^*$ as follows:

$\underline{\Theta}(c) = c$ if c is a variable or constant

$\underline{\Theta}(MN) = \underline{\Theta}(M)\underline{\Theta}(N)$

$\underline{\Theta}(S(M,N,L)) = \underline{\Theta}(M)\underline{\Theta}(L)(\underline{\Theta}(N)\underline{\Theta}(L))$

$\underline{\Theta}(\underline{S(M,N,L)}) = S(\underline{\Theta}(M),\underline{\Theta}(N),\underline{\Theta}(L))$

$|c| = c$ if c is a variable or constant

$|MN| = |M||N|$

$|S(M,N,L)| = S(|M|,|N|,|L|)$

$|\underline{S(M,N,L)}| = |S(M,N,L)|$

$|M|$ is apart from the underlining the same as M.

1.5.21 Lemma

1) $\Theta(\underline{\Theta}(M)) = \Theta(|M|)$ for all terms M of $\underline{CL}^*$.

2) $\underline{\Theta}(M) = \Theta(M)$ if M is a term of CL^*.

Proof.

Induction on the structure of M. ☒

1.5.22 Lemma

If $CL^* \vdash M_1 \geqslant_1 M_2$ or $CL^* \vdash M_1 \geqslant M_2$, then there exists a term M_2' of $\underline{CL}^*$ such that $|M_2'| = M_2$ and $\underline{CL}^* \vdash M_1 \geqslant M_2'$.

Proof.

Induction on the length of proof of $M_1 \geqslant_1 M_2$ or $M_1 \geqslant M_2$. ☒

1.5.23 Lemma

If $\underline{CL}^* \vdash M_1 \geqslant_1 M_2$ or $\underline{CL}^* \vdash M_1 \geqslant M_2$, then $CL^* \vdash \underline{\Theta}(M_1) \geqslant \underline{\Theta}(M_2)$.

Proof.

Induction on the length of proof of $M_1 \geqslant_1 M_2$ or $M_1 \geqslant M_2$. ☒

Now we are able to prove the main lemma.

1.5.13 Main Lemma.

If $M \geqslant^* N$, then there exists a term N^* such that

$CL^* \vdash M \geqslant N^*$ and $\Theta(N^*) = N$.

Proof.

Since $M \geqslant^* N$, there are terms M_1, N_1 of CL^* such that

$CL^* \vdash M_1 \geqslant N_1$ and $\Theta(M_1) = M$, $\Theta(N_1) = N$.

By 1.5.22 there exists a term N_1' such that $|N_1'| = N_1$, and $\underline{CL}^* \vdash M_1 \geq N_1'$.

By 1.5.23 it follows that $CL^* \vdash \underline{\Theta}(M_1) \geq \underline{\Theta}(N_1')$.

Take $N^* = \underline{\Theta}(N_1')$.

By 1.5.21 2) we have $\underline{\Theta}(M_1) = \Theta(M_1) = M$, hence

$CL^* \vdash M \geq N^*$.

By 1.5.21 1) we have $\Theta(N^*) = \Theta(\underline{\Theta}(N_1')) = \Theta(|N_1'|) = \Theta(N_1) = N$. ⊠

Remarks.

The idea of using CL^*, Θ and the main lemma is taken from Mitschke [1970] . (He formulated them for the λ-calculus.) The proof of the main lemma is new.

More extensive use of auxiliary theories like $\underline{CL}^*$ will be made several times in the sequel.

CHAPTER II

The ω-rule for combinatory logic and λ-calculus

§2.1. The ω-rule.

2.1.1 Definition

A term M of the λ-calculus is called closed if FV(M) = ∅.
A term M of CL is called closed if no variable occurs in M.

2.1.2 Definition

We can extend the λ-calculus or CL with the following rule, which we call the ω-rule,

$$\omega\text{-rule} \qquad \frac{MZ = NZ \quad \text{for all closed } Z}{M = N}$$

We write λω or CLω for the λ-calculus or CL extended with the ω-rule.

It is clear that the ω-rule implies extensionality. For this reason it does not matter whether we consider λω or CLω, because the λ-calculus and CL are equivalent when we have extensionality (1.4.11). In general we will formulate and prove results about the ω-rule in CL. However when it is easier or even necessary we do this in the λ-calculus.

2.1.3 Definition

1. CL is ω-consistent if CLω is consistent.
2. CL is ω-complete if the ω-rule is derivable in CL + ext (i.e. if CL + ext ⊢ MZ = NZ for all closed Z ⇒ CL + ext ⊢ M = N).

In a personal communication professor Curry suggested the possibility that CL is ω-complete.

In this chapter we will prove:

1. CL is ω-consistent (§§2.2, 2.3).
2. The ω-rule is derivable in λ + ext for a large class of terms M,N (in fact for all terms which are not universal generators) (§§2.4, 2.5).

It is still an open question whether CL is ω-complete [1].

As a corollary to the following theorem of Böhm [1968] which we state here without a proof, we can show that the ω-rule holds in λ + ext for terms having a normal form. This was suggested to us by R.Hindley.

2.1.4 Theorem (Böhm [1968]. Cf. Curry, Hindley, Seldin [1971] Ch.11 F.)

Let M,N be closed λ-terms in $\beta\eta$-normal form such that $M \not\equiv_{\alpha} N$. Then there exists closed terms $Z_1, \ldots, Z_n$ $(n \geqslant 1)$ such that for variables x,y

$$\lambda \vdash MZ_1 \ldots Z_n xy = x \quad \text{and}$$
$$\lambda \vdash NZ_1 \ldots Z_n xy = y \ .$$

2.1.5 Corollary

For closed λ-terms M,N which have a β-normal form the ω-rule is provable i.e. if $\lambda + \text{ext} \vdash MZ = NZ$ for all closed Z, then $\lambda + \text{ext} \vdash M = N$.

---

1) However there is a rumour that CL is not ω-complete.

Proof.

By 1.2.8 it follows that both M,N have a βη-normal form

hence $\lambda + ext \vdash M \geqslant M_1$, $\lambda + ext \vdash N \geqslant N_1$ where M_1, N_1 are closed and in normal forms.

Suppose that $M_1 \not\equiv_\alpha N_1$.

Then by the theorem of Böhm it follows that there exists closed terms $Z_1, \ldots, Z_n$ such that

$$\lambda \vdash M_1 Z_1 \ldots Z_n xy = x \quad \text{and}$$

$$\lambda \vdash N_1 Z_1 \ldots Z_n xy = y \ .$$

From the assumption $\lambda + ext \vdash MZ = NZ$ for all closed Z it follows that $\lambda + ext \vdash M_1 Z_1 = N_1 Z_1$. Hence $\lambda + ext \vdash x = M_1 Z_1 \ldots Z_n xy = N_1 Z_1 \ldots Z_n xy = y$ which contradicts the consistency of $\lambda + ext$.

Hence $M_1 \equiv_\alpha N_1$, therefore $\lambda \vdash M_1 = N_1$, and hence $\lambda + ext \vdash M = N$. ⊠

Corollary 2.1.5 will be included in the result of §2.5.

A priori we cannot state a similar result for CL because the theorem of Böhm does not extend to CL:

Let $M = S[K(SII)][K(SII)]$

$N = K$

M and N are closed terms both in normal form. But then the conclusion of 2.1.4 does not hold, because $CL \vdash MZ_1 = (SII)(SII)$ for all Z_1, hence $MZ_1 \ldots Z_n$ does not have a normal form for all $Z_1 \ldots Z_n$.

§2.2. The ω-consistency of combinatory logic.

In order to prove the ω-consistency of CL we introduce a theory CLω' which is a conservative extension of CLω. In the object language of CLω' itself something like "the length of a proof in CLω" is formulated. Because the ω-rule is an infinitary rule, this length can be a transfinite (however countable) ordinal. Ordinals will be denoted by α,β ... etc.

2.2.1 Definition

CLω' has the following language: Alphabet = $\text{Alphabet}_{CL} \cup \{\approx_\alpha | \alpha \text{ countable}\} \cup \{\sim_\alpha | \alpha \text{ countable}\} \cup \{=_\alpha | \alpha \text{ countable}\}$.

The terms are those of CL.

Formulas: If M,N are terms, then

$M \geqslant N$, $M = N$, $M \approx_\alpha N$, $M \sim_\alpha N$ and $M =_\alpha N$ are formulas.

2.2.2 Definition

CLω' has the following axioms and rules (see appendix).

I Same as in 1.4.2.

II 1. $M =_\alpha M$, $M \approx_\alpha M$, $M \sim_\alpha M$

2. $\dfrac{M =_\alpha N}{N =_\alpha M}$, $\dfrac{M \approx_\alpha N}{N \approx_\alpha M}$, $\dfrac{M \sim_\alpha N}{N \sim_\alpha M}$

3. $\dfrac{M =_\alpha N,\ N =_\alpha L}{M =_\alpha L}$

4. $\dfrac{M =_\alpha M'}{ZM =_\alpha ZM'}$, $\dfrac{M =_\alpha M'}{MZ =_\alpha M'Z}$, $\dfrac{M \sim_\alpha M'}{ZM \sim_\alpha ZM'}$, $\dfrac{M \sim_\alpha M'}{MZ \sim_\alpha M'Z}$

5. $\dfrac{M =_\alpha M',\ \alpha \leqslant \alpha'}{M =_{\alpha'} M}$, $\dfrac{M =_\alpha M'}{M = M'}$

III 1. $M \geqslant M$

2. $\dfrac{M \geqslant N,\ N \geqslant L}{M \geqslant L}$

3. $\dfrac{M \geqslant M'}{ZM \geqslant ZM'}$, $\dfrac{M \geqslant M'}{MZ \geqslant M'Z}$

4. $\dfrac{M \geqslant M'}{M \approx_0 M'}$; $\dfrac{M \approx_\alpha M'}{M \sim_\alpha M'}$, $\dfrac{M \sim_\alpha M'}{M =_\alpha M'}$

IV ω'-rule $\dfrac{\forall Z \text{ closed } \exists \beta < \alpha \quad MZ =_\beta NZ}{M \approx_\alpha N}$

In the above M, M', N, L, Z are arbitrary terms, and α,α' arbitrary countable ordinals.

The intuitive interpretation of

$M =_\alpha N$ is: M = N is provable using the ω-rule at most α times.

$M \sim_\alpha N$ is: $M =_\alpha N$ is provable without use of transitivity.

$M \approx_\alpha N$ is: $M =_\alpha N$ follows directly from the ω-rule (or is provable in CL in case α = 0).

2.2.3 Lemma

CL ⊢ $M \geqslant N$ ⟺ CLω ⊢ $M \geqslant N$ ⟺ CLω' ⊢ $M \geqslant N$.

Proof.

Induction on the length of proof of $M \geqslant N$. ⊠

2.2.4 Lemma

CLω' ⊢ M = N ⟺ ∃α CLω' ⊢ $M =_\alpha N$.

Proof. Trivial ⊠

2.2.5 Lemma

CLω ⊢ M = N ⟺ CLω' ⊢ M = N

Proof.

Show by induction (on the length of proof):

1. $CL\omega \vdash M = N \Rightarrow \exists\alpha \ CL\omega' \vdash M =_\alpha N$ and

2. $CL\omega' \vdash M =_\alpha N \Rightarrow CL\omega \vdash M = N$

   $CL\omega' \vdash M \sim_\alpha N \Rightarrow CL\omega \vdash M = N$

   $CL\omega' \vdash M \approx_\alpha N \Rightarrow CL\omega \vdash M = N$

Then the result follows from 2.2.4. ⊠

2.2.3 and 2.2.5 state that CLω' is a conservative extension of CLω.

2.2.6 Lemma

$CL \vdash M = N \Leftrightarrow CL\omega' \vdash M =_0 N$

Proof.

Show by induction

1. $CL \vdash M = N \Rightarrow CL\omega' \vdash M =_0 N$ and

2. $CL\omega' \vdash M =_0 N \Rightarrow CL \vdash M = N$

   $CL\omega' \vdash M \sim_0 N \Rightarrow CL \vdash M = N$

   $CL\omega' \vdash M \approx_0 N \Rightarrow CL \vdash M = N$ ⊠

2.2.7 Lemma

$CL\omega' \vdash M =_\alpha N \Leftrightarrow \exists N_1,\ldots,N_k \ \exists\beta_1,\ldots,\beta_k \leqslant \alpha$

$$CL\omega' \vdash M \sim_{\beta_1} N_1 \sim_{\beta_2} N_2 \sim\ldots\sim_{\beta_k} N_k \equiv N$$

Proof.

⇐ Trivial.

⇒ Induction on the length of proof of $M =_\alpha N$. ⊠

2.2.8 Lemma

1) If $CL\omega' \vdash M \sim_\alpha N$ and M,N are closed, then $\exists M',N',Z$ closed, $[CL\omega' \vdash ZM' =_0 M,\ CL\omega' \vdash ZN' =_0 N$ and $CL\omega' \vdash M' \approx_\alpha N']$.

2) $CL\omega' \vdash M \approx_\alpha N \quad \alpha \neq 0 \Leftrightarrow \forall Z$ closed $\exists\beta < \alpha \ CL\omega' \vdash MZ =_\beta NZ$.

Proof.

1. Induction on the length of proof of $M \sim_\alpha N$ (as an illustration we give the full proof):

case 1. $M \sim_\alpha N$ is an instance of II 1.

Take $M' = N' = M$ ($\equiv N$) and $Z \equiv I$.

case 2. $M \sim_\alpha N$ is a direct consequence of $N \sim_\alpha M$.

By the induction hypothesis there are N', M', Z closed such that

$CL\omega' \vdash ZN' =_0 N$, $CL\omega' \vdash ZM' = M$ and $CL\omega' \vdash N' \approx_\alpha M'$.

This is what we had to prove.

case 3. $M \sim_\alpha N$ is $Z_1M_1 \sim_\alpha Z_1N_1$ (hence Z_1 is closed) and is a direct consequence of $M_1 \sim_\alpha N_1$.

By the induction hypothesis there are closed M_1', N_1', Z_0 such that

$CL\omega' \vdash Z_0M_1' =_0 M_1$, $CL\omega' \vdash Z_0N_1' =_0 N_1$ and $CL\omega' \vdash M_1' \approx_\alpha N_1'$.

Define $Z \equiv \lambda^*a.Z_1(Z_0a)$, then the conclusion holds for M_1', N_1', Z as follows from 1.4.7.

case 4. $M \sim_\alpha N$ is $M_1Z_1 \sim_\alpha N_1Z_1$. This case is treated analogous to case 3.

case 5. $M \sim_\alpha N$ is a direct consequence of $M \approx_\alpha N$. Take $M' \equiv M$, $N' \equiv N$ and $Z \equiv I$.

2. Induction on the length of proof of $M \approx_\alpha N$. ⊠

2.2.9 Main Lemma

If $CL\omega' \vdash ZM \geqslant K$ and $CL\omega' \vdash M \approx_\alpha N$, where $\alpha \neq 0$ and M,N and Z are closed, then

$\exists\beta < \alpha[CL\omega' \vdash ZNKK =_\beta K]$.

We will carry out the proof of the main lemma in §2.3.

2.2.10 Notation

MK_n stands for $M\underbrace{K\ldots K}_{n \text{ times}}$.

Note that K_n is not a term, because MK...K stands for (..((MK)K)...K)..).

2.2.11 Lemma

If $CL\omega' \vdash M =_\alpha K$ and M is closed, then

(*) $\exists n \in \omega\ CL \vdash MK_{2n} \geqslant K$

Proof.

Induction on α. Because we will make use of a double induction we call the induction hypothesis with respect to this induction the α-ind.hyp.

case 1. α=0. Then $CL\omega' \vdash M =_\alpha K$ implies that $CL \vdash M = K$ by 2.2.6, hence $CL \vdash M \geqslant K$ by 1.5.1. So we can take $n = 0$.

case 2. α>0. From 2.2.7 it follows that

$CL\omega' \vdash M =_\alpha K \iff \exists M_1 \ldots M_k\ \exists \beta_1, \ldots, \beta_k \leqslant \alpha$

(**) $CL\omega' \vdash M \sim_{\beta_1} M_1 \sim_{\beta_2} M_2 \sim \ldots \sim_{\beta_k} M_k \geqslant K.$

We can suppose that the M_i, $i=1,\ldots,k$ are all closed. Because if they were not, we could substitute some constant for the free variables of the M_i and then also (**) would hold.

Now we prove with induction on k that (**) ⇒ (*). The induction hypothesis w.r.t. this induction is called the k-ind.hyp.

If $k = 0$ then there is nothing to prove, so suppose that $k > 0$.

subcase 2.1. $\beta_k < \alpha$.

Then $CL\omega' \vdash M_{k-1} \sim_\beta M_k \geqslant K$ with $\beta = \beta_k$

therefore $CL\omega' \vdash M_{k-1} =_\beta K$.

Hence by the α-ind.hyp.

$\exists n \in \omega \quad CL \vdash M_{k-1}K_{2n} \geqslant K$, because we assumed that M_{k-1} is closed.

Thus

$\exists n \in \omega \; CL\omega' \vdash MK_{2n} \sim_{\beta_1} M_1K_{2n} \sim \ldots \sim_{\beta_{k-1}} M_{k-1}K_{2n} \geqslant K$,

hence by the k-ind.hyp.

$\exists n,n' \in \omega \; CL \vdash MK_{2n}K_{2n'} \geqslant K$, which is

$\exists n,n' \in \omega \; CL \vdash MK_{2(n+n')} \geqslant K$.

subcase 2.2. $\beta_k = \alpha$.

Then $CL\omega' \vdash M_{k-1} \sim_\alpha M_k \geqslant K$.

By 2.8.1 it follows that there are

M'_{k-1}, M'_k, Z such that

$CL\omega' \vdash ZM'_{k-1} =_0 M_{k-1}$, $CL\omega' \vdash ZM'_k =_0 M_k$ and

$CL\omega' \vdash M'_{k-1} \approx_\alpha M'_k$.

Hence by 2.2.6 and 1.5.1 it follows that

$CL\omega' \vdash ZM'_k \geqslant K$.

By the main lemma 2.2.9 it follows that

$\exists \beta < \alpha[\, CL\omega' \vdash ZM'_{k-1}KK =_\beta K]$, thus

$\exists \beta < \alpha[\, CL\omega' \vdash M_{k-1}KK =_\beta K]$. Hence by the α-ind.hyp. $\exists n \in \omega \quad CL \vdash M_{k-1}KKK_{2n} \geqslant K$, thus

$\exists n \in \omega \; CL\omega' \vdash MKKK_{2n} \sim_{\beta_1} M_1KKK_{2n} \sim \ldots \sim_{\beta_{k-1}} M_{k-1}KKK_{2n} \geqslant K$.

Therefore by the k-ind.hyp. we have

$\exists n,n' \in \omega \quad CL \vdash MKKK_{2n}K_{2n'} \geqslant K$ i.e.

$\exists n,n' \in \omega \quad CL \vdash M\,K_{2(n+n'+1)} \geqslant K$. ⊠

2.2.12 Corollary

If CLω ⊢ M = K , M is closed, then $\exists n \in \omega$ CL ⊢ MK_{2n} = K.

Proof.

This follows immediately from 2.2.11 by 2.2.4 and 2.2.5. ⊠

2.2.13 Theorem

CL is ω-consistent.

Proof.

Suppose CLω were inconsistent, then

CLω ⊢ KK = K. Therefore by 2.2.12

$\exists n \in \omega$ CL ⊢ KKK_{2n} = K. Hence CL ⊢ KK = K.

This contradicts the Church-Rosser theorem for CL. ⊠

Theorem 2.2.13 implies in particular that λω, CL + ext and the λ-calculus + ext are consistent.

§2.3. The theory CL.

The most convenient way to carry out the proof of the main lemma 2.2.9, is to develop a new theory CL.

The intuitive idea behind the proof is the following.

Definition. An occurrence M' of a subterm of M is said to be active if this occurrence is in a part (M'N) of M, otherwise it is passive.

In the theory CL we keep track of the occurrences of the residuals of M in the reduction ZM ⩾ K by underlining them. Then we substitute N for the underlined subterms (this is done by ϕ_N of 2.3.8) and we obtain a reduction of ZN. When an occurrence of a residual of M is active, we omit the underlining, because subterms like MN sometimes have to be evaluated. (This is the essence of axiom VI). This is not in conflict with the substitution of N for the underlined subterms, because by 2.2.8.2) it follows that if $M \approx_\alpha N$, active occurrences of M in the reduction $ZM \geqslant K$ can be replaced by N up to equality of a lower level (i.e. $\beta < \alpha$).

If in the reduction of ZM to K it happens that all the residuals of M are active sooner or later, we are done, because then $ZN =_\beta K$. In the opposite case K is a residual of M, hence $M \geqslant K$ and $ZN =_\beta N$. Therefore

$ZNKK =_\beta NKK =_{\beta'} MKK \geqslant KKK \geqslant K$, with $\beta, \beta' < \alpha$.

2.3.1 <u>Definition</u>

<u>CL</u> is a theory defined in the following language:

$\text{Alphabet}_{\underline{CL}} = \text{Alphabet}_{CL'} \cup \{\_, \simeq\}$.

Simple terms are defined inductively by

1) Any variable or constant is a simple term.

2) If M,N are simple terms, then (MN) is a simple term.

Terms are defined inductively by

1) Any simple term is a term.

2) If M is a simple term, then $\underline{M}$ is a term.

3) If M,N are terms, then (MN) is a term.

Formulas: If M,N are terms, then

$M \geqslant_1 N$, $M \geqslant N$, $M = N$ and $M \simeq N$ are formulas.

Remark: The simple terms of <u>CL</u> are exactly the terms of CL.

2.3.2 Definition

CL has the following axioms and rules (see appendix):

I Same as in 1.5.2.

II Same as in 1.5.2.

III Same as in 1.5.2.

IV Same as in 1.5.2 plus $\dfrac{M \geqslant_1 M'}{\underline{M} \geqslant_1 \underline{M}'}$

V
1. $M \approx M$
2. $\dfrac{M \approx M'}{M' \approx M}$
3. $\dfrac{M \approx N,\ N \approx L}{M \approx L}$
4. $\dfrac{M \approx M'}{ZM \approx ZM'}$, $\dfrac{M \approx M'}{MZ \approx M'Z}$
5. $M \approx \underline{M}$

VI $\underline{M}N \geqslant_1 MN$.

In the above the restrictions on the terms are clear.

Remarks: Axiom VI is essential for $\underline{\text{CL}}$ as will become clear later on.

If CL $\vdash M \approx M'$, then M and M' are, except for the underlining, equal.

2.3.3 Lemma

1) $\underline{\text{CL}} \vdash M \geqslant M' \iff \text{CL} \vdash M \geqslant M'$ if M,M' are simple terms

2) $\underline{\text{CL}} \vdash M \geqslant M' \iff \underline{\text{CL}} \vdash \underline{M} \geqslant \underline{M}'$ if M,M' are simple terms

3) $[\underline{\text{CL}} \vdash M \geqslant_1 M'$ and $\underline{N}'$ sub $M'] \Rightarrow \exists N[\underline{N}$ sub M and CL $\vdash N \geqslant_1 N']$.

N sub M means that N is a subterm of M.

Proof.

1) Induction on the length of proof of $M \geqslant M'$.

2) Immediate.

3) Immediate using 2) and 1). ☒

It follows from 2.3.3 1) that $\underline{CL}$ is a conservative extension of CL.

2.3.4 Lemma

$\underline{CL} \vdash M \geqslant M' \Longleftrightarrow \exists N_1 \ldots N_k \quad \underline{CL} \vdash M \equiv N_1 \geqslant_1 \ldots \geqslant_1 N_k \equiv M'$.

Proof.

Immediate. ☒

2.3.5 Lemma

If $\underline{CL} \vdash Z\underline{M} \geqslant M'$, where Z is simple, and $\underline{N}$ sub M', then

(*) $\quad$ CL $\vdash M \geqslant N$.

Proof.

By 2.3.4 $\underline{CL} \vdash Z\underline{M} \geqslant M' \Longleftrightarrow \exists N_1 \ldots N_k \quad \underline{CL} \vdash Z\underline{M} \equiv N_1 \geqslant_1 \ldots \geqslant_1 N_k \equiv M'$.

From lemma 2.3.3 it follows by induction on k that (*) holds. ☒

2.3.6 Lemma

Let M, M', N be terms such that

1) M and M' are simple,

2) $\underline{CL} \vdash M \geqslant M'$ and

3) $\underline{CL} \vdash M \simeq N$,

then there exists a term N' such that

4) $\underline{CL} \vdash N \geqslant N'$ and

5) $\underline{CL} \vdash M' \simeq N'$ (see figure 7).

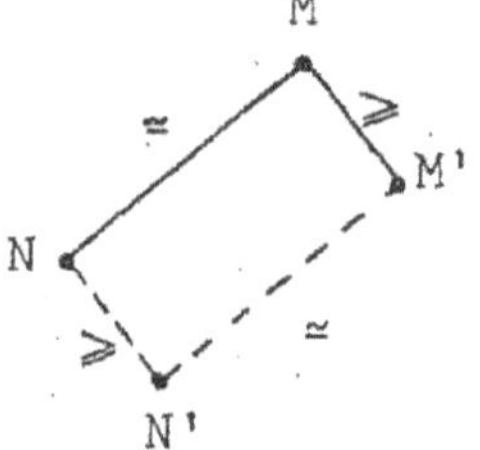

Figure 7

Proof.

Induction on the length of proof of $M \geqslant M'$ with the use of axiom VI and the sublemma:

$\underline{CL} \vdash M \simeq N \Longleftrightarrow M \equiv N$ or $[M \equiv \underline{M_1}$ and $\underline{CL} \vdash M_1 \simeq N]$ or
$[N \equiv \underline{N_1}$ and $\underline{CL} \vdash M \simeq N_1]$ or
$[M \equiv M_1 M_2$ and $N \equiv N_1 N_2$ and $\underline{CL} \vdash M_1 \simeq N_1$ and $\underline{CL} \vdash M_2 \simeq N_2]$. ⊠

2.3.7 Definition

Let A be a simple term of $\underline{CL}$.

We define a mapping ϕ_A: $\underline{CL} \to CL$ (in fact from the set of terms of $\underline{CL}$ onto the set of terms of CL).

$\phi_A(c) = c$ if c is a constant or variable.

$\phi_A(MN) = \phi_A(M)\phi_A(N)$

$\phi_A(\underline{M}) = A$

2.3.8 Lemma

If $\underline{CL}$ - {VI} $\vdash M \geqslant_1 M'$, then $CL \vdash \phi_N(M) \geqslant \phi_N(M')$ for simple terms N.

Proof.

Immediate. ⊠

2.3.9 Lemma

If $\underline{CL} \vdash Z\underline{M} \geqslant M'$, where Z is simple, Z,M,M' are closed and $CL\omega' \vdash M \approx_\alpha N$, then $\exists \beta < \alpha$ $CL\omega' \vdash \phi_N(Z\underline{M}) =_\beta \phi_N(M')$.

Proof.

Suppose $\underline{CL} \vdash Z\underline{M} \geqslant M'$ and $CL\omega' \vdash M \approx_\alpha N$.

Then $\exists N_1 \ldots N_k$ $\underline{CL} \vdash Z\underline{M} \equiv N_1 \geqslant_1 \ldots \geqslant_1 N_k \equiv M'$.

We claim that

(*) $\forall i \leqslant k \ \exists \beta_i < \alpha \quad CL\omega' \vdash \phi_N(N_i) =_{\beta_i} \phi_N(N_{i+1})$

We will prove this with induction on the length of proof of $N_i \geqslant_1 N_{i+1}$.

case 1. $N_i \geqslant_1 N_{i+1}$ is an axiom.

subcase 1.1. $N_i \geqslant_1 N_{i+1}$ is not an instance of axiom VI.
Then it follows from 2.3.8 and 2.2.6 that
$CL\omega' \vdash \phi_N(N_i) =_0 \phi_N(N_{i+1})$.

subcase 1.2. $N_i \geqslant_1 N_{i+1}$ is an instance of axiom VI,
say $\underline{M}_1 M_2 \geqslant_1 M_1 M_2$.
Then we have to show that

(**) $\exists \beta < \alpha \quad CL\omega' \vdash N\phi_N(M_2) =_\beta M_1\phi_N(M_2)$

because M_1 is simple and hence $\phi_N(M_1) \equiv M_1$.
Since $\underline{CL} \vdash Z\underline{M} \geqslant \underline{M}_1 M_2$ it follows from 2.3.5 that $CL \vdash M \geqslant M_1$. α≠0 and M is closed
Hence since $CL\omega' \vdash M \approx_\alpha N$, it follows from 2.2.8. 2) and 2.2.6 that

$\exists \beta < \alpha \quad CL\omega' \vdash N\phi_N(M_2) =_\beta M\phi_N(M_2) =_0 M_1\phi_N(M_2)$.

This implies (**).

case 2. $N_i \geqslant_1 N_{i+1}$ is $ZM_1 \geqslant_1 ZM_2$ and is a direct consequence of $M_1 \geqslant_1 M_2$. By the induction hypothesis
$\exists \beta < \alpha \quad CL\omega' \vdash \phi_N(M_1) =_\beta \phi_N(M_2)$ hence
$CL\omega' \vdash \phi_N(Z)\phi_N(M_1) =_\beta \phi_N(Z)\phi_N(M_2)$ which is
$CL\omega' \vdash \phi_N(N_i) =_\beta \phi_N(N_{i+1})$.

case 3. $N_i \geqslant_1 N_{i+1}$ is $M_1 Z \geqslant_1 M_2 Z$. This case is analogous to case 2.

Now we have established (*). Let $\beta = \mathrm{Max}\{\beta_0, \ldots, \beta_k\}$, then $\beta < \alpha$ and $CL\omega' \vdash \phi_N(Z\underline{M}) =_\beta \phi_N(N_1) =_\beta \cdots =_\beta \phi_N(N_k) =_\beta \phi_N(M')$. ⊠

Now we are able to prove the main lemma.

2.2.9 Main Lemma

If $CL\omega' \vdash ZM \geqslant K$ and $CL\omega' \vdash M \approx_{\alpha} N$, where $\alpha \neq 0$ and M, N and Z are closed, then $\exists\beta < \alpha\ [CL\omega' \vdash ZNKK =_{\beta} K]$.

Proof.

If $CL\omega' \vdash ZM \geqslant K$, then by 2.2.3 $CL \vdash ZM \geqslant K$, hence by 2.3.3 $\underline{CL} \vdash ZM \geqslant K$ and therefore by 2.3.6 $\underline{CL} \vdash Z\underline{M} \geqslant K'$ with $\underline{CL} \vdash K' \simeq K$ hence $K' \equiv K$ or $K' \equiv \underline{K}$.

case 1. $K' \equiv K$.

By 2.3.9 it follows that $\exists\beta < \alpha$ $CL\omega' \vdash ZN =_{\beta} K$, hence $\exists\beta < \alpha$ $CL\omega' \vdash ZNKK =_{\beta} KKK =_{0} K$.

case 2. $K' \equiv \underline{K}$.

Then $\underline{CL} \vdash Z\underline{M} \geqslant \underline{K}$ hence by 2.3.5

(1) $CL \vdash M \geqslant K$

Again by 2.3.9 we have $\exists\beta < \alpha$ $CL\omega' \vdash ZN =_{\beta} N$. Hence

(2) $CL\omega' \vdash ZNKK =_{\beta} NKK$.

Because $CL\omega' \vdash M \approx_{\alpha} N$, it follows from 2.2.8.2) that

(3) $\exists\beta' < \alpha$ $CL\omega' \vdash NKK =_{\beta'} MKK$.

From (1), (2) and (3) it follows that

$$\exists\beta,\beta' < \alpha\ CL\omega' \vdash ZNKK =_{\beta} NKK =_{\beta'} MKK \geqslant KKK \geqslant K.$$

Hence $\exists\beta'' < \alpha$ $CL\omega' \vdash ZNKK =_{\beta''} K$. ⊠

§2.4. Universal generators.

The motivation of the contents of this § will be stated in 2.4.6.

2.4.1 Definition

The λ-family of a term M of the λ-calculus, notation $\mathcal{F}_{\lambda}(M)$ is the following set of λ-terms

$\mathcal{F}_\lambda(M) = \{N \mid \exists M' \ \lambda \vdash M \geq M' \text{ and } N \text{ sub } M'\}$.

Analogously we define $\mathcal{F}_{CL}$ and $\mathcal{F}_{\lambda+ext}$.

2.4.2 Definition

U is a universal generator (u.g.) for the λ-calculus if $\mathcal{F}_\lambda(U)$ consists of all closed λ-terms.

Analogously we define the universal generators for CL.

Remark: If U is a universal generator for the λ-calculus then $\mathcal{F}_\lambda(U)$ even consists of all λ-terms, since every λ-term M is sub-term of a closed λ-term (take the closure $\lambda x_1 \ldots x_n.M$).

2.4.3 Lemma

There exists a closed term E such that

$\forall M[FV(M) = \emptyset \Rightarrow \exists n \ \lambda \vdash E\underline{n} \geq M]$.

Proof.

This follows from inspection of the proof of 1.3.13.

See for details Barendregt [1970].

2.4.4 Theorem

There exists a closed universal generator for the λ-calculus.

Proof.

We give here a modification of our original construction, due to Scott.

Let E be as in lemma 2.4.3, let [...,...] be the pairing function as in 1.3.6 and let $\underline{S}^+$ be the λ-defining term of the successor function (1.3.4.3)).

Define $A = \lambda bn.[En, b(\underline{S}^+ n)]$.

$B = FP\ A$ (see 1.1.8)

Then $\lambda \vdash B\underline{n} \geqslant AB\underline{n} \geqslant [E\underline{n}, B\ \underline{n+1}]$. Hence

$$\lambda \vdash B\underline{0} \geqslant [E\underline{0}, B\underline{1}] \geqslant [E\underline{0}, [E\underline{1}, B\underline{2}]] \geqslant$$
$$\geqslant [E\underline{0}, [E\underline{1}, [E\underline{2}, B\underline{3}]]] \geqslant \dots .$$

Because E enumerates all closed terms, $B\underline{0}$ is a universal generator. Since E is closed, $B\underline{0}$ is closed too. ⊠

The above considerations also hold for CL. In particular Kleene's E (2.4.3) is given for CL by a term GD^{-1} in Curry, Hindley, Seldin [1971], Ch 13. The name GD^{-1} is used because it is the inverse of the Gödel numbering.

Therefore we have

2.4.5 Theorem

There exists a universal generator for CL.

2.4.6 Remark

The motivation for the introduction of universal generators is the following:

In the next § we will prove that, if M and N are not u.g.'s and if $\lambda + ext \vdash MZ = NZ$ for all closed Z, then $\lambda + ext \vdash M = N$.

At the moment of discovery of this theorem, we were still unaware of the existence of u.g.'s. We hoped to prove that they did not exist in order to obtain, as corollary, the ω-completeness of the λ-calculus.

However we subsequently found a proof of the existence of u.g.'s. The proof of the existence of u.g.'s was presented first, because the above mentioned theorem is easier to prove with their application.

§2.5. The provability of the ω-rule for non universal generators.

In this § we will prove a result on partial ω-completeness. We present the proof for the λ-calculus because there extensionality can be axiomatized by η-reduction for which the Church-Rosser property holds (1.2.11). We do not know whether a similar result holds for CL, but probably we can prove it using strong reduction.

2.5.1 Definition

A λ-term Z is said to be of order 0 if there is no term P such that $\lambda \vdash Z \geqslant (\lambda x\ P)$.

2.5.2 Lemma

Let Z be of order 0, then:

1) For no term P we have $\lambda + ext \vdash Z \geqslant \lambda x\ P$
2) If $\lambda + ext \vdash Z \geqslant Z'$, then Z' is of order 0
3) If $\lambda + ext \vdash ZM \geqslant N$, then there exist terms Z',M' such that $N \equiv Z'M'$, $\lambda + ext \vdash Z \geqslant Z'$ and $\lambda + ext \vdash M \geqslant M'$
4) For all terms M, ZM is of order 0.

Proof.

For this proof let us call a term of the first kind if it is a variable, of the second kind if it is of the form (MN) and of the third kind if it is of the form (λx M).

1) Suppose $\lambda + ext \vdash Z \geqslant \lambda x\ P$ for some P. By Curry, Feys [1958] Ch 4D, theorem 2 pg 132, it follows that there exists a term Z' such that $\lambda \vdash Z \geqslant Z'$ and $\lambda + ext - I\ 2 \vdash Z' \geqslant (\lambda x\ P)$ (i.e.

without using β-reduction). Because Z is of order 0 Z' is of the first or of the second kind. Z' cannot be a variable because λ + ext ⊢ Z' ≥ λx P. Hence Z' is of the second kind. By induction on the length of proof in λ + ext - I 2 of a reduction M ≥ N we can show that if M is of the second kind, then N is of the second kind.

This would imply that (λx P) is of the second kind; a contradiction.

2) Immediate, using 1).

3) By induction on the length of proof of ZM ≥ N using 2).

4) By 3) it follows that if λ + ext ⊢ ZM ≥ N, then N is of the second kind. Hence ZM is of order 0. ⊠

2.5.3 Examples

1. Any variable is of order 0.

2. $\Omega_2 = \omega_2\omega_2$ with ω_2 = (λa.aa) is of order 0.

Terms of order 0 behave in some sense like variables. Namely, if λ + ext ⊢ MZ ≥ L where Z is of order 0, we can substitute x for the residuals of Z in this reduction and we obtain λ + ext ⊢ Mx ≥ L'.

Because Ω_2 is at the same time closed and of order 0 it will play an important role in connection with the ω-rule. If λ + ext ⊢ MZ = NZ for all closed Z we have in particular λ + ext ⊢ $M\Omega_2 = N\Omega_2$. We hoped that this would imply λ + ext ⊢ Mx = Nx, by substituting everywhere x for Ω_2 in the proof. The problem is that there <u>is</u> a difference between variables and terms of order 0. In a reduction, variables can never be generated whereas closed terms can. Therefore we have to find a term of order 0 $Z_0 \notin \mathcal{F}_\lambda(M) \cup \mathcal{F}_\lambda(N)$

(see 2.4.1). This is only possible if M and N are not universal generators. Then it follows from λ + ext $\vdash MZ_0 = NZ_0$ that λ + ext $\vdash Mx = Nx$ and hence λ + ext $\vdash M = N$.
In order to follow the residuals of a subterm in a reduction we again make use of the underlining technique.

An outline of what happens is the following (see fig. 8).
In 2.5.4 - 2.5.14 we define and develop a theory $\underline{\lambda}$.
In 2.5.15 - 2.5.16 we consider a mapping ϕ_x which replaces a term of order 0 by a variable x as is mentioned above.
In 2.5.21 - 2.5.24 we define the concept of closed terms which are variable like and prove their existence.
Then, to prove the main result, we assume that λ + ext $\vdash M\Xi = N\Xi$. It follows from the Church-Rosser theorem that, for some term L, λ + ext $\vdash M\Xi \geqslant L$ and λ + ext $\vdash N\Xi \geqslant L$. From this it follows, by the results of the theory $\underline{\lambda}$ that $\underline{\lambda}$ + ext $\vdash M\underline{\Xi} \geqslant L'$ and $\underline{\lambda}$ + ext $\vdash N\underline{\Xi} \geqslant L''$. The main difficulty is then to prove that $L' \equiv L''$. If we have $L' \equiv L''$, then it follows by a homomorphism argument that λ + ext $\vdash Mx = \phi_x(L') \equiv \phi_x(L'') = Nx$.
In order to prove that $L' \equiv L''$, we need proposition 2.5.20, a statement about $\mathcal{F}_{\lambda+ext}(M\underline{\Xi})$ and lemma 2.5.27, a statement about variable like terms.

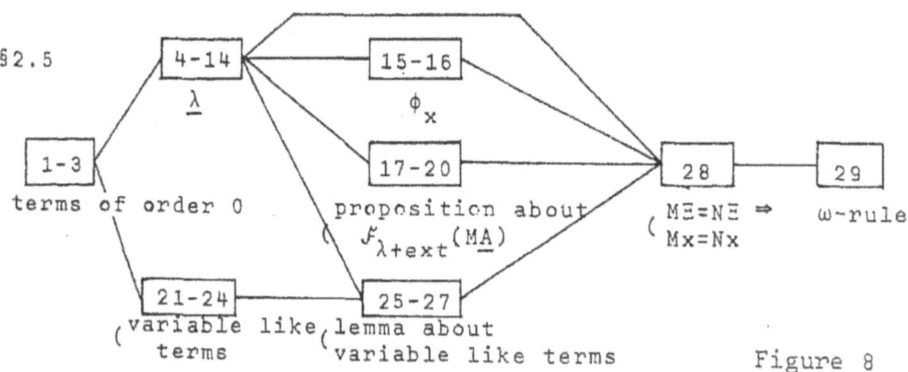

Figure 8

2.5.4 Definition

We will define a theory $\underline{\lambda}$ + ext formulated in the following language (see appendix).

$\text{Alphabet}_{\underline{\lambda} + \text{ext}} = \text{Alphabet}_{\lambda} \cup \{\geqslant_1, \_, \simeq\}$

Simple terms of the theory $\underline{\lambda}$ are exactly the terms of the λ-calculus.

Terms are defined inductively by

1) Any simple term is a term.
2) If M is a simple term and FV(M) = ∅, then $\underline{M}$ is a term.
3) If M,N are terms, then (MN) is a term.
4) If M is a term, then (λx M) is a term (x is an arbitrary variable).

Formulas: if M,N are terms, then

$M \geqslant_1 N$, $M \geqslant N$, $M = N$ and $M \simeq N$ are formulas.

A term of the theory $\underline{\lambda}$ + ext is called $\underline{\lambda}$-term.

The operations BV, FV and [x\N] can be extended to $\underline{\lambda}$-terms in the obvious way.

(Note that: BV($\underline{M}$) = BV(M), FV($\underline{M}$) = ∅ and [x\N]$\underline{M}$ = $\underline{M}$.)

2.5.5 Definition

The relation "...is subterm of ..." is defined in such a way that only $\underline{M}$ is a subterm of $\underline{M}$. To be explicit:

Sub(x) = {x} for any variable x.

Sub(MN) = Sub(M) ∪ Sub(N) ∪ {MN}

Sub(λx M) = Sub(M) ∪ {λx M}

Sub($\underline{M}$) = {$\underline{M}$}

N sub M ⟺ N ∈ Sub M

2.5.6 Definition

We define the theory $\underline{\lambda}$ + ext by the following axioms and rules (see appendix).

I 1. $\lambda x\ M \geqslant_1 \lambda y[x \backslash y]M$ if $y \notin FV(M)$

2. $(\lambda x\ M)N \geqslant_1 [x\backslash N]M$ if $BV(M) \cap FV(N) = \emptyset$

3. $\lambda x(Mx) \geqslant_1 M$ if $x \notin FV(M)$

II Same as in 1.1.4.

III Same as in 1.2.3.

IV 1. $M \geqslant_1 M$

2. $$\frac{M \geqslant_1 M'}{ZM \geqslant_1 ZM'}\ ,\quad \frac{M \geqslant_1 M'}{MZ \geqslant_1 M'Z}\ ,\quad \frac{M \geqslant_1 M'}{\lambda x\ M \geqslant_1 \lambda x\ M'}\ ,\quad \frac{M \geqslant_1 M'}{\underline{M} \geqslant_1 \underline{M}'}$$

3. $$\frac{M \geqslant_1 M'}{M \geqslant M'}$$

V 1. $M \simeq M$

2. $$\frac{M \simeq N}{N \simeq M}$$

3. $$\frac{M \simeq N, N \simeq L}{M \simeq L}$$

4. $$\frac{M \simeq M'}{ZM \simeq ZM'}\ ,\quad \frac{M \simeq M'}{MZ \simeq M'Z}\ ,\quad \frac{M \simeq M'}{\lambda x\ M \simeq \lambda x\ M'}$$

5. $M \simeq \underline{M}$

In the above the restriction on the terms is clear.

Note that we do not have a counterpart for axiom VI of 2.3.2.

$\underline{\lambda}$ is the theory which results from the above axioms and rules, omitting I 3.

2.5.7 Lemma

1) $\underline{\lambda}$ + ext $\vdash M \geqslant M' \Leftrightarrow \lambda$ + ext $\vdash M \geqslant M'$ if M, M' are simple terms

2) $\underline{\lambda}$ + ext $\vdash M \geqslant M' \Leftrightarrow \underline{\lambda}$ + ext $\vdash \underline{M} \geqslant \underline{M}'$ if M, M' are simple terms

3) [$\underline{\lambda}$ + ext $\vdash M \geqslant_1 M'$ and $\underline{N}'$ sub M'] $\Rightarrow$

[$\exists N$ $\underline{N}$ sub M and λ + ext $\vdash N \geqslant_1 N'$].

Proof.

1) Induction on the length of proof of $M \geqslant M'$

2) Immediate

3) Immediate, using 1) and the following sublemma

$\underline{N}$ sub$[x\backslash Q]P \Leftrightarrow \underline{N}$ sub P or $\underline{N}$ sub Q.

The proof of the sublemma proceeds by induction on the structure of P. ⊠

2.5.8 Lemma

$\underline{\lambda} + \text{ext} \vdash M \geqslant M' \Leftrightarrow \exists N_1 \ldots N_k \;\; \underline{\lambda} + \text{ext} \vdash M \equiv N_1 \geqslant_1 \ldots \geqslant_1 N_k \equiv M'$.

Proof.

Immediate. ⊠

2.5.9 Lemma

$[\underline{\lambda} + \text{ext} \vdash M \geqslant M'$ and $\underline{N}'$ sub $M'] \Rightarrow$

$[\exists N \;\; \underline{N}$ sub M and $\lambda + \text{ext} \vdash N \geqslant N']$.

Proof.

By 2.5.8

$\underline{\lambda} + \text{ext} \vdash M \geqslant M' \Leftrightarrow \exists N_1 \ldots N_k \;.\; \underline{\lambda} + \text{ext} \vdash M \equiv N_1 \geqslant_1 \ldots \geqslant_1 N_k \equiv M'$.

From lemma 2.5.7,3) it follows by induction on k that the conclusion holds. ⊠

2.5.10 Lemma

~~Let M,N be simple terms.~~

1) $\underline{\lambda} \vdash L \simeq \underline{M} \Leftrightarrow$ ~~[L ≡ M or L ≡ M]~~ $L \simeq M$

2) $\underline{\lambda} \vdash L \simeq \lambda x\, M \Leftrightarrow [\exists M' \;\; L \equiv \lambda x\, M'$ and $\underline{\lambda} \vdash M \simeq M']$ or $L \equiv \underline{\lambda x\, M}$

3) $\underline{\lambda} \vdash L \simeq MN \Leftrightarrow [\exists M'N' \;\; L \equiv M'N'$ and $\underline{\lambda} \vdash M \simeq M'$, $\underline{\lambda} \vdash N \simeq N']$ or $L \equiv \underline{MN}$

4) $\underline{\lambda} \vdash M \simeq M'$ and $\underline{\lambda} \vdash N \simeq N' \Rightarrow \underline{\lambda} \vdash [x\backslash N]M \simeq [x\backslash N']M'$.

Use $\underline{\lambda} \vdash M \simeq M' \Leftrightarrow |M| \equiv |M'|$,

$|..|$ like in A_{11}

Proof.

1) Induction on the proof of $L \simeq \underline{M}$, making for the induction hypothesis the statement slightly stronger.

$[\underline{\lambda} \vdash L \simeq \underline{M}$ or $\underline{\lambda} \vdash \underline{M} \simeq L] \iff]L \equiv M$ or $L \equiv \underline{M}]$

2) 3) Similarly, making use of 1).

4) Induction on the structure of M, making use of 1), 2) and 3). ⊠

2.5.11 Lemma

Let M,N be simple terms such that $M \geqslant_1 N$ is an axiom of $\underline{\lambda}$ + ext but not an instance of I 2.

Let $\underline{\lambda} \vdash M \simeq M'$. Then $\exists N'[\underline{\lambda} + \text{ext} \vdash M' \geqslant N'$ and $\underline{\lambda} \vdash N \simeq N']$.

(See fig. 9.)

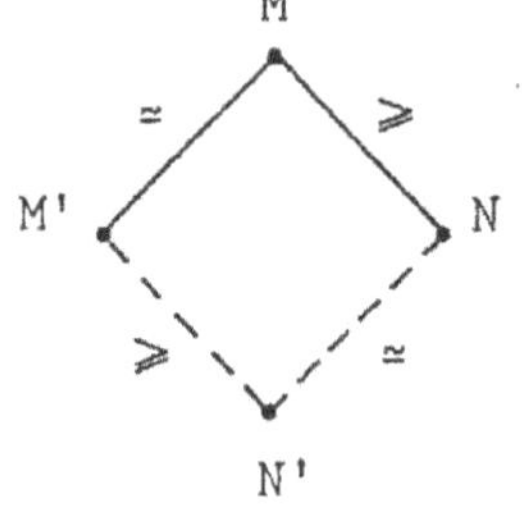

Figure 9

Proof.

By distinguishing cases and using the previous lemma. ⊠

2.5.12 Lemma

Let M,N be simple terms such that $M \geqslant_1 N$ is an instance of axiom I 2. Let $\underline{\lambda} \vdash M \simeq M'$, where M' is such that if $\underline{Z}$ sub M', then Z is of order 0.

Then $\exists N'[\underline{\lambda} + \text{ext} \vdash M' \geqslant N'$ and $\underline{\lambda} \vdash N \simeq N']$ (see fig. 9).

Proof.

Let $M \geqslant N$ be $(\lambda x\ P)Q \geqslant [x\backslash Q]P$.

As $\underline{\lambda} \vdash (\lambda x\ P)Q \simeq M'$ we can distinguish by 2.5.10 several cases.

case 1. $M' \equiv \underline{(\lambda x\ P)Q}$. Take $N' \equiv \underline{[x\backslash Q]P}$

case 2. $M' \equiv M''Q'$ with $\underline{\lambda} \vdash \lambda x\ P \simeq M''$ and $\underline{\lambda} \vdash Q \simeq Q'$.

subcase 2.1. $M'' \equiv \lambda x\ P'$ with $\underline{\lambda} \vdash P \simeq P'$.
Take $N' \equiv [x\backslash Q']P'$, then the result follows from 2.5.10,4).

subcase 2.2. $M'' \equiv \underline{\lambda x\ P}$. This case cannot occur, because then $\underline{\lambda x\ P}$ sub M', and $\lambda x\ P$ is not of order 0, contrary to our assumption. ⊠

2.5.13 Lemma

Let M,N be simple terms such that $\underline{\lambda}$ + ext $\vdash M \geqslant N$.
Let $\underline{\lambda} \vdash M \simeq M'$, where M' is such that if $\underline{Z}$ sub M', then Z is of order 0. Then $\exists N'[\underline{\lambda}$ + ext $\vdash M' \geqslant N'$, $\underline{\lambda} \vdash N \simeq N'$ and $[\underline{Z}$ sub $N' \Rightarrow Z$ is of order 0]] (see fig. 9).

Proof.

Induction on the length of proof of $M \geqslant N$.
If $M \geqslant N$ is an axiom we are done by 2.5.11 or 2.5.12, since by lemma's 2.5.9 and 2.5.2.2) it follows from the assumptions that Z is of order 0 if $\underline{Z}$ sub N'. (We need this fact for the induction step in rule III 3 (transitivity).) ⊠

2.5.14 Proposition

Let λ + ext $\vdash MZ \geqslant L$, where M,Z and L are simple and Z is of order 0. Then $\exists L'[\underline{\lambda}$ + ext $\vdash M\underline{Z} \geqslant L'$, $\underline{\lambda} \vdash L \simeq L'$ and $[\underline{Z}'$ sub $L' \Rightarrow \lambda$ + ext $\vdash Z \geqslant Z']]$ (see fig. 10).

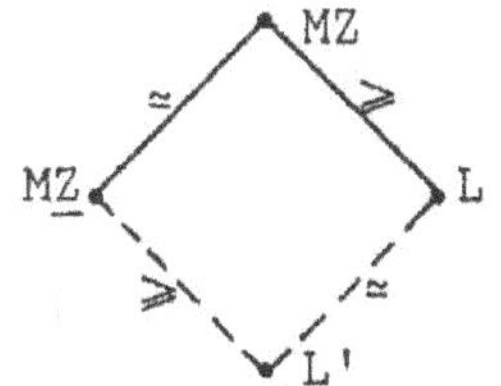

Figure 10

Proof.

This follows immediately from lemma 2.5.13 and 2.5.9. ⊠

2.5.15 Definition

Let x be any variable. We define a mapping ϕ_x: $\underline{\lambda} \to \lambda$ (i.e. from the set of $\underline{\lambda}$-terms into the set of λ-terms) as follows:

$$\phi_x(y) = y$$

$$\phi_x(MN) = \phi_x(M)\phi_x(N)$$

$$\phi_x(\lambda y\ M) = \lambda y\ \phi_x(M)$$

$$\phi_x(\underline{M}) = x$$

2.5.16 Lemma

If $\underline{\lambda}$ + ext ⊢ M ⩾ N and if x is a variable not occurring in this proof, then λ + ext ⊢ $\phi_x(M) \geqslant \phi_x(N)$.

Proof.

Induction on the length of proof of M ⩾ N, using the following sublemma

If $z \neq x$, then $\phi_z([x\backslash N]M) = [x\backslash\phi_z(N)]\phi_z(M)$.

The proof of the sublemma proceeds by induction on the structure of M. ⊠

2.5.17 Lemma

Let M,N be simple and $x \notin FV(M)$.

If λ + ext ⊢ Mx ⩾ N, then ∃M' simple [$x \notin FV(M')$, λ + ext ⊢ M ⩾ M' and $\underline{\lambda}$ + ext ⊢ M'x $\geqslant_1$ N].

Proof.

Because λ + ext ⊢ Mx ⩾ N we have by 2.5.7.1) and 2.5.8 that $\exists N_1 \ldots N_k$ $\underline{\lambda}$ + ext ⊢ $Mx \equiv N_1 \geqslant_1 \ldots \geqslant_1 N_k \equiv N$.

If all N_i, $i < k$ are of the form Px with $x \notin FV(P)$, then we are done.

Otherwise let N_{i+1} be the first term not of the form Px with $x \notin FV(P)$.

Then N_i is of the form $(\lambda z\ N_i')x$.

By α-reduction this reduces to $(\lambda x\ [z\backslash x]N_i')x$ which is $(\lambda x\ N_{i+1})x$.

Hence $\underline{\lambda}$ + ext $\vdash Mx \geq (\lambda z\ N_i')x \geq (\lambda x\ N_{i+1})x \geq (\lambda x\ N)x \geq_1 N$.

So we can take $M' \equiv \lambda x\ N$. ⊠

2.5.18 <u>Lemma</u>

1) Let L,L' be $\underline{\lambda}$-terms such that $\phi_x(L) = \phi_x(L')$ where $x \notin FV(LL')$. Let Z be a simple term such that Z sub L. Then Z sub L'.

2) If M,N are simple terms, then we have $\phi_x([x\backslash\underline{N}]M) = \phi_x(M) = M$.

Proof.

Induction on the structure of L resp. M. ⊠

2.5.19 <u>Lemma</u>

Let $\underline{\lambda}$ + ext $\vdash M\underline{A} \geq L$ and Z sub L, where M,A and Z are simple and A is closed. Let L satisfy: $\underline{A}'$ sub L $\Rightarrow \underline{A}' \equiv \underline{A}$.

Then $Z \in \mathscr{F}_{\lambda+ext}(M)$.

Proof.

By lemma 2.5.16 we have λ + ext $\vdash Mx \geq \phi_x(L)$ where x does not occur in the proof of $M\underline{A} \geq L$. Hence by lemma 2.5.17 there exists a simple term M' such that λ + ext $\vdash M \geq M'$ and $\underline{\lambda}$ + ext $\vdash M'x \geq_1 \phi_x(L)$. Hence $\underline{\lambda}$ + ext $\vdash M'\underline{A} \geq_1 L$. $[x/\underline{A}]\phi_x(L) = L$

Suppose now Z sub L and Z simple. By distinguishing the different possibilities for the proof of $M'\underline{A} \geq_1 L$ we can then show that Z sub M' hence $Z \in \mathcal{F}_{\lambda+ext}(M)$. ☒

2.5.20 <u>Proposition</u>

Let $\underline{\lambda}$ + ext ⊢ $M\underline{A} \geqslant L$ and Z sub L, where M,A and Z are simple and A is closed.

Then $Z \in \mathcal{F}_{\lambda+ext}(M)$.

Proof.

Let x not occur in the proof of $\underline{\lambda}$ + ext ⊢ $M\underline{A} \geqslant L$.

Then by 2.5.16 we have λ + ext ⊢ $Mx \geqslant \phi_x(L)$. Hence

$\underline{\lambda}$ + ext ⊢ $M\underline{A} \geqslant [x\backslash\underline{A}]\phi_x(L) \equiv L'$, say. By 2.5.18 it follows that Z sub L ⟺ Z sub L' for simple terms Z. Furthermore, L' satisfies the assumptions of 2.5.19.

Hence if Z sub L and Z is simple, then Z sub L' and therefore $Z \in \mathcal{F}_{\lambda+ext}(M)$ by 2.5.19. ☒

2.5.21 <u>Definition</u>

1) A term M is called an <u>Ω_2-term</u> if M is of the form $\Omega_2 M'$.
2) A subterm occurrence Z of M is called <u>non-Ω_2 in M</u> if Z has no Ω_2 subterm and Z is not a subterm of an Ω_2 subterm of M.
3) A term U is called a <u>heriditarily non-Ω_2 universal generator</u> if U is a closed u.g. and if λ + ext ⊢ $U \geqslant U'$, then there is a subterm occurrence Z of U' which is a u.g. and which occurs non-Ω_2 in U'.

Example: Only the second occurrence of Z in the term $x(\Omega_2(MZ))Z$ is non-Ω_2 (if Z does not have an Ω_2 subterm).

2.5.22 <u>Lemma</u>

If U is a heriditarily non-Ω_2 u.g. and if λ + ext ⊢ $U \geqslant U'$, then U' is a u.g. which is not an Ω_2-term.

Proof.

By definition it follows that some subterm Z of U' is a u.g. Then U' itself is a u.g. That U' is not an Ω_2-term follows from the fact that Z occurs non-Ω_2 in U'. ⌧

2.5.23 Proposition

There exists a heriditarily non-Ω_2 universal generator.

Proof.

We introduce ordered triples as follows

$[M,N,L] = \lambda z.zMNL$.

Define $A = \lambda bn[b\underline{0}, En, b(\underline{S}^+n)]$, where E and $\underline{S}^+$ are as in 2.4.4,

$B = FPA$ and $U = B\underline{0}$.

We will prove that U is a heriditarily non-Ω_2 u.g.

As in 2.4.4 we see that U is a closed u.g.:

$\lambda \vdash U \equiv B\underline{0} \geqslant AB\underline{0} \geqslant [B\underline{0}, E\underline{0}, B\underline{1}] \geqslant [B\underline{0}, E\underline{0}, [B\underline{0}, E\underline{1}, B\underline{2}]] \geqslant \ldots$

Let us define $U \geqslant_k U'$ to mean

$\exists N_1 \ldots N_k \;\; \underline{\lambda} + ext \vdash U \equiv N_1 \geqslant_1 \ldots \geqslant_1 N_k \equiv U'$.

(Here we need $\underline{\lambda}$ only to express one step reduction $\geqslant_1$.)

Suppose now that $\lambda + ext \vdash U \geqslant U'$. Then for some k we have $U \geqslant_k U'$.

With induction on k we can show that U' is of the form

1) $A^pB\underline{0}$ (remember that $M^pN = \underbrace{M(\ldots(M(MN))..)}_{p \text{ times}}$)

or 2) $A^p(\lambda n[U'', \ldots, \ldots])\underline{0}$ where

$B \geqslant_{k'} \lambda n[U'', \ldots, \ldots]$ and $U \geqslant_{k''} U''$ with $k', k'' < k$,

or 3) $[U''', \ldots, \ldots]$ where $U \geqslant_{k'} U'''$ with $k' < k$.

Now we prove with induction on k that if $U \geqslant_k U'$, then there exists a subterm occurrence $Z_{U'}$ of U' which is a u.g. and is non-Ω_2 in U':

If U' is of the form (1) we take $Z_{U'} \equiv A^p B\underline{0}$.

If U' is of the form (2) we take $Z_{U'} \equiv Z_{U''}$.

Finally if U' is of the form (3) we take $Z_{U'} \equiv Z_{U'''}$. ⊠

2.5.24 Definition

A term Ξ is called variable like if $\Xi \equiv \Omega_2 U$, where U is a heriditarily non-Ω_2 universal generator.

2.5.25 Definition

Let L,L' be $\underline{\lambda}$-terms such that L is simple and $\underline{\lambda} \vdash L \simeq L'$. Then L and L' are equal except for the underlining and we can give the following informal definitions:

1) If Z' is a subterm occurrence of L', then there is a unique subterm occurrence Z of L which corresponds to Z', such that $\underline{\lambda} \vdash Z \simeq Z'$.

Instead of giving a formal definition we illustrate this concept with an example.

Let L ≡ S(KS)(SKK) and L' ≡ S($\underline{\text{KS}}$)($\underline{\text{SKK}}$), then $\underline{\lambda} \vdash L \simeq L'$.

S corresponds to S, KS corresponds to $\underline{\text{KS}}$ and (SKK) corresponds to ($\underline{\text{SKK}}$).

2) Let L" be another $\underline{\lambda}$-term with $\underline{\lambda} \vdash L \simeq L''$. Then we say that L" has more line than L', notation L' ⊂ L", if for all subterm occurrences $\underline{Z}'$ of L' there is a subterm occurrence $\underline{Z}''$ of L" such that Z' sub Z" where Z',Z" are the subterm occurrences of L corresponding to $\underline{Z}'$, $\underline{Z}''$ respectively.

For example, let L" ≡ S($\underline{\text{KS}}$)($\underline{\text{SKK}}$) then L' ⊂ L" where L' is as in the above example.

3) Let Z be a subterm occurrence of L.

   Z is <u>exactly underlined in</u> L' if $\underline{Z}$ is a subterm occurrence of L' and Z corresponds to $\underline{Z}$.

4) Let Z be a subterm occurrence of L.

   Z is <u>underlined in</u> L' if Z is a subterm of Z_1(sub L) which is exactly underlined in L'.

For instance the first occurrence of K in L of the above example is underlined in L'.

5) Let Z be a subterm occurrence of L.

   Z <u>has some line in</u> L' if Z is underlined in L' or if there is a subterm occurrence Z_1 of Z which is exactly underlined in L'.

For instance SKK sub L has some line in L' in the above example.

2.5.26 <u>Lemma</u>

Let L,L',L" be $\underline{\lambda}$-terms such that L is simple and $\underline{\lambda} \vdash L' \simeq L \simeq L''$

1) If L' ⊂ L" and L" ⊂ L', then L' ≡ L".

2) If for all subterm occurrences $\underline{Z}$ of L', the corresponding subterm occurrence Z of L is underlined in L", then L' ⊂ L".

3) If Z is a subterm occurrence of L such that the~~re is no~~ corresponding subterm occurrence Z' of L' ~~which~~ is not simple, then Z has some line in L'.

Proof.

This is clear from the definitions. ☒

2.5.27 Lemma

Let L,L' be $\underline{\lambda}$-terms such that L is simple and $\underline{\lambda} \vdash L = L'$. Let Ξ be a variable like λ-term.

Suppose that

1) If Z is a subterm occurrence of L which is eactly underlined in L', then Z is an Ω_2-term.

2) If Z is a subterm occurrence of L which is a u.g. then Z has some line in L'.

Suppose further that $\lambda + ext \vdash \Xi \geqslant \Xi'$ and Ξ' is a subterm occurrence of L.

Then Ξ' is underlined in L'.

Proof.

Ξ is variable like, hence $\Xi \equiv \Omega_2 U$, where U is a heriditarily non-Ω_2 universal generator.

Since Ω_2 is of order 0 it follows from 2.5.2.3) that $\Xi' \equiv \Omega_2 U'$, where $\lambda + ext \vdash U \geqslant U'$.

Since U is a heriditarily non-Ω_2 u.g. there is a subterm occurrence Z of U' which is a u.g. and a non-Ω_2 subterm occurrence of U' (see fig.11). By our assumption 2), Z has some line in L'. The possibility that some subterm occurrence Z_1 of Z is exactly underlined in L' is excluded, since by 1) then Z_1 would be an Ω_2-term whereas Z is a non-Ω_2 subterm occurrence of L. Therefore Z is underlined in L', i.e. there is a subterm occurrence Z_2 of L which corresponds to $\underline{Z}_2$ sub L' and such that Z sub Z_2.

We claim that $\Omega_2 U'$ sub Z_2 (see fig.11).

First note that, since $\underline{Z}_2$ sub L', it follows from 1) that Z_2 is an

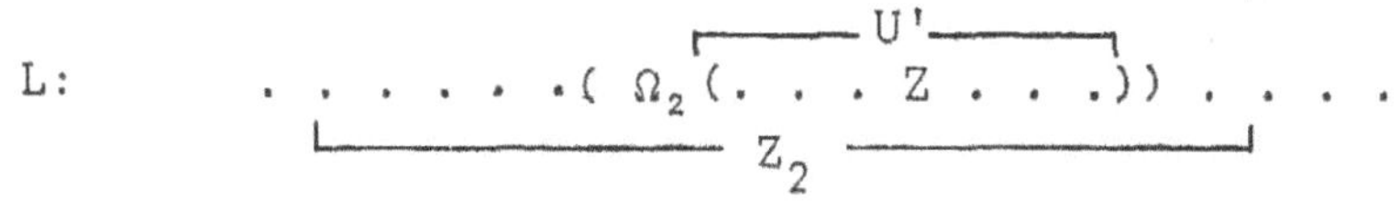

$$L: \quad \ldots\ldots(\overbrace{\Omega_2(\ldots Z \ldots)}^{U'})\ldots$$

(bracket Z_2 spanning the term)

Figure 11

Ω_2 term.

Hence since Z is a non-Ω_2 subterm occurrence of U', Z_2 is not a subterm of U'. Therefore U' sub Z_2, since subterms are either disjoint or comparable with respect to the relation sub.

Since by 2.5.22 U' is not an Ω_2-term U' is a proper subterm of Z_2.

Hence indeed $\Omega_2 U'$ sub Z_2.

Therefore $\Xi' \equiv \Omega_2 U'$ is underlined in L'. ⊠

2.5.28 <u>Theorem</u>

Let M,N be λ-terms which are not universal generators and let Ξ be a variable like λ-term.

If $\lambda + ext \vdash M\Xi = N\Xi$, then $\lambda + ext \vdash Mx = Nx$ for some variable $x \notin FV(MN)$.

Proof.

It follows from the Church-Rosser theorem 1.2.11 and the assumption $\lambda + ext \vdash M\Xi = N\Xi$, that there exists a term L such that $\lambda + ext \vdash M\Xi \geqslant L$ and $\lambda + ext \vdash N\Xi \geqslant L$.

Since $\Xi \equiv \Omega_2 U$ it follows from 2.5.3 and 2.5.2.4) that Ξ is of order 0. Hence from 2.5.14 it follows that there are terms L', L'' such that $\underline{\lambda} + ext \vdash M\underline{\Xi} \geqslant L'$, $\underline{\lambda} + ext \vdash N\underline{\Xi} \geqslant L''$ and $\underline{\lambda} \vdash L' \simeq L \simeq L''$ (see fig. 12).

82

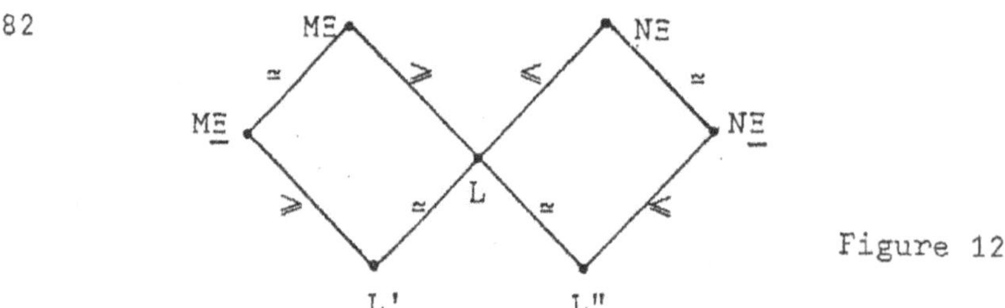

Figure 12

Now we claim that L' ≡ L".

In order to prove this, it is sufficient to show that L' ⊂ L", since by symmetry argument then also L" ⊂ L' and hence by 2.5.26.1) L' ≡ L".

We will show that for every subterm occurrence $\underline{Z}$' of L', Z' is underlined in L", where Z' is the subterm occurrence of L corresponding to $\underline{Z}$'. Then it follows by 2.5.26.2) that L' ⊂ L".

Suppose therefore that $\underline{Z}$' is a subterm occurrence of L'. By 2.5.14 it follows that $\lambda + ext \vdash \Xi \geqslant Z'$.

We verify the conditions 1) and 2) of 2.5.27 for L,L".

1) If Z is a subterm occurrence of L which is exactly underlined in L", then $\underline{Z}$ sub L", hence it follows by 2.5.14, that $\lambda + ext \vdash \Xi \geqslant Z$, hence Z is an Ω_2-term.

2) If Z is a subterm occurrence of L which is a u.g. then $Z \notin \mathcal{F}_{\lambda+ext}(N)$ (otherwise N would be a u.g.). Hence by 2.5.20 Z is not the corresponding subterm occurrence of a simple subterm of L".

   Therefore Z has some line in L', by 2.5.26.3).

Therefore it follows from 2.5.27 that Z' is underlined in L".

Hence we have proved that L' ≡ L".

Let x be a variable not occuring in the reductions represented in fig. 12. Then it follows from 2.5.16 that

$\lambda + \text{ext} \vdash Mx = \phi_x(M) \geqslant \phi_x(L')$

$\lambda + \text{ext} \vdash Nx = \phi_x(N) \geqslant \phi_x(L'')$.

Hence $\lambda + \text{ext} \vdash Mx = Nx$ since $\phi_x(L') \equiv \phi_x(L'')$. ⊠

Remark. We also have

Let M,N be λ-terms which are not u.g.'s and let Ξ be a variable like λ-term.

If $\lambda \vdash M\Xi = N\Xi$, then $\lambda \vdash Mx = Nx$ for some variable $x \notin FV(MN)$.

2.5.29 Theorem

Let M,N be λ-terms which are not universal generators. Then the ω-rule for M and N is derivable in the λ-calculus with extensionality.

Proof.

Suppose that $\lambda + \text{ext} \vdash MZ = NZ$ for all closed Z.

Then $\lambda + \text{ext} \vdash M\Xi = N\Xi$, for variable like terms Ξ, since they are closed.

Hence by 2.5.28 it follows that $\lambda + \text{ext} \vdash Mx = Nx$ for some variable $x \notin FV(MN)$.

Therefore, by extensionality, $\lambda + \text{ext} \vdash M = N$. ⊠

Chapter III

Consistency results and term models

§3.1. Modeltheoretic notions for combinatory logic and some of its extensions.

A combinatory structure is an algebraical structure for a reduct of the language of CL, in which we drop the relation $\geqslant$. $=$ is always interpreted as the real equality.

A combinatory structure is called trivial if its domain consists of a single element.

A combinatory model is a non trivial combinatory structure $\mathfrak{C} = \langle C, i, k, s, \cdot \rangle$ such that $i \cdot x = x$, $k \cdot x \cdot y = x$ and $s \cdot x \cdot y \cdot z = x \cdot z \cdot (y \cdot z)$ for all $x, y, z \in C$ (as usual we associate to the left).

A combinatory structure $\mathfrak{C}$ assigns homomorphically to each closed CL-term M an element of C which we will denote by $¤_C(M)$.

If $\mathfrak{C}$ is a combinatory model, its interior $\mathfrak{C}^0$ is by definition the restriction of $\mathfrak{C}$ to

$C^0 = \{x \in C \mid x = ¤_C(M)$ for some closed CL-term $M\}$.

A combinatory model is called hard if it coincides with its own interior.

A combinatory model is an extensional model if it satisfies the axiom of extensionality i.e. if $\forall x, y \in C\ [\forall z \in C\ (x \cdot z = y \cdot z) \Rightarrow x = y]$.

Note that the axiom of extensionality cannot be expressed in CL, since CL has no logical connectives.

A combinatory model $\mathfrak{C}$ is an ω-model if it satisfies the axiom corresponding to the ω-rule, i.e. if

$\forall x,y \in C\ [\forall z \in C^0 (x \cdot z = y \cdot z) \Rightarrow x = y]$.

It is clear that an ω-model is extensional.

From the completeness of predicate logic it follows that for every consistent extension of CL we can define a canonical model. Since the language of CL is logic free, this model is a particularly simple one, namely a term model.

3.1.1 Definition

Let & be a consistent extension of CL (in the same language). The term model of & consists of all CL-terms (closed and open) where terms that are provably equal in & are equated and application is defined as juxta position.

Hence the term model consists of the set of terms with the minimal equality which satisfies &. The non-triviality of the term model follows by the consistency of &.

An extensional model or an ω-model can be obtained as term model of CL + ext resp. CLω.

The restriction of an ω-model to its interior is again an ω-model. But the restriction of an extensional model to its interior is not necessarily extensional.

The notion of ω-completeness should be distinguished from a stronger one. Let us call an consistent extension & of CL strongly ω-complete, if all extensional models of & are in fact ω-models. Strong ω-completeness implies ω-completeness, as follows by considering the term model of & + ext.

The converse is not necessarily true.

The rumour mentioned in the footnote on page 49 was not quite justified. Apparently Jacopini [1971] has proved that CL is not strongly ω-complete. Hence the question of the ω-completeness of CL still remains open.

3.1.2 Theorem (Grzegorczyk [1971])

There is no recursive model for CL.

Proof.

If © would be a recursive model, then Th(©) would form a consistent recursive extension of CL, contradicting 1.3.17. ⊠

Since it is not clear how to interpret the λ-operation in a model we restricted ourselves to models of combinatory logic. It is nevertheless possible to define λ-abstraction in a model. This is done in the later versions of Scott [1970].

§3.2. Term models

In this § we will answer negatively the question whether Scott's lattice theoretic method provides us with all extensional models for CL. We do this by equating all the unsolvable CL-terms and obtain an extensional term model in which there is only one fixed-point(an element x such that for all y $x \cdot y = x$ is called a fixed-point). In Scott's models there are at least two fixed-points.

Further it is shown that Con, the set of equations that can be added consistently to the λ-calculus, is complete Π_1^0 (after Gödelisation). This is not an immediate consequence of the fact that λ-calculus is a complete Σ_1^0 theory, since there is no negation. Unsolvable terms will play the role of negation. Finally we construct a term model for CL which cannot be embedded into nor mapped onto an extensional model.

3.2.1 Definition

1. A CL-term M is called CL-solvable if $\exists N_1 \ldots N_k$ CL $\vdash MN_1 \ldots N_k = K$.
2. A λ-term M is called λ-solvable if $\exists N_1 \ldots N_k$ $MN_1 \ldots N_k$ has a β-normal form.
3. A λ-term M is called $\lambda\eta$-solvable if $\exists N_1 \ldots N_k$ $MN_1 \ldots N_k$ has a $\beta\eta$-normal form.

In 3.2.20½ we will give an alternative characterization of solvable terms.

3.2.2 Lemma

Let Z be a λ-term. Then Z is λ-solvable iff Z is $\lambda\eta$-solvable.

Proof.

By the remark following 1.2.8. ⊠

3.2.3 Theorem

1) If CL $\vdash$ ZM = K, then M is CL-solvable or CL $\vdash$ Zx = K for any variable x.
2) If ZM has a $\beta\eta$-normal form N, then M is $\lambda\eta$-solvable or λ + ext $\vdash$ Zx = N for any variable x.

The proof which, in the CL case, makes use of an auxiliary theory CL' similar to CL is postponed until §3.3.

3.2.4 Definition (Morris)

Let M, M' be λ-terms.

$M \subset M'$ if $\forall Z$ [ZM has a $\beta\eta$-normal form $\Rightarrow \lambda + ext \vdash ZM = ZM'$].

In his thesis Morris [1968] proved

3.2.5 Theorem

If $\lambda + ext \vdash MA = A$, then $FP\ M \subset A$.

Hence $FP\ M$ is the minimal fixedpoint (in the sense of $\subset$).

3.2.6 Theorem

If M is an unsolvable λ-term (i.e. if M is not λ-solvable) then $M \subset M'$ for all terms M'. Hence M is minimal (in the sense of $\subset$) in the set of all terms.

Proof.

This follows immediately from 3.2.3 2) and lemma 3.2.2. ⊠

As many fixedpoints are unsolvable, e.g. $FP\ K$, $FP\ S$ etc., 3.2.6 is for those terms a sharpening of 3.2.5.

3.2.7 Definition

$\mathcal{H}_{CL} = \{M = M' \mid M, M'$ are unsolvable CL-terms$\}$

$\mathcal{H}_{\lambda} = \{M = M' \mid M, M'$ are unsolvable λ-terms$\}$.

We will prove now that $CL + \mathcal{H}_{CL}$ is consistent. The most convenient way to prove this is to develop a theory CL^+ which is a conservative extension of $CL + \mathcal{H}_{CL}$. CL^+ will play the same role as $CL\omega'$ in the consistency proof of CL + ω-rule.

3.2.8 Definition

CL^+ has the following language:

Alphabet = $\text{Alphabet}_{CL} \cup \{\approx, \sim\}$.

The terms are those of CL.

Formulas: If M,N are terms, then

$M \geqslant N$, $M = N$, $M \approx N$ and $M \sim N$ are formulas.

3.2.9 Definition

CL^+ has the following axioms and rules (see appendix).

I Same as in 1.4.2.

II 1. $M = M$ $\qquad M \approx M \qquad M \sim M$

2. $\dfrac{M = N}{N = M} \qquad \dfrac{M \approx N}{N \approx M} \qquad \dfrac{M \sim N}{N \sim M}$

3. $\dfrac{M = N,\ N = L}{M = L}$

4. $\dfrac{M = M'}{ZM = ZM'}, \dfrac{M = M'}{MZ = M'Z} \qquad \dfrac{M \sim M'}{ZM \sim ZM'}, \dfrac{M \sim M'}{MZ \sim M'Z}$

III 1. Same as in 1.4.2

2. Same as in 1.4.2

3. Same as in 1.4.2

4. $\dfrac{M \geqslant M'}{M \approx M'} \qquad \dfrac{M \approx M'}{M \sim M'} \qquad \dfrac{M \sim M'}{M = M'}$

IV $M \approx M'$ if M, M' are unsolvable terms.

Now we proceed as in §2.2 to prove that $CL + \mathcal{H}_{CL}$ is consistent. If the proofs are similar to those in §2.2 or easy, we omit them.

3.2.10 Lemma

1) $CL \vdash M \geqslant N \iff CL + \mathcal{H}_{CL} \vdash M \geqslant N \iff CL^+ \vdash M \geqslant N$.

2) $CL + \mathcal{H}_{CL} \vdash M = N \iff CL^+ \vdash M = N$.

Hence CL^+ is a conservative extension of $CL + \mathcal{H}_{CL}$.

3.2.11 Lemma

$CL^+ \vdash M = N \iff \exists N_1 \ldots N_k \;\; CL^+ \vdash M \sim N_1 \sim \ldots \sim N_k \equiv N$.

3.2.12 Lemma

If $CL^+ \vdash M \sim N$, then $\exists M'.N',Z$
$[CL^+ \vdash ZM' \geqslant M,\; CL^+ \vdash ZN' \geqslant N$ and $CL^+ \vdash M' \approx N']$.

3.2.13 Lemma

If $CL^+ \vdash M \approx N$, then either 1) M,N are unsolvable or
2) $CL^+ \vdash M \geqslant N$ or $CL^+ \vdash N \geqslant M$.

3.2.14 Theorem

If $CL^+ \vdash M = K$, then

(*) $\quad CL \vdash M = K$.

Proof.

From 3.2.11 it follows that $CL^+ \vdash M = K$

(**) $\quad \exists N_1 \ldots N_k \;\; CL^+ \vdash M \sim N_1 \sim \ldots \sim N_k \geqslant K$.

By induction on k we prove that (**) ⇒ (*).

If $k = 0$, then there is nothing to prove. So suppose that $k > 0$.

Since $CL^+ \vdash M_{k-1} \sim M_k$ it follows by 3.2.12 that $\exists M'_{k-1}, M'_k, Z$ such that

$CL^+ \vdash ZM'_{k-1} \geqslant M_{k-1}$, $CL^+ \vdash ZM'_k \geqslant M_k$ and $CL^+ \vdash M'_{k-1} \approx M'_k$.

By 3.2.13 we can distinguish the following cases:

case 1. M'_{k-1}, M'_k are unsolvable.

then, since $CL^+ \vdash ZM'_k \geq M_k \equiv K$ it follows from 3.2.10 and 3.2.3 1) that

$CL \vdash Zx = K$ for any x.

Hence $CL \vdash ZM'_{k-1} = K$ and therefore

$CL^+ \vdash M_{k-1} \geq K$ as follows from

$CL^+ \vdash ZM'_{k-1} \geq M_{k-1}$, 3.2.10 and 1.5.1.

Thus $CL^+ \vdash M \sim M_1 \sim \ldots \sim M_{k-1} \geq K$, hence by the induction hypothesis

$CL \vdash M = K$.

case 2. $CL^+ \vdash M'_{k-1} \geq M'_k$ or $CL^+ \vdash M'_k \geq M'_{k-1}$.

In both cases we have

$CL \vdash M_{k-1} = ZM'_{k-1} = ZM'_k = M_k = K$ by 3.2.10.

Hence $CL^+ \vdash M_{k-1} \geq K$ by 1.5.1 and 3.2.10.

Then $CL \vdash M = K$ follows as above from the induction hypothesis. ⊠

3.2.15 Corollary

$CL + \mathcal{H}_{CL}$ is consistent.

Proof.

Suppose that $CL + \mathcal{H}_{CL} \vdash KK = K$, then by 3.2.10 $CL^+ \vdash KK = K$ and hence by 3.2.14 $CL \vdash KK = K$. This contradicts the Church-Rosser theorem for CL. ⊠

3.2.16 Remark

In the same way we can prove $Con(\lambda + \mathcal{H}_\lambda)$. With a more involved argument we can show that Con $(CL + \mathcal{H}_{CL} + ext)$ and $Con(\lambda + \mathcal{H}_\lambda + ext)$. The idea is to use the language of $CL\omega'$ (where $\approx_\alpha, \sim_\alpha, =_\alpha$ are only used for finite α) and to add the rule

$$\frac{Mx =_n Nx, \quad x \notin FV(MN)}{M \approx_{n+1} N}$$

The consistency of CL + $\mathcal{H}_{CL}$ + ext is not automatically a consequence of the consistency of CL + $\mathcal{H}_{CL}$, as will be seen in 3.2.24 where it is shown that Con(CL + $\mathfrak{M}$) ⇒ Con(CL + $\mathfrak{M}$ + ext), where $\mathfrak{M}$ is a set of equations, does not hold in general.

3.2.17 Remark

Let us call an element x of a combinatory model a fixed-point if xy = x holds for all y in the model.
In every combinatory model ©, $¤_C$(FP K) is a fixed-point. Since fixed-points in a term model correspond to unsolvable terms, it is clear that in the term model of CL + $\mathcal{H}_{CL}$(+ ext) there is only one fixed-point.
In Scott's lattice theoretic models there are always at least two fixed-points: all the elements of the initial lattice D_o become fixed-points in the limit D_∞. See Scott [1970], p.41 theorem 2.14.
Hence Scott's method does not provide us with all models for CL + ext. This was suggested to us by professor Gross. His suggestion had inspired us to prove 3.2.15.

With the help of Con(λ + $\mathcal{H}_\lambda$) we can classify in the Kleene-Mostowski hierarchy the set of equations which can be added consistently to the λ-calculus.

3.2.18 Lemma

K = FP K is not consistent with CL or the λ-calculus.

Proof (for CL).

Let $Z = \mathrm{FP}\ K$, then $CL \vdash Z = KZ$.

Hence $CL + K = Z \vdash K = Z = KZ = KK$, and therefore for arbitrary M,N $\quad CL + K = Z \vdash KIMN = KKIMN$, thus $\quad CL + K = Z \vdash N = M$. ⊠

3.2.19 Theorem

$Con_\lambda = \{\ulcorner M = N \urcorner \mid Con(\lambda + M = N)\}$ is a complete Π^0_1 set.

(As in §1.3. $\ulcorner ... \urcorner$ denotes the Gödel number of ... in some Gödelisation.)

Proof.

$\ulcorner M = N \urcorner \notin Con_\lambda \iff \lambda + M = N \vdash K = KK$.

Hence the complement of Con_λ is r.e., therefore Con is Π^0_1.

To prove that Con_λ is complete Π^0_1, let X be an arbitrary Π^0_1 set. Let $Y = \omega - X$, the complement of X. Then Y is r.e.

Define $f(n) = \begin{cases} 0 & \text{if } n \in Y \\ \uparrow & \text{else} \end{cases}$

then f is partial recursive.

Hence there is a λ-term F which strongly defines f. Note that if $f(n)\ \uparrow$, then by 1.3.3 $F\underline{n}$ is unsolvable. Then

$n \in Y \iff f(n) = 0 \iff \lambda \vdash F\underline{n} = \underline{0} \Rightarrow \lambda \vdash F\underline{n}IK = K \Rightarrow$

$\qquad \ulcorner F\underline{n}IK = \mathrm{FP}\ K \urcorner \notin Con_\lambda \qquad$ by lemma 3.2.18

$n \notin Y \iff f(n)\uparrow \iff F\underline{n}$ is unsolvable $\Rightarrow$

$\qquad \ulcorner F\underline{n}IK = \mathrm{FP}\ K \urcorner \in Con_\lambda \qquad$ by 3.2.16 since FP K is unsolvable.

Hence

$$n \in X \iff n \notin Y \iff \ulcorner F\underline{n}IK = \mathrm{FP}\ K \urcorner \in Con_\lambda.$$

Thus $X \leqslant_1 Con_\lambda$ via the function

$h(n) = \ulcorner F\underline{n}IK = \mathrm{FP}\ K \urcorner$, i.e. Con_λ is complete Π^0_1. ⊠

3.2.20 Remark

The same result holds for $Con_{\lambda+ext}$ and also for Con_{CL} and Con_{CL+ext}. In the CL-case this is proved using the strong definability (in our sense) in CL of the partial recursive functions. This CL-definability is essentially proved in Curry, Hindley, Seldin [1971], Ch 13 A.

The proof of 3.2.19 suggests the following result (from which 3.2.19 follows more directly).

3.2.20½ Theorem

Let M be a closed term of CL or the λ-calculus.

1) M is CL- (λη-, λ-) solvable $\iff \exists N_1 \ldots N_k \ MN_1 \ldots N_k = K$ is provable in CL(λ + ext, λ).

2) M is CL- (λη-, λ-) solvable $\iff$ $M = FP\ K$ is inconsistent with CL (λ + ext, λ).

Proof.

1) i) For CL this is just the definition.

ii) $\Rightarrow$: If M is λη-solvable, then

$\exists N_1 \ldots N_k \ \lambda + ext \vdash MN_1 \ldots N_k = N$, where N is in βη-normal form.

By a theorem of Böhm [1968] there exists closed terms $P_1, \ldots, P_m, Z_1, \ldots, Z_n$ such that for

$N' \equiv [x_1/P_1] \ldots [x_m/P_m] N$

(here $FV(N) = \{x_1, \ldots, x_m\}$)

we have

$\lambda + ext \vdash N'Z \ldots Z_n xy = x$.

Define $N_i' \equiv [x_1/P_1] \ldots [x_m/P_m] N_i$, then

$\lambda + ext \vdash MN_1' \ldots N_k' = N'$.

Hence $\lambda + \text{ext} \vdash MN_1' \ldots N_k' \; Z_1 \ldots Z_p KK = K$.

⇐: By definition.

iii) ⇒: If M is λ-solvable, then by 3.2.2 M is λη-solvable and therefore by ii) $\exists N_1 \ldots N_k \;\; \lambda + \text{ext} \vdash MN_1 \ldots N_k = K$.
Since the ω-rule implies the rule of extensionality, we have

$\exists N_1 \ldots N_k \;\; \lambda\omega \vdash MN_1 \ldots N_k = K$.

Hence by the analogue of 2.2.12 (which follows from the CL ⇌ λ-calculus translation 1.4.11) for the λ-calculus

$\exists N_1 \ldots N_k \;\; \exists n \in \omega \;\; \lambda \vdash MN_1 \ldots N_k \, K_{2n} = K$

⇐: By definition.

2) ⇒: Let M be --- solvable, then by 1)

$\exists N_1 \ldots N_k$ --- $\vdash MN_1 \ldots N_k = K$.

Hence --- + $M = \text{FP } K \vdash K = MN_1 \ldots N_k = \text{FP } K \; N_1 \ldots N_k = \text{FP } K$.
(remember that --- $\vdash \text{FP } K \, x = \text{FP } K$).

This yields according to 3.2.18 a contradiction.

⇐: If M would be unsolvable, then M = FP K were consistent with --- by 3.2.15 and 3.2.16 (FP K is unsolvable). ⊠

3.2.21 Definition

Let M,N be CL-terms.

M and N are separable if $\exists Z[\mathrm{CL} \vdash ZM = K$ and $\mathrm{CL} \vdash ZN = KK]$.

Trivial is

3.2.22

Con(CL + M = N) $\Rightarrow$ M and N are not separable

but

3.2.23 Theorem

The converse of 3.2.22 is not true.

Proof.

Let M = FP K and N = K. Then, by 3.2.18, not Con(CL + M = N). But M and N are not separable, for suppose $\mathrm{CL} \vdash ZM = K$, then by 3.2.3 $\mathrm{CL} \vdash Zx = K$ since M = FP K is unsolvable. Hence also $\mathrm{CL} \vdash ZN = K$, which implies that $\mathrm{CL} \vdash ZN = KK$ is impossible. ⊠

The rest of this § is devoted to establishing the following theorem.

3.2.24 Theorem

There is a set $\mathfrak{M}$ of equations such that Con(CL + $\mathfrak{M}$) but not Con(CL + $\mathfrak{M}$ + ext).

If $\mathfrak{M}$ is such a set of equations, then the term model of CL + $\mathfrak{M}$ can neither be embedded in nor mapped homomorphically onto an extensional model.

We will show by a Church-Rosser technique

that CL + K = Ω_2(KI) + KK = Ω_2(SK) is consistent (here we use par abus de langage Ω_2 as an abbreviation for SII(SII)). If we add extensionality however, this theory becomes inconsistent, since CL + ext $\vdash$ KI = SK.

3.2.25 Definition

CL" is a theory with the same language as CL' (see appendix).

CL" is defined by the following axioms and rules (see appendix)

I Same as in 1.5.2.

II Same as in 1.4.2.

III Same as in 1.4.2.

IV 1. $M \geqslant_1 M$

2. $\dfrac{M \geqslant_1 M',\ N \geqslant_1 N'}{MN \geqslant_1 M'N'}$ (!)

3. $\dfrac{M \geqslant_1 M'}{M \geqslant M'}$

V 1. $\Omega_2'(KI) \geqslant_1 K$ where CL" $\vdash \Omega_2 \geqslant \Omega_2'$

2. $\Omega_2'(SK) \geqslant_1 KK$ where CL" $\vdash \Omega_2 \geqslant \Omega_2'$

In the above M,M',N,L denote arbitrary terms and $\Omega_2 \equiv$ SII(SII).

3.2.26 Lemma

CL" $\vdash$ M = N $\iff$ CL + K = Ω_2(KI) + KK = Ω_2(SK) $\vdash$ M = N.

Proof.

Show by induction

1. CL" $\vdash M \geqslant_1 N \Rightarrow$ CL + $\mathfrak{M} \vdash$ M = N

CL" $\vdash M \geqslant N \Rightarrow$ CL + $\mathfrak{M} \vdash$ M = N

CL" $\vdash$ M = N $\Rightarrow$ CL + $\mathfrak{M} \vdash$ M = N

2. CL + $\mathfrak{M} \vdash$ M = N $\Rightarrow$ CL" $\vdash$ M = N

where $\mathfrak{M}$ = {K = Ω_2(KI), KK = Ω_2(SK)}. ⊠

3.2.27 Lemma

$CL'' \vdash M \geqslant N \iff \exists N_1 \ldots N_k \quad CL'' \vdash M \geqslant_1 N_1 \geqslant_1 \ldots \geqslant_1 N_k \geqslant N.$

Proof.

Induction on the length of proof of $M \geqslant N$. ⊠

3.2.28 Lemma

If $CL'' \vdash MN \geqslant_1 L$, then

1) $L \equiv M'N'$ and $CL'' \vdash M \geqslant_1 M'$, $CL'' \vdash N \geqslant_1 N'$ or

2) $M \equiv I$ and $L \equiv N$ or

3) $M \equiv KM_1$ and $L \equiv M_1$ or

4) $M \equiv SM_1M_2$ and $L \equiv M_1N(M_2N)$ or

5) $M \equiv \Omega_2'$, where $CL'' \vdash \Omega_2 \geqslant \Omega_2'$, $N \equiv KI$ and $L \equiv K$ or

6) $M \equiv \Omega_2'$,, where $CL'' \vdash \Omega_2 \geqslant \Omega_2'$, $N \equiv SK$ and $L \equiv KK$.

Proof.

Induction on the length of proof of $MN \geqslant_1 L$. ⊠

3.2.29 Lemma

If $CL'' \vdash \Omega_2 \geqslant \Omega_2'$, then $CL \vdash \Omega_2' \geqslant \Omega_2$, hence Ω_2' is not of the form I, K, KM, S, SM_1 or SM_1M_2.

Proof.

By induction on the length of proof of $\Omega_2 \geqslant \Omega_2'$ one shows that Ω_2 is of the form $I^n(SII)[I^m(SII)]$. Hence $CL \vdash \Omega_2' \geqslant \Omega_2$. ⊠

3.2.30 Lemma

If $CL'' \vdash M_1 \geqslant_1 M_2$ and $CL'' \vdash M_1 \geqslant_1 M_3$, then there exists a term M_4 such that $CL'' \vdash M_2 \geqslant_1 M_4$ and $CL'' \vdash M_3 \geqslant_1 M_4$. (See fig.1, p.38.)

Proof.

Induction on the length of proof of $M_1 \geqslant_1 M_2$.

case 1. $M_1 \geqslant_1 M_2$ is an axiom.

subcase 1.1. $M_1 \geqslant_1 M_2$ is $IM \geqslant_1 M$.

By 3.2.28 and 3.2.29 it follows that either

a) $M_3 \equiv IM'$ with $CL'' \vdash M \geqslant_1 M'$, then we can take $M_4 \equiv M'$, or

b) $M_3 \equiv M$, then we can take $M_4 \equiv M$.

subcase 1.2,1.3. $M_1 \geqslant_1 M_2$ is $KMN \geqslant_1 M$ or $SMNL \geqslant_1 ML(NL)$.

Analogous to subcase 1.1.

subcase 1.4. $M_1 \equiv M_2$. Then we can take $M_4 \equiv M_3$.

subcase 1.5. $M_1 \geqslant_1 M_2$ is $\Omega_2'(KI) \geqslant_1 K$.

By 3.2.28 and 3.2.29 it follows that either

a) $M_3 \equiv K$, then we can take $M_4 \equiv K$, or

b) $M_3 \equiv \Omega_2''(KI)$ with $CL'' \vdash \Omega_2' \geqslant_1 \Omega_2''$ hence we can take $M_4 \equiv K$.

subcase 1.6. $M_1 \geqslant_1 M_2$ is $\Omega_2'(SK) \geqslant_1 KK$.

Analogous to subcase 1.5 .

case 2. $M_1 \geqslant_1 M_2$ is $MN \geqslant_1 M'N'$ and is a direct consequence of $CL'' \vdash M \geqslant_1 M'$ and $CL'' \vdash N \geqslant_1 N'$.

If $M_1 \geqslant_1 M_3$ is an axiom, then we are done by case 1.

Otherwise $M_1 \geqslant_1 M_3$ is $MN \geqslant_1 M''N''$ and is a direct consequence of $CL'' \vdash M \geqslant_1 M''$ and $CL'' \vdash N \geqslant_1 N''$.

By the induction hypothesis there exist M''', N''' such that $CL'' \vdash M' \geqslant_1 M'''$, $CL'' \vdash M'' \geqslant_1 M'''$ and the same for N.

Hence we can take $M_4 \equiv M''' N'''$. ⊠

3.2.31 Lemma

If $CL'' \vdash M_1 \geqslant M_2$ and $CL'' \vdash M_1 \geqslant M_3$, then there exists a term M_4 such that $CL'' \vdash M_3 \geqslant M_4$.

Proof.

This follows from 3.2.30 and 3.2.27 (trivially, in the same way as 1.5.8 follows from 1.5.7). ⊠

3.2.32 <u>Theorem</u> (Church-Rosser theorem for CL")

If CL" $\vdash$ M = N, then there exists a term Z such that CL" $\vdash$ M $\geqslant$ Z and CL" $\vdash$ N $\geqslant$ Z.

Proof.

Induction on the length of proof of M = N (as 1.5.16 follows from 1.5.15). ⊠

3.2.33 <u>Corollary</u>

1) CL" is consistent.
2) CL + K = Ω_2(KI) + KK = Ω_2(SK) is consistent.
3) Conjecture 3.2.24 is false.

Proof.

1) If CL" $\vdash$ K = KK, then there would be a Z such that CL" $\vdash$ K $\geqslant$ Z and CL" $\vdash$ KK $\geqslant$ Z, a contradiction.
2) This follows immediately from 1) and 3.2.26.
3) Since CL + ext $\vdash$ KI = SK,
   CL + K = Ω_2(KI) + KK = Ω_2(SK) + ext $\vdash$ K = Ω_2(KI) = Ω_2(KS) = KK.
   Hence: CL + $\mathfrak{M}$ is consistent $\not\Rightarrow$ CL + $\mathfrak{M}$ + ext is consistent. ⊠

§3.3. The theory <u>CL'</u>.

In this § we will prove theorem 3.2.3. We restrict ourselves to 1) (the CL-case), since the proof of 2) (the λ-case) is similar.

The most convenient way to carry out the proof is to develop an auxiliary theory <u>CL'</u> similar to <u>CL</u>.

3.3.1 Definition

CL' is a theory with the same language as CL.

We define a mapping $|\ldots| : \underline{CL}' \to CL$ as follows

$$|c| = c \quad \text{if c is a constant or variable}$$

$$|MN| = |M||N|$$

$$|\underline{M}| = M$$

CL' is defined by the following axioms and rules (see appendix).

I, II, III, IV and V are as in 2.3.2.

VI $\quad \underline{M}\, N \geq_1 \underline{M\ |N|}$

In the above the restrictions on the terms are clear.

Axiom VI is essential for CL'; compare it with axiom VI for CL.

3.3.2 Definition

Let M,M' be CL-terms.

M' is in the CL-solution of M, notation $M \gg M'$ if

$\exists N_1 \ldots N_k \quad CL \vdash MN_1 \ldots N_k \geq M' \quad$ (k = 0 is allowed).

Note that $\gg$ is transitive. M is CL solvable iff $M \gg K$.

Now we proceed as in §2.3. When the proofs are similar to those in §2.3 we omit them.

3.3.3 Lemma

1) $\underline{CL}' \vdash M \geq M' \iff CL \vdash M \geq M'$ if M,M' are simple terms

2) $\underline{CL}' \vdash M \geq M' \iff \underline{CL}' \vdash \underline{M} \geq \underline{M}'$ if M,M' are simple terms

3) $[\underline{CL}' \vdash M \geq_1 M'$ and $\underline{N}'$ sub $M'] \Rightarrow \exists N[\underline{N}$ sub M and $N \gg N']$

3.3.4 Lemma

$\underline{CL}' \vdash M \geq M' \iff \exists N_1 \ldots N_k \quad \underline{CL}' \vdash M \equiv N_1 \geq_1 \ldots \geq_1 N_k \equiv M'$.

3.3.5 Lemma

$[\underline{CL}' \vdash M \geqslant M'$ and $\underline{N}'$ sub $M'] \Rightarrow \exists N[\underline{N}$ sub M and $N \geqslant N']$.

3.3.6 Lemma

Let M, M', N be terms such that

1) M and M' are simple

2) $CL \vdash M \geqslant M'$

3) $\underline{CL}' \vdash M \approx N$,

then there exists a term N' such that

4) $\underline{CL}' \vdash N \geqslant N'$

5) $\underline{CL}' \vdash M' \approx N'$ (see fig. 7, page 60).

3.3.7 Definition

Let M be a CL-term. An x substitution of M is the result of replacing some occurrences of x in M by other terms.

3.3.8 Lemma

If $CL \vdash M \geqslant M'$ and N is an x substitution of M, then there exists a term N' which is an x substitution of M' such that $CL \vdash N \geqslant N'$.

Proof.

Induction on the length of proof of $M \geqslant M'$. ⊠

3.3.9 Lemma

If $\underline{CL}' \vdash M \geqslant_1 M'$, then $CL \vdash \phi_x(M) \geqslant M''$, where M'' is an x substitution of $\phi_x(M')$ (ϕ_x is defined in 2.3.7 with $A \equiv x$).

Proof.

Induction on the length of proof of $M \geqslant_1 M'$.

case 1. $M \geqslant_1 M'$ is an axiom.

subcase 1.1. $M \geqslant_1 M'$ is not an instance of axiom VI 1 or 2. Then since CL − {VI} = CL' − {VI} it follows from 2.3.8 that $CL \vdash \phi_x(M) \geqslant \phi_x(M')$. Hence we can take $M'' \equiv \phi_x(M')$.

subcase 1.2. $M \geqslant_1 M'$ is an instance of axiom VI, say $\underline{M_1} M_2 \geqslant_1 \underline{M_1 \ |M_2|}$. Then $\phi_x(M) \equiv x\ \phi_x(M_2)$ and $\phi_x(M') \equiv x$. Hence we can take $M'' \equiv x\ \phi_x(M_2)$ which is an x variant of $\phi_x(M')$.

case 2. $M \geqslant_1 M'$ is $ZM_1 \geqslant_1 ZM_1'$ and is a direct consequence of $M_1 \geqslant_1 M_1'$.

By the induction hypothesis we have $CL \vdash \phi_x(M_1) \geqslant M_1''$,

where M'' is an x substitution of $\phi_x(M')$.

Therefore

$CL \vdash \phi_x(M) \equiv \phi_x(Z)\phi_x(M_1) \geqslant \phi_x(Z)M_1''$.

Hence we can take $M'' \equiv \phi_x(Z)M_1''$

since this is an x substitution of $\phi_x(M') \equiv \phi_x(Z)\phi_x(M_1')$.

case 3. $M \geqslant_1 M'$ is $M_1 Z \geqslant_1 M_1' Z$. This case is analogous to case 2. ⊠

3.3.10 Lemma

Let M,M' be CL'-terms such that M' is simple and $CL' \vdash M \geqslant M'$.

Let $x \notin M'$.

Then $CL \vdash \phi_x(M) \geqslant M'$.

Proof.

Suppose $CL' \vdash M \geqslant M'$, then $\exists N_1 \ldots N_k\ \ CL' \vdash M \equiv N_1 \geqslant_1 \ldots \geqslant_1 N_k \equiv M'$.

Hence $\exists N_1 \ldots N_k\ \ CL' \vdash M \equiv N_k \geqslant_1 \ldots \geqslant_1 N_1 \equiv M'$.

With induction on $i \leqslant k$ we will prove $CL \vdash \phi_x(N_i) \geqslant M'$.

If $i = 1$ we are done.

By lemma 3.3.9 it follows that $CL \vdash \phi_x(N_{i+1}) \geqslant N_i'$ where N_i' is an x substitution of $\phi_x(N_i)$. Since by induction hypothesis $CL \vdash \phi_x(N_i) \geqslant M'$ there exists by lemma 3.3.8 a M" which is an x variant of M' such that $CL \vdash N_i' \geqslant M''$. But $x \notin M'$, hence $M'' \equiv M'$.

Therefore $CL \vdash \phi_x(N_{i+1}) \geqslant N_i' \geqslant M'' \equiv M'$. ⊠

Now we are able to prove the CL part of theorem 3.2.3.

3.2.3 <u>Theorem</u>

If $CL \vdash ZM = K$, then M is CL-solvable or $CL \vdash Zx = K$ for any variable x.

Proof.

If $CL \vdash ZM = K$, then $CL \vdash ZM \geqslant K$ by 1.5.1, hence by 3.3.6 $\underline{CL}' \vdash Z\underline{M} \geqslant K'$ with $\underline{CL}' \vdash K' = K$, hence $K' \equiv K$ or $K' \equiv \underline{K}$.

case 1. $K' \equiv K$. Thus $\underline{CL}' \vdash Z\underline{M} \geqslant K$

By 3.3.10 it follows that

$CL \vdash \phi_x(Z\underline{M}) \geqslant K$ i.e. $CL \vdash Zx \geqslant K$.

case 2. $K' \equiv \underline{K}$. Thus $\underline{CL}' \vdash Z\underline{M} \geqslant \underline{K}$.

Hence by 3.3.5 $M \geqslant K$ i.e. M is CL solvable. ⊠

Appendix I

Survey of the theories used in the text.

This appendix presents a full description of the theories considered.

In order to facilitate the locating of those descriptions we list them here with a reference to the place where they were introduced and their page in the appendix.

Theory	Introduced in	Page
λ-calculus (with ⩾)	1.2.2	A1
CL	1.4.1	A2
CL'	1.5.2	A3
CL*	1.5.4	A4
$\underline{CL}^*$	1.5.18	A5
CLω'	2.2.2	A6
$\underline{CL}$	2.3.1	A7
$\underline{\lambda}$ + ext	2.5.4	A8
CL^+	3.2.8	A9
CL"	3.2.25	A10
$\underline{CL}'$	3.3.1	A11

A1. The λ-calculus

Language

Alphabet:	a,b,c,...	variables
	λ,(,)	improper symbols
	=	equality
	⩾	reduction

Terms: Terms are defined inductively by

1) Any variable is a term.
2) If M,N are terms, then (MN) is a term.
3) If M is a term, then (λxM) is a term

Formulas: If M,N are terms, then
M=N and M ⩾ N are formulas.

To be able to formulate the axioms we define inductively:

The set of free variables of a term:

$FV(x) = \{x\}$

$FV(MN) = FV(M) \cup FV(N)$

$FV(\lambda xM) = FV(M) - \{x\}$

The set of bound variables of a term:

$BV(x) = \emptyset$

$BV(MN) = BV(M) \cup BV(N)$

$BV(\lambda xM) = BV(M) \cup \{x\}$

Substitution of a term N in the free occurrences of the variable x in M:

$[x/N]x = N$

$[x/N]y = y$

$[x/N](M_1M_2) = [x/N]M_1)([x/N]M_2)$

$[x/N](\lambda xM) = \lambda xM$

$[x/N](\lambda yM) = \lambda y([x/N]M)$

In the above x is an arbitrary variable and y is a variable different from x.

Note. In the text [x/N] sometimes was confused with [x\N]

The λ-calculus (+ extensionality, + ω-rule)

Axioms and rules

I 1. $\lambda x M \geqslant \lambda y[x/y]M$ if $y \notin FV(M)$

2. $(\lambda x M)N \geqslant [x/N]M$ if $BV(M) \cap FV(N) = \emptyset$.

II 1. $M = M$

2. $\dfrac{M = N}{N = M}$

3. $\dfrac{M = N,\ N = L}{M = L}$

4. $\dfrac{M = M'}{ZM = ZM'}$, $\dfrac{M = M'}{MZ = M'Z}$, $\dfrac{M = M'}{\lambda x M = \lambda x M'}$

III 1. $M \geqslant M$

2. $\dfrac{M \geqslant N,\ N \geqslant L}{M \geqslant L}$

3. $\dfrac{M \geqslant M'}{ZM \geqslant ZM'}$, $\dfrac{M \geqslant M'}{MZ \geqslant M'Z}$, $\dfrac{M \geqslant M'}{\lambda x M \geqslant \lambda x M'}$

4. $\dfrac{M \geqslant M'}{M = M'}$

In λ + ext we add

I 3. $\lambda x(Mx) \geqslant M$ if $x \notin FV(M)$

In λω we add

ω-rule

$$\frac{MZ = NZ \quad \text{for all } Z \text{ with } FV(Z) = \emptyset}{M = N}$$

In the above M,M',N,L and Z denote arbitrary terms and x and y arbitrary variables.

A2. Combinatory logic (CL)

Language

Alphabet:	a,b,c,...	variables
	I,K,S	constants
	(,)	improper symbols
	=	equality
	$\geqslant$	reduction

Terms: Terms are defined inductively by

1) Any variable or constant is a term.
2) If M,N are terms, then (MN) is a term.

Formulas: If M,N are terms, then

$M = N$ and $M \geqslant N$ are formulas.

$M_1M_2\ldots M_n$ stands for $(..(M_1M_2)\ldots M_n)$

CL (+ extensionality, + ω-rule)

Axioms and rules

I
1. $IM \geq M$
2. $IMN \geq M$
3. $SMNL \geq ML(NL)$

II
1. $M = M$
2. $\dfrac{M = N}{N = M}$
3. $\dfrac{M = N,\ N = L}{M = L}$
4. $\dfrac{M = M'}{ZM = ZM'}$, $\dfrac{M = M'}{MZ = M'Z}$

III
1. $M \geq M$
2. $\dfrac{M \geq N,\ N \geq L}{M \geq L}$
3. $\dfrac{M \geq M'}{ZM \geq ZM'}$, $\dfrac{M \geq M'}{MZ \geq M'Z}$
4. $\dfrac{M \geq M'}{M = M'}$

In CL + ext we add

ext $\dfrac{Mx = M'x}{M = M'}$ if $x \notin FV(MM')$

In CLω we add

ω-rule

$$\frac{MZ = NZ \quad \text{for all } Z \text{ without free variables}}{M = N}$$

In the above M,M',N,L and Z denote arbitrary terms.

A3. CL'

Language

Alphabet:	a,b,c,...	variables
	I,K,S	constants
	(,)	improper symbols
	=	equality
	$\geqslant$	reduction
	$\geqslant_1$	one step reduction

Terms: Terms are defined inductively by

1) Any variable or constant is a term.

2) If M,N are terms, then (MN) is a term.

Formulas: If M,N are terms, then
$M = N$, $M \geqslant N$ and $M \geqslant_1 N$ are formulas.

$M_1M_2...M_n$ stands for $(..(M_1M_2)...M_n)$

CL'

Axioms and rules

I 1. IM M

2. KMN M

3. SMNL ML(NL)

II 1. $M = M$

2. $\dfrac{M = N}{N = M}$

3. $\dfrac{M = N,\ N = L}{M = L}$

4. $\dfrac{M = M'}{ZM = ZM'}$, $\dfrac{M = M'}{MZ = M'Z}$

III 1. $M \geqslant M$

2. $\dfrac{M \geqslant N,\ N \geqslant L}{M \geqslant L}$

3. $\dfrac{M \geqslant M'}{ZM \geqslant ZM'}$, $\dfrac{M \geqslant M'}{MZ \geqslant M'Z}$

4. $\dfrac{M \geqslant M'}{M = M'}$

IV 1. $M \geqslant_1 M$

2. $\dfrac{M \geqslant_1 M'}{ZM \geqslant_1 ZM'}$, $\dfrac{M \geqslant_1 M'}{MZ \geqslant_1 M'Z}$

3. $\dfrac{M \geqslant_1 M'}{M \geqslant M'}$

In the above M,M',N,L and Z denote arbitrary terms.

A4. CL*

<u>Language</u>

Alphabet:	a,b,c,....	variables
	I,K,S	constants
	(,), ,	improper symbols
	=	equality
	$\geqslant$	reduction
	$\geqslant_1$	one step reduction

Terms: Terms are defined inductively by

1) Any variable or constant is a term.
2) If M,N are terms, then (MN) is a term.
3) If M,N and L are terms, then S(M,N,L) is a term.

Formulas: If M,N are terms, then $M = N$, $M \geqslant N$ and $M \geqslant_1 N$ are formulas.

$M_1M_2 \ldots M_n$ stands for $(..(M_1M_2)...M_n)$

CL*

Axioms and rules

I . 1. $IM \geqslant_1 M$

2. $KMN \geqslant_1 M$

3. $SMNL \geqslant_1 S(M,N,L)$

II 1. $M = M$

2. $\dfrac{M = N}{N = M}$

3. $\dfrac{M = N,\ N = L}{M = L}$

4. $\dfrac{M = M'}{ZM = ZM'}$, $\dfrac{M = M'}{MZ = M'Z}$

III 1. $M \geqslant M$

2. $\dfrac{M \geqslant N,\ N \geqslant L}{M \geqslant L}$

3. $\dfrac{M \geqslant M'}{ZM \geqslant ZM'}$, $\dfrac{M \geqslant M'}{MZ \geqslant M'Z}$

IV 1. $M \geqslant_1 M$

2. $\dfrac{M \geqslant_1 M'}{ZM \geqslant_1 ZM'}$, $\dfrac{M \geqslant_1 M'}{MZ \geqslant_1 M'Z}$

3. $\dfrac{M \geqslant_1 M'}{M \geqslant M'}$

4. $\dfrac{M \geqslant_1 M'}{S(M,N,L) \geqslant_1 S(M',N,L)}$, $\dfrac{N \geqslant_1 N'}{S(M,N,L) \geqslant_1 S(M,N',L)}$

$\dfrac{L \geqslant_1 L'}{S(M,N,L) \geqslant_1 S(M,N,L')}$

In the above M,M',N,N',L,L' and Z denote arbitrary terms.

A5. CL*

Language

Alphabet:	a,b,c,....	variables
	I,K,S	constants
	(,),',–	improper symbols
	=	equality
	$\geqslant$	reduction
	$\geqslant_1$	one step reduction

Terms: Terms are defined inductively by

1) Any variable or constant is a term.
2) If M,N are terms, then (MN) is a term.
3) If M,N and L are terms, then S(M,N,L) and <u>S(M,N,L)</u> are terms.

Formulas: If M,N are terms, then $M = N$, $M \geqslant N$ and $M \geqslant_1 N$ are formulas.

$M_1M_2...M_n$ stands for $(..(M_1M_2)...M_n)$

CL*

Axioms and rules (We give an equivalent version which is slightly different from the original one.)

I 1. $IM \geqslant_1 M$

2. $KMN \geqslant_1 M$

3. $SMNL \geqslant_1 \underline{S(M,N,L)}$

II 1. $M = M$

2. $\dfrac{M = N}{N = M}$

3. $\dfrac{M = N,\ N = L}{M = L}$

4. $\dfrac{M = M'}{ZM = ZM'}$, $\dfrac{M = M'}{MZ = M'Z}$

III 1. $M \geqslant M$

2. $\dfrac{M \geqslant N,\ N \geqslant L}{M \geqslant L}$

3. $\dfrac{M \geqslant M'}{ZM \geqslant ZM'}$, $\dfrac{M \geqslant M'}{MZ \geqslant M'Z}$

IV 1. $M \geqslant_1 M$

2. $\dfrac{M \geqslant_1 M'}{ZM \geqslant_1 ZM'}$, $\dfrac{M \geqslant_1 M'}{MZ \geqslant_1 M'Z}$

3. $\dfrac{M \geqslant_1 M'}{M \geqslant M'}$

4. $\dfrac{M \geqslant_1 M'}{S(M,N,L) \geqslant_1 S(M',N,L)}$, $\dfrac{N \geqslant_1 N'}{S(M,N,L) \geqslant_1 S(M,N',L)}$

$\dfrac{L \geqslant_1 L'}{S(M,N,L) \geqslant_1 S(M,N,L')}$

5. $\dfrac{M \geqslant_1 M'}{\underline{M} \geqslant_1 \underline{M'}}$

In the above M,M',N,N',L,L' and Z denote arbitrary terms, except in IV 5, where M,M' denote terms of the form S(P,Q,R).

A6. CLω'

Language

Alphabet:	$a, b, c, \ldots$	variables
	I, K, S	constants
	(,)	improper symbols
	$=$	equality
	$\geqslant$	reduction
	$\approx_\alpha, \sim_\alpha, =_\alpha$	special equalities, for every countable ordinal α.

Terms: Terms are defined inductively by

1) Any variable or constant is a term.

2) If M,N are terms, then (MN) is a term.

Formulas: If M,N are terms, then $M = N$, $M \geqslant N$, $M \approx_\alpha N$, $M \sim_\alpha N$ and $M =_\alpha N$ are formulas.

$M_1 M_2 \ldots M_n$ stands for $(..(M_1 M_2) \ldots M_n)$

CLω'

Axioms and rules

I

1. $IM \geqslant M$

2. $KMN \geqslant M$

3. $SMNL \geqslant ML(NL)$

II

1. $M =_\alpha M$, $M \approx_\alpha M$, $M \sim_\alpha M$

2. $\dfrac{M =_\alpha N}{N =_\alpha M}$, $\dfrac{M \approx_\alpha N}{N \approx_\alpha M}$, $\dfrac{M \sim_\alpha N}{N \sim_\alpha M}$

3. $\dfrac{M =_\alpha N,\ N =_\alpha L}{M =_\alpha L}$

4. $\dfrac{M =_\alpha M'}{ZM =_\alpha ZM'}$, $\dfrac{M =_\alpha M'}{MZ =_\alpha M'Z}$, $\dfrac{M \sim_\alpha M'}{ZM \sim_\alpha ZM'}$, $\dfrac{M \sim_\alpha M'}{MZ \sim_\alpha M'Z}$

5. $\dfrac{M =_\alpha M',\ \alpha \leqslant \alpha'}{M =_{\alpha'} M'}$, $\dfrac{M =_\alpha M'}{M = M'}$

III

1. $M \geqslant M$

2. $\dfrac{M \geqslant N,\ N \geqslant L}{M \geqslant L}$

3. $\dfrac{M \geqslant M'}{ZM \geqslant ZM'}$, $\dfrac{M \geqslant M'}{MZ \geqslant M'Z}$

4. $\dfrac{M \geqslant M'}{M \approx_0 M'}$, $\dfrac{M \approx_\alpha M'}{M \sim_\alpha M'}$, $\dfrac{M \sim_\alpha M'}{M =_\alpha M'}$

IV

$$\dfrac{\forall Z \text{ closed } \exists \beta < \alpha \quad MZ =_\beta NZ}{M \approx_\alpha N}$$

In the above M,M',N,L and Z denote arbitrary terms, and α,α' arbitrary countable ordinals.

A7. CL

Language

Alphabet:	a,b,c,...	variables
	I,K,S	constants
	(,), _	improper symbols
	$=$	equality
	$\geqslant$	reduction
	$\geqslant_1$	one step reduction
	$\simeq$	intrinsic equality

Simple terms: Simple terms are defined inductively by

1) Any variable or constant is a simple term.
2) If M,N are simple terms, then (MN) is a simple term.

Terms: Terms are defined inductively by

1) Any simple term is a term.
2) If M is a simple term, then $\underline{M}$ is a term.
3) If M,N are terms, then (MN) is a term.

Formulas: If M,N are terms, then $M = N$, $M \geqslant N$, $M \geqslant_1 N$ and $M \simeq N$ are formulas.

$M_1M_2...M_n$ stands for $(..(M_1M_2)...M_n)$

CL

Axioms and rules

I

1. $IM \geqslant_1 M$
2. $KMN \geqslant_1 M$
3. $SMNL \geqslant_1 ML(NL)$

II

1. $M = M$
2. $\dfrac{M = N}{N = M}$
3. $\dfrac{M = N,\ N = L}{M = L}$
4. $\dfrac{M = M'}{ZM = ZM'}$, $\dfrac{M = M'}{MZ = M'Z}$

III

1. $M \geqslant M$
2. $\dfrac{M \geqslant N,\ N \geqslant L}{M \geqslant L}$
3. $\dfrac{M \geqslant M'}{ZM \geqslant ZM'}$, $\dfrac{M \geqslant M'}{MZ \geqslant M'Z}$
4. $\dfrac{M \geqslant M'}{M = M'}$

IV

1. $M \geqslant_1 M$
2. $\dfrac{M \geqslant_1 M'}{ZM \geqslant_1 ZM'}$, $\dfrac{M \geqslant_1 M'}{MZ \geqslant_1 M'Z}$
3. $\dfrac{M \geqslant_1 M'}{M \geqslant M'}$
4. $\dfrac{M \geqslant_1 M'}{\underline{M} \geqslant_1 \underline{M}'}$

V

1. $M \simeq M$
2. $\dfrac{M \simeq N}{N \simeq M}$
3. $\dfrac{M \simeq N,\ N \simeq L}{M \simeq L}$
4. $\dfrac{M \simeq M'}{ZM \simeq ZM'}$, $\dfrac{M \simeq M'}{MZ \simeq M'Z}$
5. $M \simeq \underline{M}$

VI

$\underline{M}N \geqslant_1 MN$

In the above M, M', N, L and Z denote arbitrary terms except in IV 4, V 5 and VI where M, M' denote simple terms.

A8. $\underline{\lambda}$ + ext

Language

Alphabet: a,b,c,... variables

λ, (,), _ improper symbols

=, ≃ equality, resp.intrinsic equality

$\geqslant$, $\geqslant_1$ reduction,resp.one step reduction

Simple terms: Simple terms are defined inductively by

1) Any variable is a simple term.
2) If M,N are terms, then (MN) is a term.
3) If M is a term, then λxM is a term (x is an arbitrary variable).

The set of free variables of a simple term is inductively defined by

$$FV(x) = \{x\}$$
$$FV(MN) = FV(M) \cup FV(N)$$
$$FV(\lambda xM) = FV(M) - \{x\}$$

Terms: Terms are defined inductively by

1) Any simple term is a term.
2) If M is a simple term and if FV(M) = ∅, then $\underline{M}$ is a term.
3) If M,$\overline{N}$ are terms,then (MN) is a term.
4) If M is a term, then λxM is a term.

Formulas: If M,N are terms then M = N, M ⩾ N, M ⩾₁ N and M ≃ N are formulas.

FV, BV, [x/N] are defined inductively by

$$FV(x) = \{x\}$$
$$FV(MN) = FV(M) \cup FV(N)$$
$$FV(\lambda xM) = FV(M) - \{x\}$$
$$FV(\underline{M}) = \emptyset$$

$$BV(x) = \emptyset$$
$$BV(MN) = BV(M) \cup BV(N)$$
$$BV(\lambda xM) = BV(M) \cup \{x\}$$
$$BV(\underline{M}) = BV(M)$$

$$[x/N]x = N$$
$$[x/N]y = y$$
$$[x/N](M_1M_2) = ([x/N]M_1)([x/N]M_2)$$
$$[x/N](\lambda xM) = \lambda xM$$
$$[x/N](\lambda yM) = \lambda y[x/N]M$$
$$[x/N]\,\underline{M} = \underline{M}$$

In the above x is an arbitrary variable and y is a variable different from x.

$\underline{\lambda}$ + ext.

Axioms and rules

I

1. $\lambda xM \geqslant_1 \lambda x[x/y]M$ if $y \notin FV(M) \cup BV(M)$
2. $(\lambda xM)N \geqslant_1 [x/N]M$ if $BV(M) \cap FV(N) = \emptyset$
3. $\lambda x(Mx) \geqslant_1 M$ if $x \notin FV(M)$.

II

1. $M = M$
2. $\dfrac{M = N}{N = M}$
3. $\dfrac{M = N,\ N = L}{M = L}$
4. $\dfrac{M = M'}{ZM = ZM'}$, $\dfrac{M = M'}{MZ = M'Z}$, $\dfrac{M = M'}{\lambda xM = \lambda xM'}$

III

1. $M \geqslant M$
2. $\dfrac{M \geqslant N,\ N \geqslant L}{M \geqslant L}$
3. $\dfrac{M \geqslant M'}{ZM \geqslant ZM'}$, $\dfrac{M \geqslant M'}{MZ \geqslant M'Z}$, $\dfrac{M \geqslant M'}{\lambda xM \geqslant \lambda xM'}$
4. $\dfrac{M \geqslant M'}{M = M'}$

IV

1. $M \geqslant_1 M$
2. $\dfrac{M \geqslant_1 M'}{ZM \geqslant_1 ZM'}$, $\dfrac{M \geqslant_1 M'}{MZ \geqslant_1 M'Z}$, $\dfrac{M \geqslant_1 M'}{\lambda xM \geqslant_1 \lambda xM'}$, $\dfrac{M \geqslant_1 M'}{\underline{M} \geqslant_1 \underline{M'}}$
3. $\dfrac{M \geqslant_1 M'}{M \geqslant M'}$

V

1. $M \simeq M$
2. $\dfrac{M \simeq N}{N \simeq M}$
3. $\dfrac{M \simeq N,\ N \simeq L}{M \simeq L}$
4. $\dfrac{M \simeq M'}{ZM \simeq ZM'}$, $\dfrac{M \simeq M'}{MZ \simeq M'Z}$, $\dfrac{M \simeq M'}{\lambda xM \simeq \lambda xM'}$
5. $M \simeq \underline{M}$

In the above M, M', N, L and Z denote arbitrary terms except in the last item of IV 2 and in V 5 where M, M' denote simple terms.

A9. CL^+

Language

Alphabet:	a,b,c,..:	variables
	I,K,S	constants
	(,)	improper symbols
	=	equality
	$\geqslant$	reduction
	$\approx$, $\sim$	special equalities

Terms: Terms are defined inductively by

1) Any variable or constant is a term.

2) If M,N are terms, then (MN) is a term.

Formulas: If M,N are terms, then $M = N$, $M \geqslant N$, $M \approx N$ and $M \sim N$ are formulas.

$M_1 M_2 \ldots M_n$ stands for $(..(M_1 M_2)\ldots M_n)$

CL^+

Axioms and rules

I 1. $IM \geqslant M$

2. $KMN \geqslant M$

3. $SMNL \geqslant ML(NL)$

II 1. $M = M$ $\quad M \approx M \quad M \sim M$

2. $\dfrac{M = N}{N = M} \qquad \dfrac{M \approx N}{N \approx M} \qquad \dfrac{M \sim N}{N \sim M}$

3. $\dfrac{M = N,\ N = L}{M = L}$

4. $\dfrac{M = M'}{ZM = ZM'}\ ,\ \dfrac{M = M'}{MZ = M'Z} \qquad \dfrac{M \sim M'}{ZM \sim ZM'}\ ,\ \dfrac{M \sim M'}{MZ \sim M'Z}$

III 1. $M \geqslant M$

2. $\dfrac{M \geqslant N,\ N \geqslant L}{M \geqslant L}$

3. $\dfrac{M \geqslant M'}{ZM \geqslant ZM'}\ ,\ \dfrac{M \geqslant M'}{MZ \geqslant M'Z}$

4. $\dfrac{M \geqslant M'}{M \approx M'} \qquad \dfrac{M \approx M'}{M \sim M'} \qquad \dfrac{M \sim M'}{M = M'}$

IV $M \approx M'$ if M,M' are unsolvable terms.

In the above M,M',N,L and Z denote arbitrary terms.

A10. CL''

Language

Alphabet:	a,b,c,...	variables
	I,K,S	constants
	(,)	improper symbols
	=	equality
	$\geqslant$	reduction
	$\geqslant_1$	one step reduction

Terms: Terms are defined inductively by

1) Any variable or constant is a term.

2) If M,N are terms, then (MN) is a term.

Formulas: If M,N, are terms, then
$M = N$, $M \geqslant N$ and $M \geqslant_1 N$ are formulas.

$M_1M_2...M_n$ stands for $(..(M_1M_2)...M_n)$

Ω_2 stands for SII(SII).

CL$^+$

Axioms and rules

I
1. $IM \geqslant M$
2. $KMN \geqslant M$
3. $SMNL \geqslant ML(NL)$

II
1. $M = M$ $\qquad M \approx M \qquad M \sim M$
2. $\dfrac{M = N}{N = M} \qquad \dfrac{M \approx N}{N \approx M} \qquad \dfrac{M \sim N}{N \sim M}$
3. $\dfrac{M = N,\ N = L}{M = L}$
4. $\dfrac{M = M'}{ZM = ZM'}\ ,\ \dfrac{M = M'}{MZ = M'Z} \qquad \dfrac{M \sim M'}{ZM \sim ZM'}\ ,\ \dfrac{M \sim M'}{MZ \sim M'Z}$

III
1. $M \geqslant M$
2. $\dfrac{M \geqslant N,\ N \geqslant L}{M \geqslant L}$
3. $\dfrac{M \geqslant M'}{ZM \geqslant ZM'}\ ,\ \dfrac{M \geqslant M'}{MZ \geqslant M'Z}$
4. $\dfrac{M \geqslant M'}{M \approx M'} \qquad \dfrac{M \approx M'}{M \sim M'} \qquad \dfrac{M \sim M'}{M = M'}$

IV $\quad M \approx M'$ if M, M' are unsolvable terms.

In the above M, M', N, L and Z denote arbitrary terms.

A10. CL"

Language

Alphabet:	a,b,c,...	variables
	I,K,S	constants
	(,)	improper symbols
	=	equality
	$\geqslant$	reduction
	$\geqslant_1$	one step reduction

Terms: Terms are defined inductively by

1) Any variable or constant is a term.

2) If M,N are terms, then (MN) is a term.

Formulas: If M,N, are terms, then $M = N$, $M \geqslant N$ and $M \geqslant_1 N$ are formulas.

$M_1M_2...M_n$ stands for $(..(M_1M_2)...M_n)$

Ω_2 stands for SII(SII).

CL"

Axiomes and rules

I 1. $IM \geqslant_1 M$

2. $KMN \geqslant_1 M$

3. $SMNL \geqslant_1 ML(NL)$

II 1. $M = M$

2. $\dfrac{M = N}{N = M}$

3. $\dfrac{M = N,\ N = L}{M = L}$

4. $\dfrac{M = M'}{ZM = ZM'}$, $\dfrac{M = M'}{MZ = M'Z}$

III 1. $M \geqslant M$

2 $\dfrac{M \geqslant N,\ N \geqslant L}{M \geqslant L}$

3. $\dfrac{M \geqslant M'}{ZM \geqslant ZM'}$, $\dfrac{M \geqslant M'}{MZ \geqslant M'Z}$

4. $\dfrac{M \geqslant M'}{M = M'}$

IV 1. $M \geqslant_1 M'$

2. $\dfrac{M \geqslant_1 M',\ N \geqslant_1 N'}{MN \geqslant_1 M'N'}$ (!)

3. $\dfrac{M \geqslant_1 M'}{M \geqslant M'}$

V 1. $\Omega_2'(KI) \geqslant_1 K$ where $CL'' \vdash \Omega_2 \geqslant \Omega_2'$

2. $\Omega_2'(SK) \geqslant_1 KK$ where $CL'' \vdash \Omega_2 \geqslant \Omega_2'$.

In the above M,M',N,L and Z denote arbitrary terms, and $\Omega_2 \equiv SII(SII)$.

A11. CL'

Language

Alphabet:	a,b,c,...	variables
	I,K,S	constants
	(,), _	improper symbols
	=	equality
	$\geqslant$	reduction
	$\geqslant_1$	one step reduction
	$\simeq$	intrinsic equality

Simple terms: Simple terms are defined inductively by

1) Any variable or constant is a simple term.
2) If M,N are simple terms, then (MN) is a simple term.

Terms: Terms are defined inductively by

1) Any simple term is a term.
2) If M is a simple term, then $\underline{M}$ is a term.
3) If M,N are terms, then (MN) is a term.

Formulas: If M,N are terms, then $M = N$, $M \geqslant N$, $M \geqslant_1 N$ and $M \simeq N$ are formulas.

$M_1M_2 \ldots M_n$ stands for $(..(M_1M_2)\ldots M_n)$

To be able to formulate the axioms we define a mapping $|\ldots|$: Terms $\rightarrow$ Simple terms.

$|c| = c$ if c is a constant or variable

$|MN| = |M||N|$

$|\underline{M}| = M$

CL'

Axioms and rules

I 1. $IM \geqslant_1 M$

2. $KMN \geqslant_1 M$

3. $SMNL \geqslant_1 ML(NL)$

II 1. $M = M$

2. $\dfrac{M = N}{N = M}$

3. $\dfrac{M = N,\ N = L}{M = L}$

4. $\dfrac{M = M'}{ZM = ZM'}$, $\dfrac{M = M'}{MZ = M'Z}$

III 1. $M \geqslant M$

2. $\dfrac{M \geqslant N,\ N \geqslant L}{M \geqslant L}$

3. $\dfrac{M \geqslant M'}{ZM \geqslant ZM'}$, $\dfrac{M \geqslant M'}{MZ \geqslant M'Z}$

4. $\dfrac{M \geqslant M'}{M = M'}$

IV 1. $M \geqslant_1 M$

2. $\dfrac{M \geqslant_1 M'}{ZM \geqslant_1 ZM'}$, $\dfrac{M \geqslant_1 M'}{MZ \geqslant_1 M'Z}$

3. $\dfrac{M \geqslant_1 M'}{M \geqslant M'}$

4. $\dfrac{M \geqslant_1 M'}{\underline{M} \geqslant_1 \underline{M'}}$

V 1. $M \approx M$

2. $\dfrac{M \approx N}{N \approx M}$

3. $\dfrac{M \approx N,\ N \approx L}{M \approx L}$

4. $\dfrac{M \approx M'}{ZM \approx ZM'}$, $\dfrac{M \approx M'}{MZ \approx M'Z}$

5. $M \approx \underline{M}$

VI $\underline{MN} \geqslant_1 \underline{M\ |N|}$

In the above M,M',N,L and Z denote arbitrary terms except in IV 4, V 5 and VI where M,M' denote simple terms.

Appendix II

The Church-Rosser theorem for the λ-calculus à la Martin-Löf

This appendix contains a proof of the Church-Rosser theorem recently discovered by Martin-Löf [1971].
This proof is strikingly simple compared to those mentioned in 1.2.18.
The idea of the proof arose from cut elimination properties of certain formal systems. In fact the Church-Rosser theorem is a kind of cut elemination theorem, the transitivity of = in the λ-calculus corresponding to the cut.
The trick is to define a relation $\geqslant_1$ between terms in such a way that

1) The transitive closure of $\geqslant_1$ is the (classical) reduction relation ($\geqslant$).
2) If $M_1 \geqslant_1 M_2$, $M_1 \geqslant_1 M_3$, then there exists a term M_4 such that $M_2 \geqslant_1 M_4$ and $M_3 \geqslant_1 M_4$.

From 1) and 2) the analogue of 2) for $\geqslant$ can be derived.
From this the Church-Rosser theorem easily follows.

<u>Definition 1.</u>

λ' is a theory formulated in the following language:

Alphabet:	a,b,c,...	variables
	λ, (,)	improper symbols
	=	equality
	$\geqslant$	reduction
	$\geqslant_1$	one step reduction

Terms: The terms are defined as in the λ-calculus (1.1.1).

Formulas: If M,N are terms, then $M = N$, $M \geqslant N$ and $M \geqslant_1 N$ are formulas.

As in 1.1.2 we define BV(M), FV(M) and $[x/N]M$.

Definition 2.

λ' is defined by the following axioms and rules.

I 1. $\dfrac{M \geqslant_1 M'}{(\lambda x M) \geqslant_1 \lambda y[x/y]M'}$ if $y \notin FV(M') \cup BV(M')$

2. $\dfrac{M \geqslant_1 M' \;,\; N \geqslant_1 N'}{(\lambda x M)N \geqslant_1 [x/N']M'}$ if $BV(M') \cap FV(N') = \emptyset$

II. 1. $M \geqslant_1 M$

2. $\dfrac{M \geqslant_1 M' \;,\; N \geqslant_1 N'}{MN \geqslant_1 M'N'}$

3. $\dfrac{M \geqslant_1 M'}{\lambda x M \geqslant_1 \lambda x M'}$

4. $\dfrac{M \geqslant_1 M'}{M \geqslant M'}$

III 1. $\dfrac{M \geqslant N,\; N \geqslant L}{M \geqslant L}$

2. $\dfrac{M \geqslant M'}{ZM \geqslant ZM'}$, $\dfrac{M \geqslant M'}{MZ \geqslant M'Z}$, $\dfrac{M \geqslant M'}{\lambda x M \geqslant \lambda x M'}$

3. $\dfrac{M \geqslant M'}{M = M'}$

IV 1. $\dfrac{M = N}{N = M}$

2. $\dfrac{M = N,\; N = L}{M = L}$

3. $\dfrac{M = M'}{ZM = ZM'}$, $\dfrac{M = M'}{MZ = M'Z}$, $\dfrac{M = M'}{\lambda x M = \lambda x M'}$

In the above M,M',N,L and Z denote arbitrary terms and x, y denote arbitrary variables.

Lemma 3.

$\lambda' \vdash M \geqslant N \iff \exists N_1 \ldots N_k \quad \lambda' \vdash M \equiv N_1 \geqslant_1 \ldots \geqslant_1 N_k \equiv N.$

Proof.

$\Leftarrow$: Immediate.

$\Rightarrow$: Induction on the length of proof of $\lambda' \vdash M \geqslant N$. ⊠

Lemma 4.

$\lambda' \vdash M \geqslant_1 N \Rightarrow \lambda \vdash M \geqslant N$

$\lambda' \vdash M \geqslant N \iff \lambda \vdash M \geqslant N$

$\lambda' \vdash M = N \iff \lambda \vdash M = N$

Proof.

In all cases induction on the length of proof. ⊠

Lemma 5.

If $\lambda' \vdash M \geqslant_1 M'$ and $\lambda' \vdash N \geqslant_1 N'$, then

$\lambda' \vdash [x/N]M \geqslant_1 [x/N']M'$.

Proof.

Induction on the length of proof of $M \geqslant_1 M'$ using the sublemma:

If $x \neq y$ then $[x/N_1]([y/N_2]M) \equiv [y/[x/N_1]N_2]([x/N_1]M)$.

The proof of the sublemma proceeds by induction on the structure of M. ⊠

Lemma 6.

1) If $\lambda' \vdash \lambda xM \geqslant_1 N$, then there exists a term M' such that $\lambda' \vdash M \geqslant_1 M'$ and $N \equiv \lambda xM'$ or $N \equiv \lambda y[x/y]M'$ with $y \notin FV(M')$.

2) If $\lambda' \vdash M_1 M_2 \geqslant_1 N$, then there exist M_1', M_2' such that $\lambda' \vdash M_i \geqslant_1 M_i'$ and $N \equiv M_1' M_2'$ or $M_1 = (\lambda x M_1')$ and $N \equiv [x/M_2']M_1''$ where $\lambda' \vdash M_1' \geqslant_1 M_1''$ and $\lambda' \vdash M_2 \geqslant_1 M_2'$.

Proof.

Induction on the length of proof. ⊠

Lemma 7.

If $\lambda' \vdash M_1 \geqslant_1 M_2$ and $\lambda' \vdash M_1 \geqslant_1 M_3$, then there exists a term M_4 such that $\lambda' \vdash M_2 \geqslant_1 M_4$ and $\lambda' \vdash M_3 \geqslant_1 M_4$.

Proof.

Induction on the sum of lengths of proof of $M_1 \geqslant_1 M_2$ and $M_1 \geqslant_1 M_3$.

case 1. $M_1 \geqslant_1 M_2$ is an axiom. Then $M_1 \equiv M_2$ and we can take $M_4 \equiv M_3$.

case 2. $M_1 \geqslant_1 M_2$ is $\lambda x M \geqslant_1 \lambda y[x/y]M'$ where $y \notin FV(M')$ and is a direct consequence of $M \geqslant_1 M'$.

By lemma 6 it follows that

$M_3 \equiv \lambda y'[x/y']M''$ where $\lambda \vdash M \geqslant_1 M''$ and $y' \notin FV(M'')$ or $y' = x$.

By the induction hypothesis there exists a M''' such that $\lambda' \vdash M' \geqslant_1 M'''$ and $\lambda' \vdash M'' \geqslant_1 M'''$. Then we can take $M_4 \equiv \lambda y''[x/y'']M'''$ with $y'' \notin FV(M''')$.

case 3. $M_1 \geqslant_1 M_2$ is $\lambda x M \geqslant_1 \lambda x M'$ and is a direct consequence of $M \geqslant_1 M'$. Analogously to case 2 we can find the required term M_4.

case 4. $M_1 \geqslant_1 M_2$ is $(\lambda x M)N \geqslant_1 [x/N']M'$ and is a direct consequence of $M \geqslant_1 M'$, $N \geqslant_1 N'$.

By lemma 6 we can distinguish the following subcases.

subcase 4.1. $M_3 \equiv (\lambda y[x/y]M'')N''$, where $\lambda' \vdash M \geqslant_1 M''$, $\lambda' \vdash N \geqslant_1 N''$.

By the induction hypothesis there exist terms M''', N''' such that $\lambda' \vdash M' \geqslant_1 M'''$;

$\lambda' \vdash M'' \geqslant_1 M'''$, $\lambda' \vdash N' \geqslant_1 N'''$ and

$\lambda' \vdash N'' \geqslant_1 N'''$.

Then by lemma 5 we can take $M_4 \equiv [x/N''']M'''$.

subcase 4.2. $M_3 \equiv [x/N'']M''$ with $\lambda' \vdash M \geqslant_1 M''$,

$\lambda' \vdash N \geqslant_1 N''$.

By the induction hypothesis there exist terms M''', N''' such that $\lambda' \vdash M' \geqslant_1 M'''$ etc.

Then by lemma 5 we can take $M_4 \equiv [x/N''']M'''$.

case 5. $M_1 \geqslant_1 M_2$ is $MN \geqslant_1 M'N'$ and is a direct consequence of $M \geqslant_1 M'$, $N \geqslant_1 N'$.

By lemma 6 we can distinguish the following subcases.

subcase 5.1. $M_3 \equiv M''N''$ with $\lambda' \vdash M \geqslant_1 M''$, $\lambda' \vdash N \geqslant_1 N''$.

By the induction hypothesis there exist terms M''', N''' such that $\lambda' \vdash M' \geqslant_1 M'''$ etc.

Then we can take $M_4 \equiv M'''N'''$.

subcase 5.2. $M_1 \geqslant M_3$ is $(\lambda x M_1)N \geqslant [x/N'']M_1'$ and is a direct consequence of $M_1 \geqslant_1 M_1'$, $N \geqslant_1 N''$.

This case is analogous to subcase 4.1. ⊠

<u>Lemma 8</u>.

If $\lambda' \vdash M_1 \geqslant M_2$ and $\lambda' \vdash M_1 \geqslant M_3$, then there exists a term M_4 such that $\lambda' \vdash M_2 \geqslant M_4$ and $\lambda' \vdash M_3 \geqslant M_4$.

Proof.

By lemma 3 $\lambda' \vdash M_1 \geqslant M_2 \iff \exists N_1 \ldots N_k \;\; \lambda' \vdash M_1 \equiv N_1 \geqslant_1 \ldots \geqslant_1 N_k \equiv N$

and similarly for $\lambda' \vdash M_1 \geqslant M_3$.

By repeated use of lemma 7 (see figure 2, page 40) it follows that the conclusion holds. ⊠

Lemma 9.

If $\lambda' \vdash M = N$, then there exists a term Z such that

$\lambda' \vdash M \geqslant Z$ and $\lambda' \vdash N \geqslant Z$.

Proof.

Induction on the length of proof of M = N, using lemma 8 in the case of transitivity of = . ⊠

Theorem 10. (Church-Rosser theorem)

If $\lambda \vdash M = N$, then there exists a term Z such that

$\lambda \vdash M \geqslant Z$ and $\lambda \vdash N \geqslant Z$.

Proof.

This follows immediately from lemma 9 and lemma 4. ⊠

Remark.

In the same way we can prove the Church-Rosser theorem for λ + ext by adding to λ' the rule

$$\frac{M \geqslant_1 M'}{\lambda x(Mx) \geqslant_1 M'}$$

References

Barendregt, Hendrik P.

[1970] A universal generator for the λ-calculus, underground Utrecht, published in ERCU publications nr.109.

[1971] On the interpretation of terms without a normal form. ERCU publications nr.111. Computer center, University of Utrecht.

Böhm, Corrado

[1968] Alcune proprieta della forme β-η-normali del λ-K-calcolo. Pubblicazioni dell'istituto per le applicazioni del calcolo, no.696, Consiglio Nazionale delle Ricerche, Roma.

Church, Alonzo

[1932] A set of postulates for the foundation of logic, Ann. of Math., ser.2, vol.33, pp.346-366.

[1933] A set of postulates for the foundation of logic (second paper), ibidem, ser.2, vol.34, pp.839-864.

[1941] The calculi of lambda-conversion, Annals of mathematics studies, no.6, Princeton.

Church, Alonzo and J.Barkley Rosser

[1936] Some properties of conversion, Trans.Amer.Math.Soc., vol.39, pp.472-482.

Curry, Haskell B.

[1930] Grundlagen der kombinatorischen Logik, Amer.J.Math. vol.52, pp.509-536, 789-834.

[1942] The inconsistency of certain formal logics, J.Symbolic Logic, vol.7, pp.115-117.

[1952] A new proof of the Church-Rosser theorem, Kon.Ned. Akad.Wetensch.Proc.Ser.A, vol.55, pp.16-23 (Indag.Math., vol.14).

Curry, Haskell B. and Robert Feys

[1958] Combinatory Logic, Amsterdam.

Curry, Haskell B., J.Roger Hindley and Jonathan P.Seldin

[1971] Combinatory Logic, vol.2, Amsterdam (in process).

Grzegorczyk, Andrzej

[1970] No existence of recursive models for theory of combinators, underground Warszawa.

Hindley, J.Roger

[1969] An abstract form of the Church-Rosser theorem I, J.Symbolic Logic, vol.34, pp.545-560.

[197?] An abstract Church-Rosser theorem, II: Applications, in preparation.

Jacopini, Giuseppe

[1971] Il principio di estensionalita nell'assiomatica del λ-calcolo, underground Roma.

Kearns, John T.

[1969] Combinatory logic with discriminators, J.Symbolic Logic, vol.34, pp.561-575.

Kleene, Stephen C.

[1934] A theory of positive integers in formal logic, Amer.J.Math., vol.57, pp.153-173, 219-244.

[1936] λ-definability and recursiveness, Duke Math.J., vol.2, pp.340-353.

[1959] Recursive functionals and quantifiers of finite types, I, Trans.Amer.Math.Soc., vol.91, pp.1-52.

[1962] Lambda-definable functionals of finite types, Fund.Math.,vol.50, pp.281-303.

Kleene, Stephen C. and J.Barkley Rosser

[1935] The inconsistency of certain formal logics, Ann.of Math., ser.2, vol.36, pp.630-636.

Martin-Löf, Per

[1971] A theory of types, underground Stockholm.

Mitschke, Gerd

[1970] Eine algebraische Behandlung von λ-K-Kalkül und kombinatorischer Logik, Ph.D.Dissertation, underground Bonn.

Newman, Maxwell H.A.

[1942] On theories with a combinatorial definition of "equivalence", Ann. of Math., ser.2, vol.43, pp.223-243.

[1952] Review of Curry [1952] , Math.Reviews, vol.13, p.715.

Rice, H.Gordon

[1953] Classes of recursively enumerable sets and their decision problems, Trans.Amer.Math.Soc., vol.74, pp.358-366.

Rogers, Hartley Jr.

[1967] Theory of recursive functions and effective computability, New York.

Rosen, Barry K.

[1971] Tree-manupulating systems and Church-Rosser theorems, underground Harvard University.

Rosser, J.Barkley

[1935] A mathematical logic without variables. Ann.of Math. ser.2, vol.36, pp.127-150, and Duke Math.J., vol.1, pp.328-355.

[1956] Review of Curry [1952] , J.Symbolic Logic, vol.21, p.377.

Sanchis, Luis Elpidio

[1967] Functionals defined by recursion, Notre Dame J. Formal Logic, vol.8, no 3, pp.161-174.

Schönfinkel, Moses

[1924] Über die Bausteine der mathematischen Logik, Math.Ann., vol.92, pp.305-316.

Schroer, David

[1965] The Church-Rosser theorem, Ph.D. dissertation, underground University of Illinois, Urbana Ill.

Shepherdson, John C.

[1965] Non standard models for fragments of number theory, in: The theory of models, eds J.W.Addison, L.Henkin and A.Tarski, pp. 342-358, Amsterdam.

Scott, Dana S.

[1963] A system of functional abstraction, underground Berkeley.

[1970] Lattice-theoretic models for the λ-calculus, underground Princeton.

Smullyan, Raymond M.

[1961] Theory of formal systems, Annals of mathematics studies, no.47, Princeton.

Tarski, Alfred, Andrzej Mostowski and Raphael M.Robinson

[1953] Undecidable theories, Amsterdam.

Troelstra, Anne S.

[1971] Notions of realizability for intuitionistic arithmetic and intuitionistic arithmetic in all finite types, Proceedings of the second Scandinavian logic symposium, ed.J.E.Fenstad, Amsterdam.

Turing, Alan M.

[1937] Computability and λ-definability, J.Symbolic Logic, vol.2, pp. 153-163.

[1937a] The *p*-function in λ-K-conversion, ibidem, p.164.

Addenda

Gödel, Kurt

[1958] Über eine bisher noch nicht benutzte Erweiterung des finiten Standpunktes, Dialectica, vol.12, pp.280-287.

Morris, James H.

[1968] Lambda-calculus models of programming languages, Ph.D.dissertation, MIT.

Strong, H.Raymond

[1968] Algebraically generalized recursive function theory, IBM J.Research and Development, vol.12, pp.465-475.

Addenda to part I.

In §3.1 we referred to a result of Jacopini [1971] which has not yet been published. Since we have not seen his argument, we give here an outline of a possibly different proof based on the results of Ch.3.

Theorem (Jacopini)

There is an extensional combinatory model which is not an ω-model.

Proof (outline)

Let Ω = SII(SII).

Define $\mathcal{E}$ = {ΩKZ = ΩSZ | Z is a closed CL-term}.

Then by 3.2.16 CL + $\mathcal{E}$ + ext is consistent since $\mathcal{E} \subset \mathcal{K}_{CL}$.

Further

CL + $\mathcal{E}$ + ω-rule $\vdash$ ΩK = ΩS, but

CL + $\mathcal{E}$ + ext $\nvdash$ ΩK = ΩS.

Hence the term model of CL + $\mathcal{E}$ + ext is an extensional model which is not an ω-model, that is, its interior is not extensional. ⊠

Corollary.

There is no set of equations (in the language of CL), in fact no set of universal formulas, that is propositional combinations of equations, whose models are exactly the extensional models of CL.

For, any submodel, in particular the interior, of a model satisfying a set $\mathcal{E}$ of universal sentences also satisfies $\mathcal{E}$.

This corollary justifies the remark on page x of the Introduction to Part I where it was stated that the concept of extensionality of models of CL cannot be expressed by equations. (Only the set of equations which are valid in all extensional models is characterized by the equational rule ext; or more interestingly by the finite number of combinatory axioms, given in Curry and Feys [1958],Ch.6 C, which axiomatize the rule ext.

The proof above of Jacopini's theorem is also of interest for our work in the ω-rule in Chapter 2. If it should turn out that CL itself is ω-complete, that is that the ω-rule is simply valid for CL + ext, the result stated in §2.2 would be completely superseded. However, the method of §2.2 can be adapted to prove the consistency of the ω-rule, for CL + & , a system which is certainly not ω-complete. Thus, whether or not CL itself is ω-complete, at least for some extensions of CL + ext we certainly cannot establish the consistency of the ω-rule simply by proving ω-completeness.

We give here a short account of CL_I introduced by Rosser [1935], which is the combinatory counterpart of the λI-calculus.

Definition

We define a theory CL_I formulated in the following language:

Alphabet: a,b,c,... variables
I,J constants
(,) improper symbols
⩾, = reduction, equality

Terms: The terms are defined inductively by

1) Any variable or constant is a term
2) If M,N are terms, then (MN) is a term.

Formulas: If M,N are terms, then M = N and M ⩾ N are formulas.

Definition

CL_I is defined by the following axioms and rules:

I 1. IM ⩾ M
2. JMNLP ⩾ MN(MPL)

II, III: Same axioms and rules as for CL (cf. appendix I, A2 of part I)

In the above M,N,L and P are arbitrary terms.

In CL_I it is possible to define an abstraction operator λ* simulating the λ-operator of the λI-calculus.

Lemma

In CL_I we can define closed terms B,C and S such that

$CL_I \vdash$ Babx = a(bx)
$CL_I \vdash$ Cabx = axb
$CL_I \vdash$ Sabx = ax(bx)

Proof.

Define

$T = JII$

$C = JT(JT)(JT)$

$B = C(JIC)(JI)$

$W = C(C(BC(C(BJT)T))T)$

$S = B(B(BW)C)(BB)$

Then B,C and S have the required properties. ⊠

Definition

For every term M such that $x \in FV(M)$ we define a term λ^*xM.

$$\lambda^*xx = I$$

$$\lambda^*x(M_1M_2) = \begin{cases} BM_1(\lambda x^*M_2) & \text{if } x \notin FV(M_1) \text{ and } x \in FV(M_2) \\ C(\lambda^*xM_1)M_2 & \text{if } x \in FV(M_1) \text{ and } x \notin FV(M_2) \\ S(\lambda^*xM_1)(\lambda^*xM_2) & \text{if } x \in FV(M_1) \text{ and } x \in FV(M_2) \end{cases}$$

Theorem

For every term M with $x \in FV(M)$ we have

1) $FV(\lambda^*xM) = FV(M) - \{x\}$

2) $(\lambda^*xM)x \geqslant M$

Hence similar to 1.4 in part

Corrections to Part I.

Introduction. On p. xxi it was stated that for a CL-term M

M has no normal form $\Leftrightarrow$ $¤_{R'}(M) = *$.

This should be (see 2.30)

1) M has no normal form $\Rightarrow$ $¤_{R'}(M) = *$

2) M is in normal form $\Rightarrow$ $¤_{R'}(M) \neq *$

Appendix II. Some statements have to be corrected by explicit reference to free and bound variables:

Lemma 5. If $FV(N) \cap BV(MM') = \emptyset$ and $FV(N') \cap BV(N') = \emptyset$ and if $\lambda' \vdash M \geqslant_1 M'$, $\lambda' \vdash N \geqslant_1 N'$, then $\lambda' \vdash [x/N]M \geqslant_1 [x/N']M'$.

To prove lemma 5 one notes:

1) If $\lambda' \vdash M \geqslant_1 M'$, then $FV(M) = FV(M')$

2) If $y \notin FV(N_1)$ and $x \neq y$, then $[x/N_1]([y/N_2]M) \equiv [y/[x/N_1]M_2]([x/N_1]M)$

3) $[x/N_1]([x/N_2]M) \equiv [x/[x/N_1]N_2]M$

Lemma 7 follows from the new version of lemma 5 and the observations:

1) If $\lambda' \vdash M \geqslant_1 N$ and $N \equiv_\alpha N'$, then $\lambda' \vdash M \geqslant_1 N'$

2) For every M there exists an M' such that

$M \equiv_\alpha M'$ and $FV(M) \cap BV(M') = \emptyset$.

Samenvatting

Dit proefschrift houdt zich bezig met de combinatorische logica, niet als basis voor de rest van de wiskunde, maar als formeel systeem voor de bestudering van berekeningsprocedures.

Hoofdstuk I geeft een overzicht en uitbreiding van reeds bekend materiaal.

In Hoofdstuk II wordt de ω-regel ingevoerd en met behulp van transfinite inductie bewezen dat de uitbreiding van de combinatorische logica met de ω-regel consistent is. Verder wordt de existentie van universele generatoren bewezen. Voor de termen die geen universele generatoren zijn, geldt dat de ω-regel een afgeleide regel is.

In Hoofdstuk III worden een aantal andere consistentie resultaten bewezen, waardoor verschillende niet elementair equivalente modellen van de combinatorische logica verkregen worden.

In de bewijzen van de hierboven vermelde resultaten wordt meestal gebruik gemaakt van conservatieve uitbreidingen van de combinatorische logica. Hierbij speelt een nieuwe bewijstechniek een belangrijke rol, te weten de methode van het onderlijnen. Deze methode formaliseert het begrip residu en vermijdt aldus de anders nogal omslachtige argumenten.

Curriculum vitae

Op 18 december 1947 werd ik geboren te Amsterdam.

In 1960 kwam ik op het Montessori lyceum aldaar. Door mijn leraar F.H.Fischer werd mijn belangstelling gewekt voor de grondslagen van de wiskunde. Onder leiding van mijn leraar C.L.Scheffer studeerde ik analyse en lineaire algebra.

Na in 1965 het eindexamen gymnasium-β gehaald te hebben, liet ik mij inschrijven als student in de wis- en natuurkunde aan de Rijksuniversiteit Utrecht.

Onder leiding van Dr.D.van Dalen legde ik mij toe op de grondslagen van de wiskunde. Daarnaast volgde ik een college van Prof.J.J.de Iongh in Nijmegen en nam ik aldaar deel aan het interuniversitaire seminarium grondslagen van de wiskunde dat samen met de Rijksuniversiteit Utrecht gegeven werd.

In 1968 kreeg ik van de Polska Akademia Nauk een studiebeurs voor een maand studie onder leiding van Prof.Mostowski in Warschau.

Van 1966 tot 1969 was ik verbonden als slagwerker aan Dansgroep Pauline de Groot, hetgeen mij financiëel in staat stelde als student deel te nemen aan diverse internationale wiskunde congressen.

In december 1968 legde ik het doctoraal examen wiskunde met groot bijvak wijsbegeerte van de wiskunde af.

Sinds 1969 ben ik verbonden aan de Centrale Interfaculteit van de Rijksuniversiteit Utrecht als wetenschappelijk medewerker in de wijsbegeerte van de wiskunde.

Door de bestudering van het proefschrift van Goodman 'The interpretation of intuitionistic arithmetic in a theory of constructions' in een interuniversitaire werkgroep samen met de afdeling grondslagen van de wiskunde van de Gemeente Universiteit van Amsterdam werd mijn belangstelling gewekt voor de combinatorische logica. Deze belangstelling werd verder gestimuleerd door de hoogleraren Curry, Scott en Grzegorczyk.

Address of the author:

Mathematical Institute
Budapestlaan 6
Utrecht
Netherlands

Future address:

Department of Philosophy
University of Stanford
Stanford, California 94305

STELLINGEN

I

De wijze waarop Rosenbloom het extensionaliteits principe formuleert geeft aanleiding tot verwarring, met name bij Rosenbloom zelf.

Rosenbloom: The elements of mathematical logic, blz.112.

II

Ten onrechte schrijft Goodman aan zijn abstractie operator λ zekere eigenschappen met betrekking tot gedefinieerdheid toe.

Goodman: Intuitionistic arithmetic as a theory of constructions, section 8.

III

In de intuïtionistische theorie der gelijkheid is het axioma

$\neg \forall z\ (z \neq x \vee z \neq y) \rightarrow x = y$

echt sterker dan het stabiliteits axioma

$\neg\neg\, x = y \rightarrow x = y$.

IV

Door de axioma's van Kearns betreffende de discriminatoren in combinatorische logica iets voorzichtiger te formuleren, is het mogelijk dat de reductie- en de gelijkheidsrelatie ook rechtsmonotoon zijn.

Kearns: Combinatory logic with discriminators, J.Symbolic Logic, vol.34(1969)

V

Het begrip 'sterk definitioneel gelijk', zoals Tait dit in heeft gevoerd, is niet helemaal adequaat. De moeilijkheid is op te lossen door een variant van Curry's sterke reductie relatie in te voeren.

Tait: Intensional interpretations of functionals of finite type I, J.Symbolic Logic, vol.32, blz.204-205.

VI

Curry's opvatting, dat de combinatorische logica een prelogica vormt die de grondslag vormt voor alle formele systemen, gaat voorbij aan de moeilijkheden in de analyse van het iteratie proces.

Curry en Feys: Combinatory logic, Introduction.

VII

Bij de vraag of post- ook propterhypnotisch gedrag is, gaat het er niet om of de proefpersoon toneel speelt, beleefd is, bedriegt of wat dan ook. Relevant is alleen van welke stimuli alternatief gedrag afhankelijk is.

VIII

De molens in Nederland draaien met hun wieken tegen de wijzers van de klok. Dit is een gevolg van de omstandigheid dat er in Nederland meer ruimende dan krimpende wind voorkomt: wanneer de molenaar tijdens werkzaamheden tengevolge van deze ruimende wind moet kruien gaat dit lichter dan met krimpende wind in verband met de gyroscopische werking van het wiekenkruis.

H.P.Barendregt 16 juni, 1971

About thesis and author

Summary

This Thesis is concerned with combinatory logic, not as a foundation for all of mathematics, but as a formal system aiming at the study of computational procedures.

Chapter I presents a survey and extension of existing background material.

In Chapter II the ω-rule is introduced and added to combinatory logic. Using transfinite induction the consistency of this extension is proved. Furthermore, the existence of universal generators is proved. For the complement of the set of these terms, it holds that the ω-rule is a derived rule.

Chapter III proves a number of other consistency results. In this way several models of combinatory logic are obtained that are not elementary equivalent.

The proofs of the results above, mostly employ conservative extensions of combinatory logic. An important role is played by the novel method of underlining. This technique formalizes the notion of residual, thus circumventing otherwise rather verbose arguments.

Curriculum Vitae

Born December 18, 1947 at Amsterdam, The Netherlands.

1952-1954 Montessori Kindergarten.

1954-1960 Montessori Elementary school.

1960-1965 Montessori Grammar School. There teacher Fred Fischer evoked my interest in the Foundations of Mathematics. With teacher Carel Scheffer I studied analysis and linear algebra.

1965-1968 Study Mathematics at Utrecht University. Specialization under Lector Dirk van Dalen: Philosophy of mathematics. Followed a Seminar on the Foundations of mathematics directed by Prof. Johan de Iongh.

1966-1969 Percussionist of modern Dance group Pauline de Groot, providing funds that enabled me to take part in several international mathematics meetings.

1968 Grant from the Polska Akademia Nauk to study a summer with Prof. Andrzej Mostowski in Warsaw.

December 1968 Master degree Mathematics with major Philosophy of Mathematics.

1969-1971 Working on PhD in the Foundations of Mathematics at Utrecht University. Thesis supervisors: Prof. Dirk van Dalen and Prof. Georg Kreisel.

Studying in a joint research group with the University of Amsterdam the PhD thesis of N. Goodman 'The interpretation of intuitionistic arithmetic in a theory of constructions', evoked interest in combinatory logic. This interest was further stimulated by Profs. Curry, Scott, and Grzegorczyk.

Propositions

I Rosenbloom's formulation of the extensionality principle is confusing, in particular to Rosenbloom himself[1].

Rosenbloom: The elements of mathematical logic, 1950, p. 112.

II Goodman attributes certain definedness properties to his abstraction operator λ, this without justification.

Goodman: Intuitionistic arithmetic as a theory of constructions, 1968, Section 8.

III In the intuitionistic theory of equality the axiom

$$\neg \forall z\, (z \neq x \vee z \neq y) \to x = y$$

is properly stronger than the stability axiom

$$\neg \neg\, x = y \to x = y.$$

IV If one formulates a bit more carefully the axioms of Kearns concerning the discriminators in combinatory logic, then it follows that the reduction and equality relations are also right monotone.

Kearns: Combinatory logic with discriminators, J. Symbolic Logic, 34, 1969.

V The notion 'strongly definitionally equal', as introduced by Tait, is not entirely adequate. The problem can be solved by introducing a variant of Curry's strong reduction relation.

Tait: Intensional interpretations of functionals of finite type I, J. Symbolic Logic, 32, 1967, 204-205.

[1] What is meant here is that extensionality is described as being the ω-rule. Moreover it is claimed that this follows from combinatory axioms, like those of Curry (Barendregt 1984, $A_{\beta\eta}$ Corollary 73.15). But although these imply the proper rule of extensionality, they do not imply the ω-rule.

VI Curry's view, that combinatory logic constitutes a prelogic providing a foundation for all formal systems, fails to take into account the difficulties in the analysis of the iteration process.

Curry and Feys: Combinatory logic, 1958, Introduction.

VII The question whether post-hypnotic behavior is also propter-hypnotic behavior, does not deal with the possibility that the subject is acting, is polite, is cheating or whatsoever. Relevant is only the needed strength of stimuli leading to alternative behavior[2].

VIII The windmills in The Netherlands turn their blades counterclockwise. This is a consequence of the circumstance that in The Netherlands a veering wind occurs more often than a shrinking wind. When during work the miller needs to wheel the wings because of a veering wind, this is easier than with shrinking wind, due to the gyroscopic action of the cross of blades[3].

---

[2][Added in 2020.] The Stanford Hypnotic Susceptibility Scale (SHSS) assigns a value to a hypnotic subject, according to the number of increasingly unlikely things that are followed up as a posthypnotic suggestion. A disadvantages of the SHSS are that in different cultures certain behavior is more accepted and that subjects may be faking. To counter the first point several local versions of the scale appeared. In the above Proposition a different approach is suggested dealing with both problems. One assesses the strength of stimuli that are needed to prevent the subject from obeying the posthypnotic suggestion.

[3][Added in 2020.] This Proposition was justly challenged in 1976 by Eric Zwijnenberg in a Proposition accompanying his PhD thesis on astronomy. He—also living in a windmill—went so far as to experimentally refute it. His Proposition 7 in

E. Zwijnenberg. Observation of brightness profiles of the soft X-ray background in Gemini, Orion and Eridanus, PhD thesis, Leiden University, 1976

is as follows

"The claim of Barendregt that the counterclockwise turning of windmills can be explained by the gyroscopic action of the cross of blades and the circumstance that in The Netherlands there are more veering than shrinking winds can be refuted both theoretically and experimentally."

Henk Barendregt 1971 *Photo by Molly Mackenzie*

Part II

Motivation & Failure

1

Motivation

1.1 The λ-calculus

Studying the PhD thesis of Goodman (1968) on Intuitionistic Arithmetic did evoke my interest in λ-terms and combinators. Browsing also in Church (1941) and Curry & Feys (1958) (specially the latter is not a book to study from cover to cover) I learned that the original version of the λ-calculus, Church (1932, 1933), was intended to be a foundation for all of mathematics: reasoning and computing. This theory turned out to be inconsistent, as shown by the paradox of Kleene & Rosser (1935). Later this inconsistency was considerably simplified by the paradox of Curry (1941), consisting of only a few lines of derivation, see Section III 1.3 (that is: Section 3 in Chapter 1 in Part III).

After that Church focused on the underlying pure system, omitting the logic. This is presently called the (type free) λ-calculus, dealing only with computing. It turned out that this system could capture surprisingly[1] well the notions 'computable' and 'decidable'. It consists of λ-terms with as only statements equations between these, there are no logical connectives or quantifiers. This theory was proved consistent, in the sense that not all equations are provable, by a syntactic argument, the *Church-Rosser Theorem*, also known as *confluence*, Church & Rosser (1936b).

This result gives an analysis of proofs in the λ-calculus. Writing

$$\begin{aligned} M =_\beta N &\iff \lambda \vdash M = N; \\ M \twoheadrightarrow_\beta N &\iff \lambda \vdash M \geqslant N. \end{aligned}$$

It is easily seen that $\twoheadrightarrow_\beta$ is the reflexive, transitive, and compatible closure of the one step reduction relation $\rightarrow$ defined by

$$(\lambda x.M)N \rightarrow [x:=N]M; \qquad (\beta)$$

[1]See Kleene (1981).

and $=_\beta$ is the symmetric and transitive closure of $\twoheadrightarrow_\beta$. Drawing $\twoheadrightarrow_\beta$ downwards, one has that $M{=_\beta}N$ holds if there is a zig-zag up-down path form M to N. The Church-Rosser theorem states that this path can be simplified to a path that first goes down and then up.

$$\lambda \vdash M = N \Rightarrow \exists L[M \twoheadrightarrow_\beta L \;\&\; N \twoheadrightarrow_\beta L].$$

This implies consistency: one has $\lambda \nvdash K = S$ as there is no downward reduction possibility from either of these two terms.

1.2 Combinatory Logic

Even simpler than the λ-calculus is its variant combinatory logic, in notation CL. It originated with Schönfinkel (1924). CL also is an equational theory, having just one binary operation *application*[2], in notation $\cdot$, but similarly to the convention in algebra usually not explicitly written: xy denotes $x \cdot y$. Moreover, xyz denotes $(xy)z$. In general one has $x_1 \ldots x_k = (..(x_1x_2) \ldots x_k),$: association to the left. In CL there are variables $x, y, z, \ldots$ and constants $\mathbf{I}, \mathbf{K}, \mathbf{S}$ forming with application the set of combinatory terms, also denoted by CL. The set of *closed* terms (without variables) is denoted by CL^o. The equational theory CL is axiomatized by equational logic extended by the schemes

$$\boxed{\begin{array}{rcl} \mathbf{I}x & = & x \\ \mathbf{K}xy & = & x \\ \mathbf{S}xyz & = & xz(yz) \end{array}} \qquad (1)$$

This has the usual meaning that the variables may be substituted by arbitrary terms; therefore equations containing variables indicate uniformly valid provable equations. The constant **I** is not strictly needed as it can be defined by $\mathbf{I} = \mathbf{SKK}$ and hence can be omitted: indeed $\mathbf{SKK}x = \mathbf{K}x(\mathbf{K}x) = x$. Consistency is proved again by confluence

$$CL \vdash P = Q \Rightarrow \exists R[P \twoheadrightarrow R \;\&\; Q \twoheadrightarrow R],$$

this time for $\twoheadrightarrow$ being $\twoheadrightarrow_w$, called *weak reduction*, coming from the axioms of CL interpreted as rewrite relation $\rightarrow_w$. A *w-normal form* is a term to which no $\rightarrow_w$ step is possible. For example $\mathbf{K}, \mathbf{S}$ are such terms, but $\mathbf{IK}$ not. From confluence it follows that $\nvdash \mathbf{K} = \mathbf{S}$. A term that *has a w-normal form* is $\mathbf{IK} \rightarrow_w \mathbf{K}$. An example of a term without w-normal form is $\Omega \triangleq \mathbf{SII}(\mathbf{SII})$

1.3 Search for a model

Work on this thesis started with the intention to construct a model of CL

$$\mathcal{A} = \langle A, i, k, s, \cdot \rangle$$

[2]Abbreviated as *app*. The apps on a smartphone are very much related to this operator, because $x \cdot y$ stands for *application* of x (seen as program) to y (seen as argument).

satisfying (the universal closure of) the axioms (1). Of course there is the trivial model $A = \{i\}$ with $i \cdot i = i$ and $i = k = s$. Finding a model for CL was easier than finding one for the λ-calculus, as one didn't need to deal with abstraction. Moreover in the presence of extensionality the two theories become equivalent, see Section III 1.2.

In a personal communication A. Grzegorczyk had shown that the first-order theory with as axioms

$$\boxed{\begin{array}{rcl} \mathbf{K}xy &=& x \\ \mathbf{S}xyz &=& xz(yz) \\ \mathbf{K} &\neq& \mathbf{S} \end{array}}$$

has no computable model and is essentially undecidable, i.e. has no consistent decidable extension. The official version of CL is just a purely equational theory. The axiom $k \neq s$ is equivalent to non-triviality of the model. Indeed, if $k = s$, then all elements are provably equal (to i):

$$x = ix = ki(ki)x = skkix = kkkix = kix = i.$$

Conversely, in a trivial model one has $k = s$. Grzegorczyk's result shows why finding a non-trivial model wasn't so easy. For one thing, there are no finite such models. This can be seen also from the fact that in $\mathcal{A}$ the elements

$$k^n k \triangleq \underbrace{k(k(k \ldots (k\,k)))}_{n\,\times},$$

for $n \in \mathbb{N}$, are all different, assuming $k \neq s$. Moreover, there are no computable models.

Computability theory

Besides the investigations of Church on computability there was the work of Turing (1937a), Turing (1937b), which described the notion in terms of deterministic steps performed by a mechanical device, now called Turing Machine. Turing showed that Church's model of computation and that of himself define the same class of (partial) computable functions. Based on this and other considerations Kleene (1952) introduces on $\mathbb{N}$ a partial operator $\{x\}(y)$, that can be interpreted as the possible result of applying the partial computable function with code x to input[3] y. Kleene translated the intuition of known results in λ-calculus into elementary computability (also known as recursion) theory. In this way he obtained the S^m_n-theorem and the recursion theorem from respectively 'Currying' (after H. B. Curry, but earlier known to Schönfinkel) and the fixed point theorem.

My intention was to do the reverse by using this binary operator $\{x\}(y)$ to construct a (total) combinatory algebra in such a way that Kleene's translation of λ-calculus results would become a simple model-theoretic interpretation. The attempts will be described in next chapter.

[3]Actually Kleene did this for partial functions of k-arguments, but here we take $k = 1$.

1.4 Combinatory algebras: total and partial

DEFINITION 1.1. (i) An *applicative structure* is of the form $\mathcal{A} = \langle A, \cdot \rangle$, a set endowed with a binary operation.

(ii) One writes $ab = a \cdot b$, omitting the $\cdot$.

(iii) As the operation $\cdot$ is always defined one speaks of a *total* applicative structure.

(iv) By convention $ab_1 \dots b_n = (..((ab_1)b_2) \cdots b_n)$, *association to the left*.

(v) $\mathcal{A}$ is *extensional* if $\forall a, a'.[\forall b.ab = a'b] \Rightarrow a = a'$ holds in $\mathcal{A}$.

(vi) $\mathcal{A}$ is called *trivial* if $A = \{a\}$ with $a = a \cdot a$, otherwise *non-trivial*.

Combinatory algebras

DEFINITION 1.2. A *combinatory algebra*, abbreviated as ca, is an applicative structure $\mathcal{A} = \langle A, \cdot, i, k, s \rangle$ such that for all $x, y, z \in \mathcal{A}$ one has

$$\begin{aligned} ix &= x; \\ kxy &= x; \\ sxyz &= xz(yz). \end{aligned}$$

These are models of CL. In the previous section it was noted that a combinatory algebra is trivial iff $k = s$. Such a ca is considered as a degenerate one.

The motivation for this notion comes from the theory of combinators beginning with Schönfinkel (1924), where it is essentially shown that in a ca all algebraic functions (i.e. expressible by an expression over the structure using variables, constants and application) are representable by an element. For example, $F(x, y) = yk$, is algebraic and one has $F(x, y) = axy$, with $a = k(si(kk))$.

DEFINITION 1.3. Let $\mathcal{A}$ be a ca.

(i) A term over $\mathcal{A}$ is built up from variables and constants for elements of $\mathcal{A}$ using application.

(ii) The set $\mathcal{A}[\vec{x}]$ consists of terms over $\mathcal{A}$ using at most variables from $\vec{x}$.

The following result states that every algebraic function over $\mathcal{A}$ is representable by one of its elements.

PROPOSITION 1.4 (Combinatory completeness). *Let $\mathcal{A}$ be a ca, For every applicative expression $t \in \mathcal{A}[\vec{x}]$ the following holds in $\mathcal{A}$*

$$\exists b \forall \vec{x}. b\vec{x} = t[\vec{x}].$$

PROOF. First one constructs for a term $t \in \mathcal{A}[x, \vec{y}]$ a term $\lambda^* x.t \in \mathcal{A}[\vec{y}]$ that simulates[4]

[4] There are several ways of doing this. The easiest way described here comes from Rosenbloom (1950) and yields an algorithm of complexity $O(n) = 2^n$. With a little effort (Curry) one can reduce this to $O(n) = n^2$. There exist algorithms with asymptotic complexity $O(n) = n \log n$, see e.g. Statman (1986). For a survey and an interesting middle way, see Broda & Damas (1997).

λ-abstraction, that is $\forall x \in \mathcal{A}.(\lambda^* x.t)x = t$.

$$\begin{array}{rcll} \lambda^* x.x & = & i; & \\ \lambda^* x.y & = & ky, & \text{if } x \neq y; \\ \lambda^* x.c & = & kc, & \text{if c is a constant;} \\ \lambda^* x.t_1 t_2 & = & s(\lambda^* x.t_1)(\lambda^* x.t_2). & \end{array}$$

By induction on the generation of t it is easy to see that

$$(\lambda^* x.t)x = t. \tag{1}$$

Now for a term $t \in \mathcal{A}[x_1, \ldots, x_n]$ define

$$b = \lambda^* x_1.(\lambda^* x_2.(\ldots(\lambda^* x_n.t)))^5.$$

Then $bx_1 \cdots x_n = t$, by repeated application of (1). □

Conversely, the existence of i, k, s in a ca are just three instances of combinatory completeness. The term *combinatory completeness* was coined by Curry.

Partial combinatory algebras

Now these notions will be loosened by allowing partial application. This will make it more easy to construct relevant structures.

DEFINITION 1.5. A *partial applicative structure* (pas) is of the form $\mathcal{A} = \langle A, \cdot \rangle$, a set endowed with $\cdot \colon A \rightharpoonup A$ a partial map. If $\cdot$ is total, then $\mathcal{A}$ is a *(total) applicative structure.*

NOTATION 1.6. For a partial or total applicative structure we use the following notations for application.

(i) $ab = a \cdot b$, which may be undefined.

(ii) $ab_1 \ldots b_n = (..((ab_1)b_2) \cdots b_n)$,

with the understanding that if e.g. $ab\uparrow$, then $abc\uparrow$.

(iii) For two expressions E_1, E_2 that may or may not be defined as element of $\mathcal{A}$, write $E_1 \simeq E_2$ to denote that if one of the two expressions is defined, then so is the other one and both are equal: $E_1 = E_1$.

Let $\mathcal{A}$ be a pca. As before we can define what is a *algebraic partial functions* over $\mathcal{A}$. Also *representable partial functions* are defined as before with one extra condition. A partial map $F \colon \mathcal{A}^k \rightharpoonup \mathcal{A}$, with $k > 0$, is *representable* if in $\mathcal{A}$

$$\exists b \forall x_1, \ldots, x_k.[bx_1 \ldots x_k \simeq F(x_1 \ldots x_k) \; \& \; bx_1 \ldots x_{k-1}\downarrow].$$

[5]This is called association to the right.

DEFINITION 1.7. Let $\mathcal{A}$ be a pas. Then this structure is a *partial combinatory algebra* pca if every algebraic partial function on $\mathcal{A}$ is representable.

PROPOSITION 1.8. *Let* $\mathcal{A} = \langle A, \cdot \rangle$ *be a pas. Then* $\mathcal{A}$ *is a pca iff there are* $i, k, s \in A$ *such that in* $\mathcal{A}$ *one has*

$$\begin{array}{rcll} ix & \simeq & x, & \textit{hence } ix = x; \\ kxy & \simeq & x, & \textit{hence } kxy = x; \\ sxyz & \simeq & xz(yz); & \end{array}$$

and for all $x, y \in A$ *one has* $kx\downarrow$, $sx\downarrow$ *and* $sxy\downarrow$.

PROOF. Similarly to the proof for the total case, noting that one always has $\lambda^*x.t\downarrow$. □

1.5 $\mathcal{K}$: Kleene's (first) pca

Turing's fundamental result about computability over $\mathbb{N}$ implies that there is a universal partial computable function of two variables $\{e\}(x)$[6] such that for every unary computable partial function ψ there exists a code e satisfying $\psi = \{e\}$. This operator turns $\mathbb{N}$ into a pca.

DEFINITION 1.9. Write for $x, y \in \mathbb{N}$

$$\begin{array}{rcll} x \cdot y & = & \{x\}(y), & \text{if defined;} \\ & = & \uparrow, & \text{else.} \end{array}$$

LEMMA 1.10. *There are* $i, k, s \in \mathbb{N}$ *such that for all* $x, y, z \in \mathbb{N}$

$$\begin{array}{rcl} ix & \simeq & x; \\ kxy & \simeq & x; \\ sxyz & \simeq & xz(yz), \end{array}$$

such that also $kx\downarrow$, $sx\downarrow$ *and* $sxy\downarrow$. *Hence* $\mathcal{K} = \langle \mathbb{N}, i, k, s, \cdot \rangle$ *is a pca.*

PROOF. We show how this is done for i and s. For k see 1.2 in Chapter 3.

Case i. This number is simply the code of the computable function I defined by $I(x) = x$. Then $\{i\}(x) = I(x) = x$.

Case s. Define the function ψ by

$$\psi(x, y, z) \simeq \{\{x\}(z)\}(\{y\}(z)).$$

[6]In Rogers Jr (1967) the notation $\varphi_e(x)$ is used for $\{e\}(x)$.

Then ψ is a partial computable function, hence $\psi(x,y,z) \simeq \{e\}^3(x,y,z)$, for some $e \in \mathbb{N}$. By the S-m-n theorem one has (omitting the precise super- and subscripts of S)

$$\begin{array}{rcll} \{\{x\}(z)\}(\{y\}(z)) & \simeq & \psi(x,y,z). & \\ & \simeq & \{e\}^3(x,y,z), & \\ & \simeq & \{S(e,x,y)\}(z), & \\ & \simeq & \{\{S(e',e,x)\}(y)\}(z), & \text{where } \forall x,y \in \mathbb{N}.\{e'\}(x,y) = S(e,x,y), \\ & \simeq & \{\{\{S(e'',e',e)\}(x)\}(y)\}(z), & \text{where } \forall x \in \mathbb{N}.\{e''\}(x) = S(e',e,x). \end{array}$$

Therefore we can take $s = S(e'', e', e)$. □

DEFINITION 1.11. $\mathcal{K}$ is called Kleene's first[7] partial combinatory algebra[8]. This is a *partial* combinatory algebra, because xy is not always defined.

There seemed to be some possibilities to turn Kleene's first model $\mathcal{K}$ into a total combinatory algebra. This will be described in the next chapter.

[7]There is also Kleene's second pca consisting of all functions in Baire space $\mathbb{B} = \mathbb{N}^{\mathbb{N}}$ with fg defined by interpreting f as 'associate' for a continuous functional $F\colon \mathbb{B} \to \mathbb{B}$. See Troelstra 1973.

[8]This pca has been used in Kreisel (1958) to define HRO, a model of the typed λ-calculus, in order to describe constructive aspects of mathematics. In Wagner (1969) a modest part of computability theory was described as a Uniformly Reflexive Structure (URS) based on $\mathcal{K}$, extended with a constant for discriminating elements, see Chapter 3.

2 Failure

In this chapter it will be explained in detail how four attempts to construct from $\mathcal{K}$ a total combinatory algebra did fail. However, the work has led to the main notions and results in the thesis:

1. the ω-rule and its consistency and partial validity;
2. the notion of solvability and the consistency of equating unsolvable terms.

These positive side-effects will be explained in more detail in Part III.

2.1 $\mathcal{K}^*$: adding undefined

My first attempt was to make the application function in Kleene's pca $\mathcal{K}$ total by extending it as follows. For this one should not be afraid of the undecidable, as was clear from Grzegorczyk's result.

DEFINITION 2.1. (i) Let $\mathbb{N}_* = \mathbb{N} \cup \{*\}$, with $* \notin \mathbb{N}$.

(ii) Write

$$\begin{aligned} x|y &= \{x\}(y), && \text{if defined;} \\ &= *, && \text{else.} \end{aligned}$$

By convention $\forall x \in \mathbb{N}_*.x|* = *|x = *|* = *$. By the undecidability of the halting problem the operation $|$ is non-computable.

It now seems that one obtains a total ca $\mathcal{K}^* = \langle \mathbb{N}_*, i, k, s, | \rangle$ with

$$\begin{aligned} i|x &= x, \\ k|x|y &= x, \\ s|x|y|z &= x|z|(y|z). \end{aligned}$$

The value of Ω

The question comes up what is the value of e|e with $e = s|i|i$ in $\mathcal{K}^*$. This corresponds to the λ-term $\Omega = \omega\omega$, with ω[1] $= \lambda x.xx$. We write $[\![\Omega]\!]$ for e|e.

Does one have $[\![\Omega]\!] = *$, or do we have $[\![\Omega]\!] = 1729$? For e one has $ex = xx$ so that $ee = ee$ and we do not get any information from this definition about the value of $[\![\Omega]\!] \in \mathbb{N}$ or its being undefined. For e' such that $e'x = xx + 1$ one knows for sure that $e'e'\uparrow$, because otherwise $e'e' = e'e' + 1$, a contradiction. Therefore $e'|e' = *$.

Comparing e|e and $e'|e'$ seems related to the comparing the Henkin sentence H and the Gödel sentence G in in Peano arithmetic. Let $\Box$ denote formalized provability inside this theory. Then one has

$$\begin{array}{lll} \mathrm{PA} \vdash \mathrm{H} \leftrightarrow \Box \mathrm{H}, & & \text{for the Henkin sentence H;} \\ \mathrm{PA} \vdash \mathrm{G} \leftrightarrow \neg\Box \mathrm{G}, & & \text{Gödel sentence G.} \end{array}$$

The Henkin sentence H, Henkin (1952), asserts its own provability, while the Gödel sentence G denies its own provability, Gödel (1931). Under natural assumptions (the Löb's axioms[2]) one has

$$\begin{array}{ll} \mathrm{PA} \vdash \mathrm{H} & \text{Löb (1955);} \\ \mathrm{PA} \nvdash \mathrm{G} & \text{provided that PA is consistent, Gödel (1931)} \end{array}$$

It is interesting that Löb's solution of Henkin's problem is closely related to Curry's paradox, mentioned earlier and derived later in Section III 1, while Gödel's result is related to the liar paradox.

In Chapter 3 it will be shown that under natural conditions imposed on $\{e\}(x)$ one has $[\![\Omega]\!] = *$. In the absence of these natural conditions one may have $[\![\Omega]\!] = 1729$, and in fact Ω can take any value in $\mathcal{K}^*$ 'it shouldn't take'[3]

For natural versions of the coding, involving a notion of length of computation, as in Moschovakis (1971), taught to us by Carl Gordon, one has

$$[\![\mathbf{O}]\!]^{\mathcal{K}^*} = *.$$

[1] In France and Italy $\lambda x.xx$ often is denoted by Δ, so that $\Omega = \Delta\Delta$.

[2] The so called Löb conditions are

$$\begin{array}{l} \text{L1.} \vdash A \Rightarrow \vdash \Box A, \\ \text{L2.} \vdash \Box A \rightarrow \Box\Box A, \\ \text{L3.} \vdash \Box(A \rightarrow B) \rightarrow \Box A \rightarrow \Box B. \end{array}$$

See Löb (1955) and Boolos (1995).

[3] This may be compared to later work of Baeten & Boerboom (1979), in a master thesis showing that Ω in the Plotkin-Scott model $P\omega$ can take any value one wants, while it was known that under natural conditions of the coding of finite sets of natural numbers one has $[\![\Omega]\!] = \emptyset$, as shown by Hyland. The title of this thesis is "*Ω can be anything it shouldn't be*" was a variant of that of Solovay (1965), called "*$2^{\aleph_0}$ can be anything it ought to be*". In fact for any $M \in \Lambda^o$ one can force $P\omega \models \Omega = M$. A similar results hold for the interpretation of Ω in webbed models Berline, Chantal (2000), which generalize the model $P\omega$ and D_A of Engeler, E. (1981).

This is shown in Chapter 3, Theorem 1.3. This length of computation notion is formalized by an extra feature of a URS, resulting in a so called *'Normed Uniformly Reflexive Structure'* (NURS), Section II 3.0. In fact Theorem II 3.3 states that for $P \in CL$ without w-nf its interpretation in a NURS $\mathcal{U}$ is undefined:

$$P \text{ has no } w\text{-normal form} \;\Rightarrow\; [\![P]\!]^{\mathcal{U}} = *.$$

A putative canonical λ-theory

Therefore, if $\mathcal{K}^*$ is indeed a combinatory algebra, it would be a model of

$$CL_{\perp} = CL + \{P = Q \mid P, Q \text{ have no } w\text{-normal form}\},$$

showing that this theory is consistent. This would complement nicely the theorem of Böhm (1968) that states that terms having different $\beta\eta$-normal forms cannot be consistently equated. Hopefully the consistency of $CL_{\perp}$ would imply that of a similar theory $\lambda_{\perp}$, equating terms without a $\beta(\eta)$-normal form[4]. This I was intending to have as goal for my thesis. But then I found out that the theory $CL_{\perp}$ was *not* consistent after all. The contradiction is easiest to explain using λ-terms. Using the abbreviation $[P, Q] = \lambda x.xPQ$ define the terms

$$\begin{aligned} M &\triangleq [K, \Omega] \\ N &\triangleq [S, \Omega] \end{aligned}$$

Both M, N don't have a β-normal form and would be equated in $\lambda_{\perp}$. But

$$\begin{aligned} MK &= K, \\ NK &= S, \end{aligned}$$

hence from $M = N$ one can derive $K = S$ and consequently, as we have seen in Section 1.3, in fact every equation. Therefore $M = N$ is inconsistent[5] and the goal was unreachable. The moral is that although both M, N don't have a β-normal form they can be 'solved' by applying them to an argument yielding different normal forms. This gave rise to the notion of *(un)solvability* of terms, see Section III 2.3.

$\mathcal{K}^*$ is not a model for CL

The failure to reach the goal of finding a canonical λ-theory like $\lambda_{\perp}$ is due to the fact that $\mathcal{K}^*$ fails to be a model of CL. The reason is actually very simple. Although $\mathcal{K}^*$ is a total

[4] In the thesis it is also shown that having a β-nf is equivalent to having a $\beta\eta$-nf, see I.1, Lemma 2.8 and the remark following, and that β-solvability and $\beta\eta$-solvability are the same, see I.3 Lemma 2.2.

[5] In CL this equation becomes $S(SI(KK))(K\Omega) = S(SI(KS))(K\Omega)$, with $\Omega = SII(SII)$.

applicative structure, it is not a total combinatory algebra, because the equation for k doesn't hold for all $x, y \in \mathbb{N}_*$: indeed,

$$* = k|0|* \neq 0$$

as it should be in a ca. For the same reason there is no another element k' that could act as interpretation of **K**.

$\mathcal{K}^*$ is a model for $\mathrm{CL}^{\mathbf{I}}$ and λI-calculus

On the other hand, the structure $\mathcal{K}^*$ does provide a model for the variant of CL without **K**, the theory $\mathrm{CL}^{\mathbf{I}}$, corresponding to the λI-calculus in which $\lambda x.M$ is only allowed if $x \in FV(M)$, the version of the λ-calculus preferred by Church. This gives a model of

$$\mathrm{CL}^{\mathbf{I}}_{\perp} = \mathrm{CL}^{\mathbf{I}} + \{P = Q \mid P, Q \text{ have no } w\text{-normal form}\},$$

showing its consistency, as shown in Chapter 3. This fits with the result that equating unsolvables is consistent and a later result Barendregt (1973) that for λI-terms M one has

$$M \text{ is I-solvable} \iff M \text{ has a normal form.}$$

Here I-solvable means solvable by using terms in Λ^{I}. Using this result in Theorem III 3.9 a 'Hilbert-Post' completion of the λI-calculus will be obtained.

2.2 $\mathcal{K}_{\sim}$: making application total

Still I had the hope to finding an appropriate combinatory algebra by modifying $\mathcal{K}$. By the method of proving the recursion theorem in theory Rogers Jr (1967) one can make the application $\cdot$ total.

DEFINITION 2.2. Define for $n, n' \in \mathbb{N}$

$$n \sim n' \iff \forall y \in \mathbb{N}. n|y = n'|y.$$

PROPOSITION 2.3. *Given a partial computable function* $\psi\colon \mathbb{N}^k \to \mathbb{N}$ *in* $\mathbb{N}$, *there exists a total computable function* $f\colon \mathbb{N}^k \to \mathbb{N}$ *such that*

$$\psi(x_1, \ldots, x_k)\downarrow \;\Rightarrow\; f(x_1, \ldots, x_k) \sim \psi(x_1, \ldots, x_k).$$

In Visser (1980) this is called 'f *makes* ψ *total*[6] *modulo* $\sim$*'.*

[6]Through Ershov's notion of *pre-complete numbered sets* it is emphasized that the existence of f holds for all partial computable functions and is in fact a property of the equivalence relation $\sim$. Building on this notion Visser (1980) has formulated a powerful result, the *Anti Diagonal Normalization Theorem*.

PROOF. Define $\chi(x_1, \ldots, x_k, y) = \psi(x_1, \ldots, x_k) \cdot y$. This χ has a partial recursive code, hence can be written as

$$\{e\}(x_1, \ldots, x_k, y) = \chi(x_1, \ldots, x_k, y).$$

By the S-n-m theorem there exists a total computable function S such that

$$S(e, x_1, \ldots, x_k) \cdot y = \chi(x_1, \ldots, x_k, y).$$

Now define $f(x_1, \ldots, x_k) = S(e, x_1, \ldots, x_k)$. □

COROLLARY 2.4. (i) *There is a total computable function* $g \colon \mathbb{N} \to \mathbb{N}$ *such that*

$$\forall n, m \in \mathbb{N}.[n \cdot m\downarrow \;\Rightarrow\; g(n, m) \sim n \cdot m].$$

This function g *is typically employed in the proof of the recursion theorem, see Rogers Jr (1967).*

NOTATION 2.5. Modify the partial map $\cdot \colon \mathbb{N}^2 \rightharpoonup \mathbb{N}$ into a total $\boxdot \colon \mathbb{N}^2 \to \mathbb{N}$ by writing

$$n \boxdot m \;=\; g(n, m).$$

COROLLARY 2.6. *For all* $n, m \in \mathbb{N}$ *such that* $n \cdot m\downarrow$ *one has* $n \boxdot m \sim n \cdot m$.

PROPOSITION 2.7. *There are* $i, k, s \in \mathbb{N}$ *such that*

$$\begin{array}{rcl} i \boxdot x & \sim & x; \\ k \boxdot x \boxdot y & \sim & x; \\ s \boxdot x \boxdot y \boxdot z & \sim & (x \boxdot z) \boxdot (y \boxdot z). \end{array}$$

PROOF. The elements i, k are as in $\mathcal{K}$. The last element s can be found by constructing an $s' \in \mathbb{N}$ such that $s'xyz = (x \boxdot z) \boxdot (y \boxdot z)$ and taking $s = s'$. □

The second attempt to find a total ca as modification of $\mathcal{K}$ was to consider

$$\mathcal{K}_\sim \triangleq \langle \mathbb{N}/\sim, [i]_\sim, [k]_\sim, [s]_\sim, \boxdot \rangle,$$

with $[x]_\sim \boxdot [y]_\sim \triangleq [x \boxdot y]_\sim$. Incomplete thinking made me believe that now one has a model of $CL_\perp$. This, however, fails because the application on equivalence classes is not well-defined: it depends on the choice of representatives.

PROPOSITION 2.8. *The relation* $\sim$ *on* $\mathbb{N}^2$ *is not a congruence: in general*

$$y \sim y' \not\Rightarrow e \boxdot y \sim e \boxdot y.$$

PROOF. Suppose $y \sim y'$, but $y \neq y'$. Then there exists a total computable function f such that $f(y) \not\sim f(y')$. Let e be a code of f. It follows that

$$\begin{array}{lll} & \forall x \in \mathbb{N}.\{e\}(x) = f(x), & \\ \Rightarrow & \forall x \in \mathbb{N}.e \boxdot x \sim f(x), & \text{as } e \boxdot x \sim \{e\}(x) = f(x)\downarrow, \\ \Rightarrow & e \boxdot y \sim f(y) \not\sim f(y') \sim e \boxdot y', & \\ \Rightarrow & e \boxdot y \not\sim e \boxdot y'. \;\square & \end{array}$$

2.3 $\mathcal{K}_\infty$: a non-trivial extensional applicative structure

The third attempt to modify $\mathcal{K}$ to a total ca was as follows. Proofs are given more detail than I do usually.

DEFINITION 2.9. Let α be an ordinal. Define by transfinite recursion a subset $\mathbb{N}_\alpha \subseteq \mathbb{N}$ and a binary relation $\sim_\alpha \subseteq \mathbb{N}^2$ as follows.

$$
\begin{array}{rcl}
\mathbb{N}_0 & = & \mathbb{N}; \\
\mathbb{N}_{\alpha+1} & = & \{x \in \mathbb{N}_\alpha \mid [\forall y \in \mathbb{N}_\alpha . x \boxdot y \in \mathbb{N}_\alpha] \ \& \\
& & \qquad [\forall y, y' \in \mathbb{N}_\alpha . [y \sim_\alpha y' \Rightarrow x \boxdot y \sim_\alpha x \boxdot y']]\}; \\
\mathbb{N}_\lambda & = & \bigcap_{\delta<\lambda} \mathbb{N}_\delta, \text{ for } \alpha = \lambda \text{ a limit ordinal.} \\
x \sim_0 x' & \iff & x \sim x', \text{ see Definition 2.2;} \\
x \sim_{\alpha+1} x' & \iff & \forall y \in \mathbb{N}_\alpha . [x \boxdot y \sim_\alpha x' \boxdot y]; \\
x \sim_\lambda x' & \iff & \exists \delta<\lambda . x \sim_\delta x', \text{ that is } \sim_\lambda = \bigcup_{\delta<\lambda} \sim_\delta, \text{ for } \lambda \text{ a limit ordinal.}
\end{array}
$$

PROPOSITION 2.10. *There exists an ordinal γ such that $\mathbb{N}_\gamma = \mathbb{N}_{\gamma+1}$ and $\sim_\gamma$ is the same relation as $\sim_{\gamma+1}$. Let γ_0 be the least ordinal where this happens.*

PROOF. The ordinal γ exists before the first uncountable ordinal ω_1, otherwise $\mathbb{N}$ and $\mathbb{N}^2$ have uncountably many elements. □

PROPOSITION 2.11. *Let α, β be ordinals.*

(i) $\alpha \leq \beta \Rightarrow \mathbb{N}_\beta \subseteq \mathbb{N}_\alpha$.

(ii) $\sim_\alpha \subseteq \sim_{\alpha+1}$.

(iii) $\alpha \leq \beta \Rightarrow \sim_\alpha \subseteq \sim_\beta$.

(iv) *For all α one has $\sim_\alpha$ is an equivalence relation.*

(v) $\forall x, x' \in \mathbb{N}_{\alpha+1} . [x \sim_{\alpha+1} x' \iff \forall y, y' \in \mathbb{N}_\alpha . [y \sim_\alpha y' \Rightarrow xy \sim_\alpha x'y']]$.

(vi) $\forall x' \in \mathbb{N} . [x' \sim_\alpha x \in \mathbb{N}_\alpha \Rightarrow x' \in \mathbb{N}_\alpha]$.

PROOF. (i) By transfinite induction on β one shows

$$\forall \alpha < \beta . \mathbb{N}_\beta \subseteq \mathbb{N}_\alpha .$$

Case $\beta = 0$. Trivial.

Case $\beta + 1$. If $\alpha < \beta + 1$, then $\alpha < \beta$ or $\alpha = \beta$. In the first case by the IH (Induction Hypothesis) one has $\mathbb{N}_\beta \subseteq \mathbb{N}_\alpha$, and we are done since clearly $\mathbb{N}_{\beta+1} \subseteq \mathbb{N}_\beta$. In the second case we are also done.

Case β limit ordinal. Let $\alpha < \beta$. Then for some $\beta' < \beta$ one has $\alpha < \beta'$. Then by definition and the IH

$$\mathbb{N}_\beta = \bigcap_{\gamma<\beta} \mathbb{N}_\gamma \subseteq \mathbb{N}_{\beta'} \subseteq \mathbb{N}_\alpha .$$

(ii) By induction on α.

Case $\alpha = 0$. If $x \sim_0 x'$, then $x \sim x'$, then by definition $x|y = x'|y$ for all $y \in \mathbb{N}$. Therefore

$$\forall y \in \mathbb{N}_0.[x \boxdot y \sim x|y = x'|y \sim x' \boxdot y],$$

which is $x \sim_1 x'$.

Case $\alpha + 1$. Then

$$\begin{array}{rcll} x \sim_{\alpha+1} x' & \Rightarrow & \forall y \in \mathbb{N}_\alpha.(x \boxdot y \sim_\alpha x' \boxdot y), & \text{by definition,} \\ & \Rightarrow & \forall y \in \mathbb{N}_\alpha.(x \boxdot y \sim_{\alpha+1} x' \boxdot y), & \text{by the IH,} \\ & \Rightarrow & \forall y \in \mathbb{N}_{\alpha+1}.(x \boxdot y \sim_{\alpha+1} x' \boxdot y), & \text{since } \mathbb{N}_{\alpha+1} \subseteq \mathbb{N}_\alpha, \text{ by (i),} \\ & \Rightarrow & x \sim_{\alpha+2} x'. & \end{array}$$

Case $\alpha = \lambda$ a limit ordinal. Then

$$\begin{array}{rcll} x \sim_\lambda x' & \Rightarrow & x \sim_\delta x', & \text{for some } \delta < \lambda, \\ & \Rightarrow & x \sim_{\delta+1} x', & \text{by the induction hypothesis,} \\ & \Rightarrow & \forall y \in \mathbb{N}_\delta.(x \boxdot y \sim_\delta x' \boxdot y), & \text{by definition,} \\ & \Rightarrow & \forall y \in \mathbb{N}_\lambda.(x \boxdot y \sim_\delta x' \boxdot y), & \text{since } \mathbb{N}_\lambda \subseteq \mathbb{N}_\delta \text{ by (i),} \\ & \Rightarrow & \forall y \in \mathbb{N}_\lambda.(x \boxdot y \sim_\lambda x' \boxdot y), & \text{since by definition } \sim_\delta \subseteq \sim_\lambda, \\ & \Rightarrow & x \sim_{\lambda+1} x'. & \end{array}$$

(iii) By induction on β one shows as in (i), but now using (ii), that

$$\forall \alpha < \beta. \sim_\alpha \subseteq \sim_\beta .$$

(iv) By transfinite induction on α. We only treat transitivity for the case α is a limit ordinal. In that case $\sim_\alpha = \bigcup_{\beta<\alpha} \sim_\beta$ and one has

$$\begin{array}{rcll} x \sim_\alpha y \;\&\; y \sim_\alpha z & \Rightarrow & x \sim_\beta y \;\&\; y \sim_\gamma z, & \text{for some } \beta, \gamma < \alpha. \text{ Wlog } \beta \leq \gamma, \text{ so} \\ & \Rightarrow & x \sim_\gamma y \;\&\; y \sim_\gamma z, & \text{by (iii),} \\ & \Rightarrow & x \sim_\gamma z, & \text{by the IH,} \\ & \Rightarrow & x \sim_\alpha z. & \end{array}$$

(v) ($\Rightarrow$) Let $x, x' \in \mathbb{N}_{\alpha+1}, y, y' \in \mathbb{N}_\alpha$. Assume $x \sim_{\alpha+1} x'$, and $y \sim_\alpha y'$ towards $x \boxdot y \sim_\alpha x' \boxdot y'$. Now

$$\begin{array}{rcll} x \boxdot y & \sim_\alpha & x' \boxdot y, & \text{since } x \sim_{\alpha+1} x' \text{ and } y \in \mathbb{N}_\alpha, \\ & \sim_\alpha & x' \boxdot y', & \text{since } x' \in \mathbb{N}_{\alpha+1}, y, y' \in \mathbb{N}_\alpha, \text{ and } y \sim_\alpha y'. \end{array}$$

($\Leftarrow$) Let $x, x' \in \mathbb{N}_{\alpha+1}$. Assume $\forall y, y' \in \mathbb{N}_\alpha.[y \sim_\alpha y' \Rightarrow x \boxdot y \sim_\alpha x' \boxdot y']$. By (ii) one has $y \sim_\alpha y$ for all y. Therefore by assumption $x \boxdot y \sim_\alpha x' \boxdot y$, which is $x \sim_{\alpha+1} x'$.

(vi) By induction on α we show that for all $x, x' \in \mathbb{N}$

$$x' \sim_\alpha x \;\&\; x \in \mathbb{N}_\alpha \Rightarrow x' \in \mathbb{N}_\alpha.$$

Case $\alpha = 0$. Trivial.
Case $\alpha + 1$. Assume $x' \sim_{\alpha+1} x \in \mathbb{N}_{\alpha+1}$ towards $x' \in \mathbb{N}_{\alpha+1}$. This is
(1) $\forall y \in \mathbb{N}_\alpha . x' \boxdot y \in \mathbb{N}_\alpha$;
(2) $\forall y, y' \in \mathbb{N}_\alpha . [y \sim_\alpha y' \Rightarrow x' \boxdot y \sim_\alpha x' \boxdot y']$.
As to (1). Since $x' \sim_{\alpha+1} x$ one has

$$x' \boxdot y \sim_\alpha x \boxdot y \in \mathbb{N}_\alpha,$$

and the IH applies.
As to (2), assume $y, y' \in \mathbb{N}_\alpha, y \sim_\alpha y'$. Then

$$\begin{array}{rcll} x' \boxdot y & \sim_\alpha & x \boxdot y, & \text{since } x' \sim_{\alpha+1} x, y \in \mathbb{N}_\alpha, \\ & \sim_\alpha & x \boxdot y', & \text{since } x \in \mathbb{N}_{\alpha+1}, y \sim_\alpha y', \\ & \sim_\alpha & x' \boxdot y', & \text{since } x \sim_{\alpha+1} x', y' \in \mathbb{N}_\alpha. \end{array}$$

Case $\alpha = \lambda$ a limit ordinal. Assume $x' \sim_\lambda x \in \mathbb{N}_\lambda = \bigcap_{\beta<\lambda} \mathbb{N}_\beta$ towards $x' \in \mathbb{N}_\lambda$. Then $x' \sim_\beta x \in \mathbb{N}_\beta$, for some $\beta < \lambda$. By the IH one has $x' \in \mathbb{N}_\beta$.

$$\begin{array}{rl} x' \sim_\delta x \in \mathbb{N}_\delta, & \text{for all } \delta \text{ with } \beta \leq \delta < \lambda, \\ x' \in \mathbb{N}_\delta, & \text{for } \beta \leq \delta < \lambda, \text{ by the IH, and also} \\ x' \in \mathbb{N}_\delta, & \text{for } \delta < \beta, \text{ by (i); therefore} \\ x' \in \bigcap_{\beta<\lambda} \mathbb{N}_\beta = \mathbb{N}_\lambda. & \end{array}$$

□

PROPOSITION 2.12. (i) *If* $x, y \in \mathbb{N}_{\gamma_0}$, *then* $x \boxdot y \in \mathbb{N}_{\gamma_0}$.
(ii) *If* $x \sim_{\gamma_0} x'$ *and* $y \sim_{\gamma_0} y'$, *then* $x \boxdot y \sim_{\gamma_0} x' \boxdot y'$.

PROOF. (i) For $x \in \mathbb{N}_{\gamma_0} = \mathbb{N}_{\gamma_0+1}$ and $y \in \mathbb{N}_{\gamma_0}$ one has $x \boxdot y \in \mathbb{N}_{\gamma_0}$.
(ii) Assume $x \sim_{\gamma_0} x'$ and $y \sim_{\gamma_0} y'$. Then $x \sim_{\gamma_0+1} x'$ and hence $x \boxdot y \sim_{\gamma_0} x' \boxdot y'$. □

DEFINITION 2.13. (Where is the flaw?) Take γ_0 as above. Define

$$\begin{array}{rcl} \mathbb{N}_\infty & = & \mathbb{N}_{\gamma_0}; \\ \sim_\infty & \Longleftrightarrow & \sim_{\gamma_0}; \\ \mathcal{K}_\infty & \triangleq & \langle \mathbb{N}_\infty/\sim_\infty, [i]_{\sim_\infty}, [k]_{\sim_\infty}, [s]_{\sim_\infty}, \boxdot \rangle, \end{array}$$

with

$$[x]_{\sim_\infty} \boxdot [y]_{\sim_\infty} \triangleq [x \boxdot y]_{\sim_\infty}.$$

Now it seems to follow from Proposition 2.11(v) that application is well defined and i, k, s satisfy the requirements. The question remains whether the model is non-trivial.

DEFINITION 2.14. A *special fixed point* is a number $o \in \mathbb{N}$ such that in the sense of Definition 2.2 one has $o|y = o$, for all $y \in \mathbb{N}$.

LEMMA 2.15. (i) *There exists a special fixed point* $o \in \mathbb{N}$.

(ii) *A fixed point* $o \in \mathbb{N}$ *satisfies* $\forall y \in \mathbb{N}. o \boxdot y \sim_0 o$.

(iii) *There exists two special fixed points* $o_1, o_2 \in \mathbb{N}$ *such that* $o_1 \neq o_2$.

PROOF. (i) There exists a total computable $k \colon \mathbb{N} \to \mathbb{N}$ such that $k(x)|y = \{k(x)\}(y) = x$. By the recursion theorem there exists a number $o \in \mathbb{N}$ such that $k(o) \sim o$. This implies that for all $y \in \mathbb{N}$ one has $o|y = k(o)|y = o$.

(ii) By Lemma 2.6 one has $o \boxdot y \sim o|y = o$, for all $y \in \mathbb{N}$, so that $o \boxdot y \sim_0 o$.

(iii) The 'padding' Lemma, II.3.2.9 below, states that there exists a total computable function P of two arguments such that for all $x, y \in \mathbb{N}$ one has $P(x,y) \sim x$ and moreover $P(x,y) = P(x',y')$ implies $x = x'$ and $y = y'$. Using P two different variants of o can be found. Indeed, define the total computable functions k_i such that $k_i(x) \cdot y = P(x,i)$, for $1 \leq i \leq 2$. Applying twice the recursion theorem there exists $e_1, e_2 \in \mathbb{N}$ such that $e_i \sim_1 k_i(e_i)$, $1 \leq i \leq 2$. Take $o_i = P(e_i, i)$. Then for all $y \in \mathbb{N}$ one has

$$\begin{array}{rcll} o_1 \boxdot y & \sim & o_1|y, & \text{by Corollary II.2.6} \\ & \triangleq & P(e_1,1)|y, & \text{by definition.} \\ & = & e_1|y, & \text{by the padding property: } P(e_1,1) \sim e_1, \\ & = & k_1(e_1)|y, & \text{as } e_1 \sim k(e_1) \text{ using the recursion theorem,} \\ & = & P(e_1,1), & \text{by choice of } k_1, \\ & \triangleq & o_1. & \end{array}$$

Therefore $o_1 \sim_0 o_1 \boxdot y$ is a special fixed point, and similarly $o_2 \sim_0 o_2 \boxdot y$. By construction $o_1 = P(e_1,1) \neq P(e_2,2) = o_2$ are different, because of the padding function P. ☐

COROLLARY 2.16. (i) *If* $o \in \mathbb{N}$ *is a special fixed point, then* $o \in \mathbb{N}_\infty$.

(ii) *For the fixed points* o_1, o_2 *one has* $o_1 \not\sim_\infty o_2$. *Therefore* $[o_1]_{\sim_\infty} \neq [o_2]_{\sim_\infty}$.

PROOF. (i) By transfinite induction on α one shows $o \in \mathbb{N}_\alpha$.

Case $\alpha = 0$ is trivial.

Case $\alpha + 1$. By the induction hypothesis $o \in \mathbb{N}_\alpha$. To show that $o \in \mathbb{N}_{\alpha+1}$, we need

(1) $\forall y \in \mathbb{N}_\alpha. o \boxdot y \in \mathbb{N}_\alpha$;

(2) $\forall y, y' \in \mathbb{N}_\alpha. [y \sim_\alpha y' \;\Rightarrow\; o \boxdot y \sim_\alpha o \boxdot y']$.

As to (1). $o \boxdot y \sim_0 o \in \mathbb{N}_\alpha$. Then $o \boxdot y \sim_\alpha o \in \mathbb{N}_\alpha$, by Proposition 2.11(iii), and we can conclude $o \boxdot y \in \mathbb{N}_\alpha$, by Proposition 2.11(vi).

As to (2), let $y, y' \in \mathbb{N}_\alpha$ towards $o \boxdot y \sim_\alpha o \boxdot y'$. Now $o \boxdot y \sim_0 o \sim_0 o \boxdot y'$, so that we are done by Proposition 2.11(iii).

Case α is a limit ordinal. By the IH $o \in \mathbb{N}_\beta$ for $\beta < \alpha$. Therefore $o \in \mathbb{N}_\alpha$.

(ii) By induction on α we show $o_1 \not\sim_\alpha o_2$.

Case $\alpha = 0$. Suppose $o_1 \sim_0 o_2$. Then $o_1 = o_1|7 = o_2|7 = o_2$, contradicting the Lemma.

Case $\alpha+1$. Suppose $o_1 \sim_\alpha o_2$. Then $o_1 \sim_0 o_1 \boxdot y \sim_\alpha o_2 \boxdot y \sim_0 o_2$, for any element $y \in \mathbb{N}_\alpha$ (for which we may take 7 again), contradicting the IH.

Case α limit ordinal. Then $o_1 \sim_\alpha o_2$ implies $o_1 \sim_\beta o_2$, for some $\beta < \alpha$, contradicting the IH. □

CONJECTURE 2.17. [Without evidence] $\mathcal{K}_\infty$ is an non-trivial extensional combinatory algebra.

In spite of the above results this conjecture doesn't follow. The problem is that although one has $[i]_\infty, [k]_\infty \in \mathcal{K}_\infty$, it is unclear whether $[s]_\infty \in \mathcal{K}_\infty$. Therefore $\mathcal{K}_\infty$ is only an extensional non-trivial total applicative structure, not necessarily a combinatory algebra. (Added April 1, 2021: $\mathcal{K}_\infty$ is not a combinatory algebra, see Appendix.)

HRO & HEO

A construction like that of $\mathcal{K}_\infty$ does work for the typed variants of the λ-calculus, the simply typed lambda calculus $\lambda_\to$, see e.g. (Barendregt 1984, Appendix A), or Barendregt et al. (2013). Built on top of $\mathcal{K}$ there is for this system without extensionality there is structure HRO and for the system with extensionality there is HEO, see Troelstra (1973). Also there is in general the possibility to make an extensional collapse (going from HRO to HRO^E). This is not possible for the untyped λ-calculus, see in Part I, Theorem 3.2.24 showing the impossibility of adding Ext to some consistent set of CL equations. HEO and HRO^E are different structures, but with the same intention. Using an involved argument it can be shown that nevertheless these two structures are isomorphic, see Bezem (1985).

2.4 $\mathcal{K}_\infty^{CL}$: an extensional combinatory algebra

The final and for the thesis significant attempt to modify $\mathcal{K}$ into a total ca was as follows.

DEFINITION 2.18. Define $\mathbb{N}^{CL}$ to be the least set $\subseteq \mathbb{N}$ such that

(i) $i, k, s \in \mathbb{N}^{CL}$;
(ii) $x, y \in \mathbb{N}^{CL} \Rightarrow x \boxdot y \in \mathbb{N}^{CL}$.

DEFINITION 2.19. By transfinite recursion on α define $\approx_\alpha \subseteq (\mathbb{N}^{CL})^2$.

$$
\begin{aligned}
x \approx_0 x' &\iff x \sim x', \text{ see Definition 2.2;}\\
x \approx_{\alpha+1} x' &\iff \Big(\forall y \in \mathbb{N}^{CL}.[x \boxdot y \approx_\alpha x' \boxdot y]\\
&\qquad \vee \exists z, y, y' \in \mathbb{N}^{CL}.[y \approx_\alpha y' \;\&\; x = z \boxdot y \;\&\; x' = z \boxdot y']\\
&\qquad \vee \exists z, y, y' \in \mathbb{N}^{CL}.[y \approx_\alpha y' \;\&\; x = y \boxdot z \;\&\; x' = y' \boxdot z]\\
&\qquad \vee \exists x'' \in \mathbb{N}^{CL}.[x \approx_\alpha x'' \;\&\; x'' \approx_\alpha x']\Big);\\
x \approx_\lambda x' &\iff \exists \delta < \lambda . x \approx_\delta x', \text{ that is } \approx_\lambda = \bigcup_{\delta<\lambda} \approx_\delta .
\end{aligned}
$$

PROPOSITION 2.20. *For all ordinals* α, β *one has*

(i) $\alpha \leq \beta \Rightarrow \approx_\alpha \subseteq \approx_\beta$.

(ii) *The relation* $\approx_\alpha$ *is reflexive and symmetric.*

(iii) $[\forall y \in \mathbb{N}^{CL}. x \boxdot y \approx_\alpha x' \boxdot y] \Rightarrow x \approx_{\alpha+1} x'$.

(iv) *For all* $x, x', z \in \mathbb{N}^{CL}.[x \approx_\alpha x' \Rightarrow z \boxdot x \approx_{\alpha+1} z \boxdot x']$.

(v) *For all* $x, x', z \in \mathbb{N}^{CL}.[x \approx_\alpha x' \Rightarrow x \boxdot z \approx_{\alpha+1} x' \boxdot z]$.

(vi) *If* λ *is a limit ordinal, then the relation* $\approx_\lambda$ *is a congruence relation on* $\mathbb{N}^{CL}$.

PROOF. (i) As for Proposition 2.11(iii).

(ii) By induction on α.

(iii) By the first disjunct in the clause defining $\approx_{\alpha+1}$ in Definition 2.19.

(iv) By the second disjunct.

(v) By the third disjunct.

(vi) Let λ be a limit ordinal. Suppose that $x \approx_\lambda x''$ and $x'' \approx_\lambda x'$. Then for some ordinals $\beta, \gamma < \lambda$ one has $x \approx_\beta x''$ and $x'' \approx_\gamma x'$. Wlog $\beta \leq \gamma$, so that by (i) it follows that $x \approx_\gamma x''$. Therefore $(x, x') \subseteq \approx_{\gamma+1} \subseteq \approx_\lambda$. Together with (ii) this shows that $\approx_\lambda$ is an equivalence relation. In a similar way it follows by (iv), (v) that $\approx_\lambda$ is a congruence. □

PROPOSITION 2.21. *There exists an ordinal* γ *such that* $\mathbb{N}_\gamma = \mathbb{N}_{\gamma+1}$ *and* $\approx_\gamma$ *is the same relation as* $\approx_{\gamma+1}$. *Let* γ_0 *be the least limit ordinal where this happens. Write* $\approx_\infty$ *for* $\approx_{\gamma_0}$ *and define* $\mathbb{N}_\infty^{CL} = \mathbb{N}^{CL} / \approx_\infty$.

PROOF. As for Proposition 2.10. □

PROPOSITION 2.22. (i) *The relation* $\approx_\infty$ *is a congruence relation.*

(ii) $\langle \mathbb{N}_\infty^{CL}, \boxdot \rangle$, *with* $[p]_{\approx_\infty} \boxdot [q]_{\approx_\infty} = [p \boxdot q]_{\approx_\infty}$, *is an extensional applicative structure.*

(iii) $\mathcal{K}_\infty^{CL} = \langle \mathbb{N}_\infty^{CL}, [i], [k], [s], \boxdot \rangle$ *is an extensional combinatory algebra.*

PROOF. (i) By Proposition 2.20 (vi).

(ii) As $\approx_\gamma$ is a congruence application is well defined.

(iii) By the fact that $\approx_\infty$ is $\approx_\gamma = \approx_{\gamma+1}$, using the first disjunct in the clause of the definition of $\approx_{\gamma+1}$. □

Although $\mathcal{K}_\infty^{CL}$ is an extensional combinatory algebra, still this did not satisfy the set goal. The point is that this ca may be trivial and I could neither refute nor establish this.

The ω-rule

As the elements of $\mathbb{N}^{CL}$ are generated by the combinators, the resulting structure is 'hard' (aka 'minimal', comparable to prime fields in which all elements are generated from $\{0, 1\}$ and the operations $\{+, -, \times, \div\}$). Therefore the equations valid in $\mathcal{K}_\infty^{CL}$ are closed under the ω-rule:

$$\frac{FZ = GZ \text{ for all } Z \in CL^o}{F = G}$$

The difference between extensionality Ext and the ω-rule is that in the assumption of Ext one has

$$\mathrm{CL} + \mathrm{ext} \vdash \mathsf{F}z = \mathsf{G}z \text{ for a fresh variable } z, \tag{2}$$

which is stronger than the assumption that

$$\mathrm{CL} + \mathrm{ext} \vdash \mathsf{F}\mathsf{Z} = \mathsf{G}\mathsf{Z}, \text{ for all } \mathsf{Z} \in \mathrm{CL}^{o} \tag{3}$$

in order to conclude $\mathsf{F} = \mathsf{G}$. Indeed, (2) states something more than (3): the equality holds *uniformly*, giving for each Z (a substitution instance of) the same proof.

DEFINITION 2.23. (i) The ω-rule is said to be *valid* for the pair F, G (often one calls this *admissible*) if (3) implies $\mathsf{F} = \mathsf{G}$.

(ii) The ω-rule is said to be *consistent* with theory $\mathcal{T}$ if

$$\mathcal{T} + \omega\text{-rule does not prove every equation.}$$

This can be applied to both CL and the λ-calculus. Under the hypothesis that the model $\mathcal{K}_{\infty}^{\mathrm{CL}}$ is non-trivial, it follows that the ω-rule is consistent with CL-calculus.

These considerations naturally led me to study the ω-rule[7]. I started to wonder whether the ω-rule could be valid for all F, G. The other extreme would be that it is inconsistent. In Chapter I.2 of this thesis the middle way was established by the following results. 1. Adding the ω-rule to the λ-calculus (or CL) with extensionality turned out to be consistent[8]. 2. For most pairs of terms (not being so-called *universal generators*, introduced in Barendregt (1970)) the ω-rule is valid.

[7] Rosenbloom 1952, an early book on combinatory logic and the lambda calculus, by accident formulates extensionality as being the ω-rule. But no consistency proof was provided.

[8] One hope was that the ω-consistency of CL+Ext could imply that $\mathcal{K}_{\infty}^{\mathrm{CL}}$ is non-trivial.

3 Normed uniformly reflexive structures

This chapter is an improvement of Barendregt (1971a) and was published as Barendregt (1975). The notion of Uniformly Reflexive Structure (URS) of Wagner (1969) is introduced, coming from his thesis in 1963. A URS is a partial applicative system $\mathcal{U}$, made total by a fresh element $*$ representing undefined, with elements $\mathsf{i}, \mathsf{k}, \mathsf{s}$ making it a partial combinatory algebra, plus an element δ that serves as test for equality for $x, y, u, v \in \mathcal{U}$

$$\begin{aligned} \delta xyuv &= u, && \text{if } x = y, \\ &= v, && \text{else.} \end{aligned}$$

Kleene's pca $\mathcal{K}$ can easily be extended by the code of the computable function representing δ. This then yields a URS. Using the notion URS a modest but basic part of computability theory has be developed by Wagner and Strong (1968, 1970).

In this chapter we introduce an equational system WS to derive results about URSs, similar to the function of CL producing equations valid in all ca's, aided by a reduction (rewrite) relation. It turns out that the equation $\mathsf{EE} = \underline{*}$, with $\mathsf{E} = \mathsf{SII}$, cannot be derived in WS. In fact in the 'intended model' $\mathcal{K}$ (enlarged with a δ, but that element doesn't play a role here) the value of ee, with $\mathsf{e} = \mathsf{sii}$, depends on how the partial computable functions are coded as natural numbers. If one adds to a URS a *norm*, that represents the natural notion of length of computation, as in Moschovakis (1971), one obtains a normed URS (NURS). In every NURS one has $\mathsf{EE} = *$. In fact for every CL-term P one has in a NURS $\mathcal{U}$ that

$$\mathsf{P} \text{ doesn't have a } w\text{-normal form} \iff [\![\mathsf{P}]\!]^{\mathcal{U}} = *.$$

We have slightly strengthened the axioms of a URS by requiring

$$\mathsf{sab} = \mathsf{sa'b'} \Rightarrow \mathsf{a} = \mathsf{a'} \;\&\; \mathsf{b} = \mathsf{b'}.$$

From this it follows that i, k, s, δ can be chosen in such a way that in the resulting URS different normal forms have different values, Corollary 2.10. This property has been exploited in Bethke & Klop (1995) and in Bethke et al. (1999, 1996). One interesting result is that a pca satisfying this result can be embedded into a total ca.

In this chapter ω stands for the smallest infinite ordinal, used for the set of natural numbers. In other places this set is denoted by $\mathbb{N}$. There is (at least) one thing to correct: in the proof of 3.3 ($\Rightarrow$), just after 3.3.10, it is written "infinite chain of descending integers." This should be "infinite descending chain of natural numbers. Contradiction."

The following text is the paper[1] Barendregt (1975) in its entirety, being an improved version of Barendregt (1971a).

[1]Reprinted by permission from Springer Nature Customer Service Center GmbH: Lecture Notes in Computer Science, vol 37, Springer, International Symposium on Lambda-Calculus and Computer Science Theory, by H. P. Barendregt, 1975.

NORMED UNIFORMLY REFLEXIVE STRUCTURES

Henk Barendregt
Mathematisch Instituut
Boedapestlaan, Utrecht
The Netherlands

§0. Introduction. The theory of Uniformly Reflexive Structures (URS) studied by Wagner and Strong ([8],[6],[1]), is an elegant axiomatization of parts of recursion theory. The theory abstracts some properties of the function $\{n\}(m)$ (i.e. the nth partial recursive function applied to m) by considering arbitrary domains with a binary operation application. The standard URS is $\mathfrak{R}$ with domain $\omega \cup \{*\}$ and application $n.m = \{n\}(m)$ if defined $*$ else.

However the URS are not completely adequate for the description of recursion theory. Real computations do have a length, a feature which is missing in the URS. In fact there are sentences in the language of URS undecided by the axioms. E.g. let $e = \lambda x.xx$, i.e. $ex = xx$ for all x, then $ee = *$ is such a sentence. But this sentence holds in the intended interpretation $\mathfrak{K}$ as follows from an argument using length of computation.

Moreover in a URS it is not always possible to represent the partial recursive functions.

To overcome these defects we introduce a concept of a norm.

A Normed Uniformly Reflexive Structure (NURS) is a URS which a norm $|..;..|$ can be defined satisfying:

1. $|x;y| \in \omega \cup \{\infty\}$
2. $|x;y| = \infty \iff x.y = *$
3. $|s.x.y;z| > |x.z;y.z| + |x;z| + |y;z|$, if $|s.x.y;z| \neq \infty$

The intended interpretation of $|x;y|$ is "the length of computation of x.y".

The following facts motivate the introduction of NURS. As was intended $\mathfrak{R}$ is a NURS. Wagners (highly) constructible URS are NURS. In every NURS $ee = *$ holds. More generally, for a NURS $\mathfrak{N}$ and a term M of the theory, M has no normal form $\iff \mathfrak{N} \models M = *$. In a NURS all splinters are semi-computable, and hence can be used to represent the partial recursive functions.

The use of length of computation in recursion theory has also been stressed by Y.Moschovakis [3]. In fact the axioms of the norm in a URS imply Moschovakis' condition on the length of computation.

Familiarity with URS is assumed. See e.g. Wagner [8] and Strong [6].

In §1 the defects of URS mentioned above are shown. A formal theory WS, convenient for the study of URS, is introduced in §2. The term model of an extension of WS provides some counter examples for the relation between semi-computable and recursively enumerable. The results about the NURS are proved in §3.

§1. The definition of a URS given below is not exactly the same as those of Wagner and Strong. The axioms are written down in a way showing the correspondence with combinatory logic. Axiom 7 is added; it implies that we may assume that terms with different normal forms are unequal in a URS (2.10).

1.1. Def. A URS is a structure $\mathfrak{U} = \langle U,*,i,k,s,\delta,\cdot\rangle$ such that the following holds where a,b,c are variables ranging over U - {*}:

1. $*.a = a.* = *.* = *$
2. $i.a = a$
3. $k.a.b = a$
4. $s.a.b.c = (a.c).(b.c)$; $s.a.b \neq *$
5. $a = b \rightarrow \delta.a.b = k$; $a \neq b \rightarrow \delta.a.b = k.i$
6. $i \neq k$
7. $s.a.b = s.a'.b' \rightarrow a = a' \wedge b = b'$.

1.2. Def. Kleenes URS, $\mathfrak{K}$, is the structure $\langle \omega^*,*,i,k,s,\delta,\cdot\rangle$ such that $\omega^* = \omega \cup \{*\}$ with, $* \notin \omega$, $n.m = \{n\}(m)$ if defined, $*$ else

$*.n = n.* = *.* = *$, and i,k,s,δ are to be found by the s-m-n theorem such that axioms 2,...,7 hold. As an example we construct k. Let $\psi(x,y) = x$. Then ψ is partial recursive. Hence

$$\begin{aligned} x &= \psi(x,y) \\ &= \{e\}(x,y) && \text{for some index } e \text{ of } \psi. \\ &= \{s_1^1(e,x)\}(y) \\ &= \{\{k\}(x)\}(y) && k \text{ index of } \lambda x.s_1^1(e,x). \\ &= k.x.y. \end{aligned}$$

By pumping up the indices, cf. Rogers [4], p.83, we can assure that axiom 7 holds.

1.3. Theorem. Let $e = s.i.i.$ Then $e.e = *$ is independent in the theory of the URS. [1)]

Proof. It will be shown that $e.e = *$ is true in $\mathcal{K}$ but false in a modification $\mathcal{K}^\circ$.

We have $\mathcal{K} \models e.a = (i.a)(i.a) = a.a$, i.e. $\{e\}(a) = \{a\}(a)$.

The computation of $\{e\}(a)$ runs as follows:

Read a; compute $\{a\}(a)$. Hence the computation of $\{e\}(e)$ is:

Read e; compute $\{e\}(e)$; Read e; compute $\{e\}(e)$; ...

Therefore $\{e\}(e)$ is undefined. Hence $\mathcal{K} \models e.e = *$.

Let $\mathcal{K}^\circ = \langle \omega^*, *, i, k, s^\circ, \delta, \circ \rangle$ be the following modification of $\mathcal{K}$.

$$a \circ b = a.b \quad \text{if } a \neq e \text{ or } b \neq e$$
$$= 0 \quad \text{else}$$

Then $\circ$ is partial recursive. Let $s^\circ.a.b.c = (a \circ c) \circ (b \circ c)$.
Again by pumping up the indices we may assume that $s^\circ \neq e$, $s^\circ.a \neq e$ for all a and $s^\circ.a.b = e$ iff $a = b = i$. Hence $s^\circ \circ a \circ b \circ c = s^\circ.a.b.c = (a \circ c) \circ (b \circ c)$, unless perhaps $s^\circ.a.b. = c = e$. But then $a = b = i$ and $(i \circ e) \circ (i \circ e) = e \bullet e$.
It is clear that $i, k, \delta \neq e$ and the axioms 2,3 and 5 follow.
Axiom 7 can be assured as in 1.2. Clearly $\mathcal{K}^\circ \not\models e.e = *$. ⊠

Another defect of the URS is the following. The partial recursive functions can be represented in a URS provided one has an infinite semi-computable (SC) splinter, Strong [6],3.2. However, H.Friedman has shown that there is a URS without infinite SC splinter.

1.4. Def. Let $\mathfrak{A}$ be a non-standard model of Peano arithmetic with universe A. Let $\mathcal{K}_{\mathfrak{A}}$ be the structure $\langle A^*, *, i, k, s, \delta, \circledast \rangle$ where $* \notin A$, i, k, s, δ are as in 1.2 and $\circledast$ is defined by

$$* \circledast a = a \circledast * = * \circledast * = *$$
$$a \circledast b = c \quad \text{if} \quad \mathfrak{A} \models \{\underline{a}\}(\underline{b}) = \underline{c} \quad \text{i.e. } \mathfrak{A} \models \exists z[T(\underline{a},\underline{b},z) \wedge U(z) = \underline{c}]$$
$$= * \quad \text{else.}$$

U and T are the components of Kleene's normal form theorem. Then $\mathcal{K}_{\mathfrak{A}}$ is a URS; e.g. $\mathcal{K}_{\mathfrak{A}} \models k.a.b = a$ holds since $\{\{k\}(a)\}(b) = a$ is provable in Peano arithmetic, hence $\mathfrak{A} \models \{\{k\}(a)\}(b) = a$.

1) Compare this with the following : Let $E = \{x | x \in x\}$. Then $E \in E$ is independent in ZF without foundation, but refusable in ZF itself.

1.5. Theorem (H.Friedman). $\mathcal{H}_{\mathfrak{A}}$ is a URS without infinite SC splinter.

Proof. If $\mathcal{H}_{\mathfrak{A}}$ would contain an infinite SC splinter, each splinter would be SC, Strong [6] 3.11. Therefore the set of standard numbers would be SC. But this is absurd since SC sets are definable ($x \in A \iff f(x) \neq \cdot$), and the set of standard numbers is not. ⊠

1.6. Cor. There exists a URS with an infinite non SC splinter on which the partial recursive functions can be represented.

Proof. Let $\mathfrak{N}$ be the standard model of Peano arithmetic. Let $\mathfrak{A} \equiv \mathfrak{N}$ be a non-standard model. For each partial recursive function ψ with index e we have

$$\mathfrak{N} \models \{\underline{e}\}(\underline{n}) = \underline{m} \iff \psi(n) = m$$

$$\mathfrak{N} \models \exists z\, T(\underline{e},\underline{n},z) \iff \psi(n) \text{ is undefined.}$$

Therefore, since $\mathfrak{A} \equiv \mathfrak{N}$, $\mathcal{H}_{\mathfrak{A}} \models \underline{e}\,\underline{n} = \underline{m} \iff \psi(n) = m$

$$\mathcal{H}_{\mathfrak{A}} \models \underline{e}\,\underline{n} = \underline{\cdot} \iff \psi(n) \text{ is undefined.}$$ ⊠

However, there exists a URS such that only partial recursive functions with recursive domain can be represented on any of the infinite splinters.

1.7. Theorem. There exists a URS such that for no infinite splinter X the partial recursive functions can be represented on X.

Proof. Let $\mathfrak{A}$ be a non-standard model of Peano arithmetic in which only the recursive r.e. sets are definable on ω, see [2], Exc.7,p123. Let ψ be a partial recursive function with non recursive domain A. Then ψ is not representable on the splinter of standard integers for otherwise A would be definable on ω. But then ψ is not representable on any infinite splinter X, since all infinite splinters are in bijective computable correspondence, [6],3-7.⊠

§2. The following theory WS is convenient for the study of URS.

2.1. Def. WS has the following language.

Alphabet:	$x_0, x_1, \ldots$	variables
	$I, K, S, \Delta, \underline{\cdot}$	constants
	$\geqslant, =$	reduction, equality
	(,)	brackets

Terms are inductively defined by

1. A variable or constant is a term
2. If M,N are terms, so is (MN).

Formulas are $M \geqslant N$ and $M = N$ where M,N are terms.

Notation: x,y,z,... denote arbitrary variables

M,N,L denote arbitrary terms

$M_1M_2\ldots M_n$ stands for $(..(M_1M_2)\ldots M_n)$

$M \subset M'$ if M is a subterm of M'

$x \in M$ if x occurs in M

M is closed if for no x $x \in M$

$\equiv$ denotes syntactic equality.

If M is a closed WS term and $\mathcal{U} = \langle U,*,i,k,s,\delta,\cdot\rangle$ is a URS, then $M^{\mathcal{U}}$ is the obvious interpretation of M in $\mathcal{U}$: $\underline{*}^{\mathcal{U}} = *$, $I^{\mathcal{U}} = i$, etc, $(MN)^{\mathcal{U}} = M^{\mathcal{U}}.N^{\mathcal{U}}$; $\mathcal{U} \models M = N$ iff $M^{\mathcal{U}} = N^{\mathcal{U}}$.

A term M is in normal form (nf) if it has no subterms of the form $\underline{*}$, IA, KAB, SABC or ΔAB.

WS is defined by the following axioms and rules:

I	0.	$\underline{*}M \geqslant \underline{*}$	$M\underline{*} \geqslant \underline{*}$
	1.	$IM \geqslant M$	
	2.	$KMN \geqslant M$	if N is in nf
	3.	$SMNL \geqslant ML(NL)$	
	4.a	$\Delta MM \geqslant K$	if M is in nf
	b	$\Delta MN \geqslant KI$	if M,N are in nf and $M \not\equiv N$
II	1.	$M \geqslant M$	
	2.	$M \geqslant M' \Rightarrow ZM \geqslant ZM'$, $MZ \geqslant M'Z$	
	3.	$M \geqslant N,\ N \geqslant L \Rightarrow M \geqslant L$	
III	1.	$M \geqslant N \Rightarrow M = N$	
	2.	$M = N \Rightarrow N = M$	
	3.	$M = N,\ N = L \Rightarrow M = L$	

2.2. (Church-Rosser theorem) If WS $\vdash M = N$, then for some term Z WS $\vdash M \geqslant Z$ and WS $\vdash N \geqslant Z$.

Proof. Well-known. See e.g. [5], T. 12, p. 144. ⊠

2.3. Def. A WS-term M has a nf if WS $\vdash M = M'$ and M' is in nf.

By 2.2 the normal form of a term is unique if it exists. If M has a nf, all its reduction sequences terminate, by the restriction in axioms I2,4.

2.4. Def. Let $\mathcal{U}$ be a URS with domain U. WS($\mathcal{U}$) is the theory WS modified as follows. For each a ∈ U, $\underline{a}$ is an additional constant. A term of WS($\mathcal{U}$) is in nf, if it does not contain a subterm $\underline{*}$, IA, etc. or $\underline{a}$M. WS($\mathcal{U}$) has the additional axioms $\underline{a}M \geqslant \underline{a.M}$. Axiom I4.b should be replaced by

$\Delta MN \geqslant KI$ if M,N are nf's and $\mathcal{U} \models M \neq N$.

Clearly $\mathcal{U} \models$ WS($\mathcal{U}$).

2.2 and 2.3 apply also to WS($\mathcal{U}$).

2.5. (Abstraction) Let M be a WS($\mathcal{U}$) term not containing *. Then there exists a WS($\mathcal{U}$) term λx.M such that

1. λx.M is in nf; $x \notin \lambda x.M$
2. WS($\mathcal{U}$) ⊢ $(\lambda x.M)N = [x/N]M$ for N in nf.

Proof. As in combinatory logic. ⊠

Note, however, that also there exists a WS term $\lambda x.\underline{*}$ in nf such that $\mathcal{U} \models (\lambda x.\underline{*})a = \underline{*}$ for all $\mathcal{U}$.
Take e.g. $\lambda x.\underline{*} = S(K\omega)(K\omega)$ with $\omega = \lambda x.\Delta(KI)(xx)$.

2.6. Def. Let $M \sim M'$ denote $Mx = M'x$ for $x \notin MM'$.

2.7. (Fixed Point Theorem) There exists a WS term FP such that

1. WS ⊢ FP f ~ f(FP f)
2. FP f is in nf.

Proof. Let $\omega_f = \lambda xz.f(xx)z$ and FP f = $\omega_f\omega_f$. ⊠

2.8. Lemma. Let M be a WS($\mathcal{U}$) term. Then M is a nf ⇒ ⇒ $\mathcal{U} \models M \neq *$.
Proof. The set of normal forms NF can be defined inductively by 1. $\underline{a}$,I,K,S,Δ ∈ NF. 2. AB ∈ NF ⇒ KA,SA,ΔA and SAB ∈ NF. Then the result follows inductively realizing that in a URS k.a, s.a, δ.a, s.a.b ≠ *. ⊠

The pumping up of indices used in 1.2 and 1.3 can be done in each URS due to axiom 7.

2.9. Lemma.
Then there exists a term P such that for all $\mathcal{U}$

1. $\mathcal{U} \models Pab \neq *$
2. $\mathcal{U} \models Pab \sim a$
3. $\mathcal{U} \models Pab = Pa'b' \rightarrow a = a' \wedge b = b'$.

Proof. Let $P \equiv \lambda abx.\ K(ax)b$. Clearly P satisfies 1 and 2. By writing out P in terms of I, K and S, one sees that P satisfies 3 due to axiom 7. ⊠

2.10. Cor. Let $M \not\equiv M'$ be WS terms in nf. Then we may assume $\mathfrak{U} \models M \neq M'$ for all $\mathfrak{U}$.
Proof. By changing if necessary the basic constants i,k,s, and δ, using P. See e.g. [9], p. 133 bottom. ⊠

What we may we will.

2.11. Cor. WS($\mathfrak{U}$) is a conservative extension of WS.
Proof. The only axiom of WS not in WS($\mathfrak{U}$) is I4b. However, this follows from the modified axiom by 2.10. Hence WS($\mathfrak{U}$) is an extension of WS. If M,N are WS terms and WS($\mathfrak{U}$) $\vdash M = N$ (or $\vdash M \geqslant N$), then the proof involves only WS terms (unless WS $\vdash M = N = \underline{*}$). The WS($\mathfrak{U}$) axioms only can hold for $A \not\equiv B$, by 2.10. Hence WS $\vdash M = N$ ($\vdash M \geqslant N$). ⊠

2.12. Theorem 1. WS($\mathfrak{U}$) $\vdash M = N \Rightarrow \mathfrak{U} \models M = N$
2. M has a nf $\Rightarrow \mathfrak{U} \models M \neq *$
Proof. 1. Induction on the length of proof of $M = N$ using 2.10.
2. By 1. and 2.6. ⊠

The converse of 2.12. 1,2 are false. E.g. in $\mathcal{K}^{\circ} \models EE \neq *$ where $E = SII$. But EE has no nf. However, if $\mathfrak{U}$ is a NURS the converse of 2.12.2 is true. See 3.3.

2.13. Def. Let WS* be WS augmented by the axioms:
$M \geqslant \underline{*}$ if M has no nf.

For each NURS $\mathfrak{U}$ we will have the completeness result:
WS* $\vdash M = N \iff \mathfrak{U} \models M = N$, for closed M,N;
see 3.5.

2.14. Def. $\mathfrak{U}(WS^*_o)$ (respectively $\mathfrak{U}(WS^*_c)$) is the term model consisting of arbitrary (respectively closed) WS terms modulo provable equality in WS*. Clearly they are URS.
Similarly we define $\mathfrak{U}(WS^*_{o,c}(\bar{\mathfrak{U}}))$.

These term models can be used for some counter-examples

2.15. Def. A subset X of a URS $\mathfrak{U}$ is RE if X = ∅ or X = Ra f = = {a | $\mathfrak{U} \models \exists x\, (\underline{f}x = \underline{a})$} for some total f in $\mathfrak{U}$ (i.e. ∀a fa ≠ •). In $\mathcal{K}$, X is RE ⟺ X is SC.

2.16. Theorem [1]. For $\mathfrak{U}(WS_o^*)$ we have

1. X is SC ⇏ X is RE
2. X is RE ⇏ X is SC
3. X is computable ⇒ X is finite or cofinite.

Proof.

2.16.1 Def. The family of F, $\mathcal{F}(F)$, is the set {N | ∃F' ⊢ F ⩾ F' ∧ N ⊂ F'} . If F has a nf, $\mathcal{F}(F)$ is finite. Each reduction of FA to a nf can be written in the form

$$FA \geqslant_\beta M_0[A] \geqslant_\delta M_0'[A] \geqslant_\beta M_1[A] \geqslant_\delta M_1'[A] \geqslant \ldots \geqslant M[A] \qquad (*)$$

where $\geqslant_\beta$ is axiomatized leaving out the Δ reduction axioms and $\geqslant_\delta$ is axiomatized leaving out the $\underline{\bullet}$,I,K,S axioms. A may not actually occur in M[A]. Referring to the sequence (•) we define:

2.16.2 Def. $Diag_n(F,A) = \{\Delta C_1[A]C_2[A] \mid \Delta C_1[A]C_2[A] \subset M_n\}$.

B satisfies $Diag_n(F,A) \iff \Delta C_1[A]C_2[A] = \Delta C_1[B]C_2[B]$, for all members of $Diag_n(FA)$.

2.16.3 Lemma. Let FA have a nf for all A. Let xa ⊄ F. Consider the sequence (•) for F(xa). Then

0. B satisfies $Diag_n(F,xa) \Rightarrow M_n[B] \geqslant_\delta M_n'[B]$.

1_n. xa is never "active" (i.e. in a subterm of the form ((xa)P)) in $M_n[xa]$, $M_n'[xa]$.

2_n. For almost all, i.e. all except finitely many, B satisfies $Diag_n(F,xa)$.

Proof. 0 is obvious.

1_0 follows by substituting for xa a nf ω such that ωP has no nf for all P.

$1_n \Rightarrow 2_n$ by realizing that the only possible exceptions are in $\mathcal{F}(F)$.

$2_n \Rightarrow 1_{n+1}$ follows as 1_0 with ω satisfying $\bigcup_0^n Diag_n(F,xa)$ and using 0. ⊠

---

1) A different example of 1. was given in Wagner [8], 6.13. 3. was proved by Strong [7] for the URS $\mathfrak{U}(WS_c^*)$.

2.16.4 <u>Cor</u>. Let FA have a nf for all A. Let xa $\not\subset$ F and xa $\not\subset$ M, the nf of F(xa). Then for almost all B
F(B) = F(xa).
Proof. Let Diag(F,xa) = $\cup$ Diag_n(F,xa) which is finite. This is satisfied by almost all B (2.16.3.2). Thus (2.16.3.0)
FB $\geqslant$ M[B]. Also F(xa) $\geqslant$ M[xa]. But then, since xa $\not\subset$ M[xa],
FB = F(xa). ⊠

More easily one can prove the following.
2.16.5 <u>Cor</u>. Let F(xa) have a nf, where xa $\not\subset$ F, xa $\not\subset$ the nf of F(xa). Then for x' $\not\subset$ F F(x'a) = F(xa).
Proof. Since x'a is a non-active term, it does not matter if it occurs in an active place. ⊠

2.16.6 <u>Cor</u>. Suppose RA F $\subset$ closed normal forms. Then Ra F is finite.
Proof. Take xa $\not\subset$ F. By the assumption, never xa $\subset$ M, the nf of FA. Hence for almost all B, FB = F(xa). ⊠

Now we can prove 2.16.
1. Take X = $\{K^n I \mid n \in \omega\}$. Then X is an infinite splinter hence SC (since $\mathcal{U}(WS_0^*)$ is a NURS, see §3). Suppose X were RE, say X = Ra F. Then F satisfies the assumption of 2.16.6, but Ra F = X is not finite. Contradiction.
2. Take X = Ra F, with Fa = xa. Suppose X were SC, i.e.

GM = I if M $\in$ X
      * else

for some G. Take a $\notin$ G. Then xa $\not\subset$ G. Also xa $\not\subset$ I which is the nf of G(xa). Hence for x' $\not\subset$ G it follows by 2.16.5 that G(x'a) =
= G(xa) = I, i.e. x'a $\in$ X, a contradiction.
3. Let X = Ø be computable. Define

GM = M if M $\in$ X
      M_0 else for some $M_0 \in$ X.

Then X = Ra G. Suppose the complement of X is not finite. Then there is a variable x $\notin$ Ra G $\cup$ $\mathcal{F}$(G). Then xa $\not\subset$ G, xa $\not\subset$ the nf of G(xa). Hence by 2.16.4 GB = G(xa) for almost all B, i.e.
X = Ra G is finite. ⊠

§3. For NURS it is convenient to define for elements of $\omega \cup \{\infty\}$: $p \gtrsim q$ iff $p = \infty \vee p > q$. Then $\gtrsim$ is transitive and axiom 3 for a norm can be stated as
$|s.a.b;c| \gtrsim |a.c;b.c| + |a;c| + |b;c|$.

3.1. Examples of NURS.

1. $\mathfrak{K}$ becomes a NURS by defining

$$|e;x| = \begin{cases} \mu z \ T(e,x,z) & \text{if defined} \\ \infty & \text{else} \end{cases}$$

Then an examination of the properties of the T predicate shows that this defines a norm on $\mathfrak{K}$.

2. $\mathcal{U}(WS^*_{o,c})$ are NURS by defining

$$|F;X| = \begin{cases} \text{the length of the inside out reduction of FX to nf} \\ \infty \quad \text{if FX has no nf.} \end{cases}$$

The inside out reduction only reduces redeces SABC,etc. when A, B and C are normal forms.

3. Let $\mathcal{U}$ be a (highly) constructible URS in the sense of [8]. Then $\mathcal{U}$ is a NURS:

Let $f(e;x) = \begin{cases} \mu n[\langle e,x\rangle \in \Lambda_n] & \text{if defined} \\ \infty & \text{else.} \end{cases}$

Take $|e;x| = 4^{f(e;n)}$. This is a norm on $\mathcal{U}$, for let $f(sxy,z) = n$, then $sxy = \phi_6(x,y)$, $n > 0$ and $\langle x,z\rangle, \langle y,z\rangle, \langle xz,yz\rangle \in \Lambda_{n-1}$ (see [8] ,p.20-21 for the notation). Then $f(x,z), f(y,z), f(xz,yz) \leqslant n-1$, and $|sxy;z| = 4^n > 3.4^{n-1} \geqslant |x;z| + |y;z| + |xz;yz|$.

4. Let $\mathfrak{A}$ be a non-standard model of Peano arithmetic. Then $\mathfrak{K}_{\mathfrak{A}}$ is not a NURS. This follows from 1.5 and 3.4. Similarly it follows from 1.3 and 3.2 that $\mathfrak{K}^\circ$ is not a NURS.

The sentence EE = *, with E = SII, which was independent in the theory of URS becomes true in all NURS.

3.2. Let E = SII and $\mathcal{U}$ be a NURS. Then
$\mathcal{U} \models EE = *$.

Proof. Suppose EE $\neq$ *. Then $|E;E| \neq \infty$. But then $|E;E| = |SII;E| > |IE;IE| = |E;E|$, a contradiction. ⊠

More general

3.3. <u>Theorem</u>. Let $\mathcal{U}$ be a NURS and M a WS($\mathcal{U}$) term. Then
M has no nf $\Longleftrightarrow$ $\mathcal{U} \models M = *$.

Proof. $\Leftarrow$ By 2.12.2.

$\Rightarrow$ This will be proved in a number of steps.

3.3.1 Def. SC(M), the set of subcomputations of M, is defined inductively by:

If M is in normal form $SC(M) = \emptyset$; else $M \equiv AB$ and $SC(AB) = SC(A) \cup SC(B) \cup \{|A^{\mathfrak{U}};B^{\mathfrak{U}}|\}$. Below we often omit the superscript $\mathfrak{U}$. Clearly SC(M) is a finite set $\subset \omega \cup \{\infty\}$ and if $M \supset M'$, then $SC(M) \supset SC(M')$.

3.3.2 Def. $\|M\| = Max\{SC(M)\}$. If SC(M) contains ∞, $\|M\| = \infty$.

3.3.3 Lemma. If $M \supset M'$, then $\|M\| \geqslant \|M'\|$.

3.3.4 Lemma. $\|M\| = \infty \iff \mathfrak{U} \models M = *$.

Proof. $\|M\| = \infty \iff \infty \in SC(M)$

$\iff$ for some $AB \subset M$ $|A;B| = \infty$

$\iff$ for some $AB \subset M$ $\mathfrak{U} \models AB = *$

$\iff \mathfrak{U} \models M = *$. ⊠

3.3.5 Lemma. Let $M \geqslant M'$ be an axiom of $WS(\mathfrak{U})$. Then $\|M\| \geqslant \|M'\|$.

Proof. Let $M \equiv SABC$ and $M' \equiv AC(BC)$.

Then $SC(M) = \{|S;A|, |SA;B|, |SAB;C|\} \cup SC(A) \cup SC(B) \cup SC(C)$.

$SC(M') = \{|A;C|, |B;C|, |AC;BC|\} \cup SC(A) \cup SC(B) \cup SC(C)$.

Since $|SAB;C| \geqslant Max\{|A;C|, |B;C|, |AC;BC|\}$

$\|M\| \geqslant \|M'\|$. Equality may occur, e.g. if SC(C) contains the largest subcomputation.

If $M \equiv KAB$, $M \equiv IA$ or $M \equiv M'$, then $M' \equiv A$ or $M' \equiv M$, hence $M \supset M'$ and the result follows by 3.3.3.

If $M \equiv \Delta AB$, then $M' \equiv K$ or $\equiv KI$, so $SC(M) \supset SC(M') = \emptyset$, hence $\|M\| \geqslant \|M'\|$. **Similarly if $M \equiv \underline{a}N$.** ⊠

3.3.6 Cor. If $WS(\mathfrak{U}) \vdash M \geqslant M'$, then $\|M\| \geqslant \|M'\|$.

Proof. Induction on the length of proof of $M \geqslant M'$.

Let us consider only the case that $M \geqslant M'$ is $ZA \geqslant ZA'$ and is a direct consequence of $A \geqslant A'$. Then $SC(ZA) = SC(Z) \cup SC(A) \cup \{|Z;A|\}$ and similarly for SC(ZA'). Now $\mathfrak{U} \models A = A'$, hence $|Z;A| = |Z;A'|$. Hence $\|ZA\| \geqslant \|ZA'\|$ by the induction hypothesis $\|A\| \geqslant \|A'\|$. ⊠

3.3.7 Def. A special redex is a $WS(\mathfrak{U})$-term SABC, where A, B and C are in normal form.

3.3.8 Lemma. If SABC is a special redex, then
$\|SABC\| \gtrsim \|AC(BC)\|$.
Proof. Since $\underline{SC}(A) = \underline{SC}(B) = \underline{SC}(C) = \emptyset$
$\|SABC\| = \text{Max}\{|S;A|,|SA;B|,|SAB;C|\} \geqslant |SAB;C| \gtrsim$
$\gtrsim \text{Max}\{|A;C|,|B;C|,|AC;BC|\} = \|AC(BC)\|$. ⊠

3.3.9 Lemma. Let M be a WS(𝔘) term without normal form. Then there exists a special redex N without normal form in the family (see 2.16.1) of M, or else $\mathfrak{U} \vdash M = *$.
Proof. Consider the finite set T of subterms of M partially ordered by ⊂. Let N be a minimal element of T without a normal form. Then all subterms of N have a normal form. Checking all possibilities it follows that N is of the form SABC. Let A^*, B^* and C^* be the normal forms of A, B and C. Now we have
$M \equiv$ ——(SABC) —— $\geqslant$ ——$(SA^*B^*C^*)$ —— and $SA^*B^*C^*$ is a special redex without normal form. ⊠

3.3.10 Cor. If M has no normal form, then there exists a term M' without normal form and $\|M\| \dot{\gtrsim} \|M'\|$.
Proof. Let N be as in 3.3.9, then $\|M\| \geqslant \|N\|$ by 3.3.6 and 3.3.3. Let $N \geqslant M'$. Then $\|N\| \gtrsim \|M'\|$ by 3.3.8. Since N has no normal form, neither has M'. ⊠

Now the proof of 3.3.⇒ can be given.
Let M be a term without normal form. Suppose $\mathfrak{U} \models M \neq *$. Then $\|M\| \neq \infty$ by 3.3.4. Hence by 3.3.10 there exists a sequence $M, M', M'', \ldots$ such that $\|M\| > \|M'\| > \|M''\| > \ldots$ is an infinite descending chain of integers. ⊠

3.4. Theorem. In a NURS $\mathfrak{U}$ all infinite splinters are SC.
Proof. Let $X = \{f^n o\}$ be an infinite splinter. Define by the fixed point lemma a WS($\mathfrak{U}$) term H such that
Hyx = I if y = x
H(fy)x else.
Then $h = (H\underline{o})^{\mathfrak{U}}$ is a semi-characteristic function of X:
If $a \in X$, clearly $H\,\underline{o}\,\underline{a} = I$, hence $ha \neq *$.
If $a \notin X$, then $H\,\underline{o}\,\underline{a} \geqslant H\,\underline{f(o)}\,\underline{a} \geqslant \ldots$, i.e.
$H\,\underline{o}\,\underline{a}$ has no nf. Hence $ha = *$ by 3.3. ⊠

WS* is a complete axiomatization for the equations true in all NURS.

3.5. <u>Theorem</u>. Let $\mathfrak{U}$ be a NURS. Then for closed WS terms:
WS* $\vdash M = N \iff \mathfrak{U} \models M = N$.
Proof. $\Rightarrow$ By 2.12.1, 3.3. $\Leftarrow$ By 2.10, 3.3. ⊠

3.6. <u>Theorem</u>. Each URS can be embedded in a NURS (cf. Wagner [8], p.31, 6.2), if the similarity type has no constants.
Proof. Clearly $\mathfrak{U} \hookrightarrow \mathfrak{U}(WS^*_{o,c}(\mathfrak{U}))$ which is a NURS by 3.1.2. ⊠

<u>Concluding remarks</u>.
A URS is almost a precomputation theory in the sense of Moschovakis [3] 1). Restricting the attention to single-valued functions, his computation theories have an additional length of computation $|e;\vec{x}|$ satisfying

$$(+) \quad |S^n_m(e,\vec{x});\vec{y}| > |e;\vec{x},\vec{y}|, \text{ if defined.}$$

Define in a NURS $|e;\vec{x}| = |e;x_1| + |e.x_1;x_2| + \ldots + |e.x_1\ldots x_{n-1};x_n|$.

Then it follows readily from the definition of S^n_m in a URS ([8], 2.6) that this norm satisfies Moschovakis' axiom (+).

As suggested in [6], there is another way of extending a URS. A <u>selection</u> 2) URS is an URS containing a "selection operator" c such that

$$\exists a[f.a \neq *] \Rightarrow f.(c.f) \neq * .$$

---

1) Not quite, because a URS does not need to contain a computable successor set.
2) In [6] such a URS is called "well-ordered". This name is a little absurd as can be argued as follows. Let $\mathfrak{A}$ be a model of Peano arithmetic of power continuum. Then $\mathfrak{N}_{\mathfrak{A}}$ is a selection URS but cannot be well-ordered in ZF. On the other hand $\mathfrak{U}(WS^*_o)$ is countable and hence well-ordered, but has no selection operator.

In a selection URS a set is computable iff it is SC and co SC, [6],3.4. This is not true in a general URS, [8],p.39 bottom.

Having a norm or a selection operator are independent of each other. $\mathfrak{X}$ has a selection operator $\{c\}(e) = (\mu x\, T(e,(x)_0,(x)_1))_0$. Since this is provably in arithmetic a selection operator, $\mathfrak{X}_{\mathfrak{A}}$ is a selection URS but not a NURS. Conversely, it is not difficult to show that $\mathfrak{U}(WS_0^*)$ is not a selection URS, although it is a NURS,

In a NURS it would be natural to require for a selection operator c

$$|c;a| \gtrsim |a;c.a|$$

cf.[3],p.225,(6-4).

Acknowledgement. The paper is an elaboration of part II of the author's dissertation. He wishes to thank his supervisor professor G.Kreisel for his stimulating personality.

References.

[1] Friedman,H. Axiomatic recursive function theory, in: R.Gandy and M.Yates (eds), Logic Colloquium '69, North Holland, Amsterdam (1971), 113-137.

[2] Kreisel,G., J. Krivine, Elements of Mathematical Logic, North-Holland, Amsterdam (1967).

[3] Moschovakis,Y. Axioms for computation theories - first draft, in: R.Gandy and M.Yates (eds), Logic Colloquium '69, North Holland, Amsterdam (1971), 199-255.

[4] Rogers,H. Theory of recursive functions and effective operations, McGrawHill (1967).

[5] Rosser,J. A mathematical logic without variables, Ann. of Math. ser.2, 36 (1936), 127-150.

[6] Strong,H. Algebraically generalized recursive function theory, IBM J.Research and Development (1968), 465-475.

[7] - . Construction of models for algebraically generalized recursive function theory, J.Symbolic Logic 35 (1970), 401-409.

[8] Wagner,E. Uniform reflexive structures: on the nature of Gödelizations and relative computability, Trans.Amer. Math.Soc.144 (1969), 1-41.

[9] Troelstra,A, et al. Metamathematical investigation of intuitionistic arithmetic and analysis, Lecture Notes in Mathematics 344, Springer (1973).

Part III

2020 Hindsight

This Part III consists of the following chapters.

III.1. Up to 1969
It sketches what was known about Combinatory Logic and λ-calculus, needed to write this thesis; for the computability part, see Section II 2.2.
III.2. The period 1969-1971
This is a commented summary of work in this thesis.
III.3. The period 1971-1980
Sketching later developments, related to this thesis or my later work.
III.4. After 1980
Sketching applications. The application of λ-calculus to functional programming and hardware construction is only briefly mentioned. More attention is given to formalizing and securing proofs, with applications in ICT and mathematics.

This Part III is not trying to give a survey of what happened later in the field. The book Barendregt (1984) is a reasonable survey of what happened to type-free λ-calculus up to 1982. As to typed versions of the theory, see Girard et al. (1989), Barendregt (1992), Sørensen & Urzyczyn (2006), Barendregt et al. (2013), and Nederpelt & Geuvers (2014) to get some impression. The distribution of the material over these chapters corresponding to the respective periods is not exact: sometimes a topic belonging to a later time slot was anticipated.

1

Up to 1969

1.1 Models of computability

The theory Combinatory Logic deals with manipulating symbols with the intention to become a foundation for logic and hence mathematics. It was initiated by Schönfinkel in 1920 and later rediscovered by Curry in the later 1920s. This theory claims to avoid the use of variables. Then there is the related original form of λ-calculus[1], Church (1932, 1933) as part of a theory intended to be a foundation for all of mathematics: reasoning and computing. This extended theory turned out to be inconsistent, as shown by Church's students Kleene & Rosser (1935). Later the inconsistency was much simplified by the paradox of Curry (1941). Because of the inconsistency in the extended λ-calculus (as foundation for mathematics) Church and his students focused on the 'pure part' dealing with computation only. The correspondence with the computational part of combinatory logic was established in Rosser (1935) and a consistency proof for pure λ-calculus was given in Church & Rosser (1936b).

In this consistent theory Church defined numerals $\mathbf{c}_0, \mathbf{c}_1, \mathbf{c}_2, \ldots$ as iterators to represent the natural numbers: $\mathbf{c}_k \triangleq \lambda fx.f^k x$, e.g. $\mathbf{c}_2 = \lambda fx.f(fx)$. Church and his students soon showed that on these the functions addition, multiplication, and exponentiation are λ-definable: for $F_+ \triangleq \lambda nmfx.nf(mfx)$, $F_\times \triangleq \lambda nmf.n(mf)$, $F_{exp} = \lambda nmf.mnf$ one has

$$\begin{aligned} F_+\mathbf{c}_n\mathbf{c}_m &= \mathbf{c}_{n+m}; \\ F_\times\mathbf{c}_n\mathbf{c}_m &= \mathbf{c}_{n\times m}; \\ F_{exp}\mathbf{c}_n\mathbf{c}_m &= \mathbf{c}_{n^m}. \end{aligned}$$

[1]A noteworthy example of how failing the goal of an intended PhD project could lead to success was told to me by Alonzo Church. His supervisor Veblen had assigned him the task to compute from an algebraically given two-dimensional surface its Betti number, which is twice its genus (number of holes in it). Church didn't succeed in doing this. He started to wonder whether the assignment could be fulfilled at all. In order to show that the goal was impossible he needed to have a precisely defined notion of computability. For this reason he invented the λ-calculus.

(The equation for exponentiation doesn't hold for $m = 0$, but Church started counting from 1. Alternatively one can take as numerals $\mathbf{c}'_n = \lambda xf.f^n x$.) At first Church and his students were not able to λ-define the predecessor function. However, during a dental treatment[2] Kleene found a way to do this, by finding a way to translate recursion into iteration. After Kleene explained to his supervisor how he had been able to represent the predecessor function, Church reportedly said: "Then all computable functions must be λ-definable." Since the converse is easy to show, Church's Thesis[3] was born.

A function is intuitively computable if and only if it is λ-definable. (Church'sThesis)

It equates the not precisely defined class of intuitively computable functions on the natural numbers with the precisely defined class of λ-definable functions. The thesis was considerably strengthened when Turing independently concluded by a conceptual analysis that the class of mechanically computable functions coincides with the Turing Machine computable functions, Turing (1937a), submitted in 1936. This is Turing's thesis.

Effective computability is equivalent to machine computability. (Turing'sThesis)

Moreover Turing proved that machine computability coincides with λ-definability, Turing (1937b). The combined theses of Church and Turing state that the classes of mechanical and effective computable functions coincide and also with the class of functions computable by a Turing machine or by λ-definability.

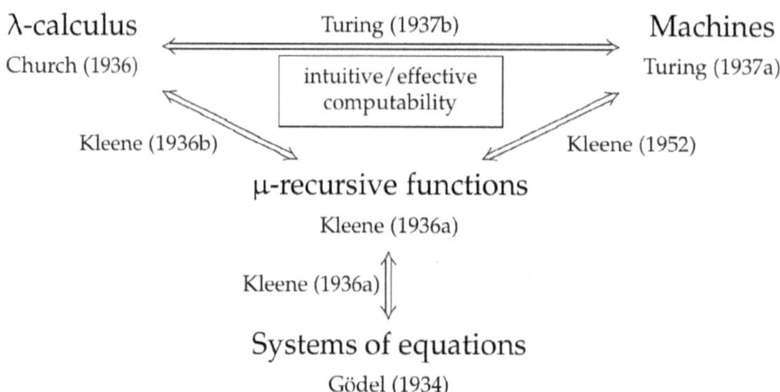

Complementing the work of Church and Turing other classes of 'computable functions' were considered by Kleene: that of Gödel consisting of functions defined by systems of equations and that of the μ-recursive functions, that starts with a set of basis functions, and is closed under substitution, primitive recursion, and minimalization.

[2]This is reported in Crossley (1975). Kleene had told me this was under the influence of laughing gas N_2O, that still is used today as anesthesia in dentistry.

[3]In his talk for the seventieth birthday of Robin Gandy it was stated by Kleene: "After I found out how to define the predecessor function I could have stated Church's thesis; but I didn't, he did."

In Kleene (1936a) it is shown that these two classes of total functions (only these were considered) are the same. Moreover that class coincides with the λ-definable functions, Kleene (1936b). In a reaction to Church's Thesis Gödel found both λ-definability and his own characterization using systems of equations not satisfactory as a characterization of the notion 'effectively computable'. The reason was that both characterizations depend on a formal deductive system. But Gödel was convinced by the analysis of Turing using machines and hence independent of a logical system. Only in Kleene (1938) the importance of partial functions was emphasized. See Davis (1982) for more historical remarks. The theory of computability and the resulting digital revolution[4] have been changing and are changing society in profound ways.

Leibniz had as ideal to design a *universal language* (Characteristica universalis) in which all scientific and even metaphysical questions could be formulated, together with a decision method (Calculus ratiocinator) to assert or refute by mere computation the validity of these. Leibniz had as motto 'Calculemus' ('let us compute') in order to settle scientific questions. Once the notion of effective or of machine computability had been formalized by Church and Turing independently, they did show also that a decision method for arithmetical sentences, leave alone for all scientific problems, is impossible for logical reasons. The same impossibility holds for sentences of the predicate calculus. In spite of this, by means of computations one may get impressively far. This is shown in systems for computer algebra, such as on the one hand Mathematica for symbolic calculations in analysis, technical applications, and more, and on the other hand in Magma for those in abstract algebra, number theory, and more.

1.2 λ-calculus and Combinatory Logic

In this chapter an introduction to λ-calculus and combinatory logic is given, somewhat more detailed than in Chapter II.1.

λ-calculus

DEFINITION 1.1. (i) Terms of the lambda calculus, in notation Λ, are defined by the following inductive definition.

$$\begin{aligned} & x \in \Lambda; \\ M \in \Lambda,\ N \in \Lambda \ \Rightarrow\ & (MN) \in \Lambda; \\ M \in \Lambda \ \Rightarrow\ & (\lambda x.M) \in \Lambda. \end{aligned}$$

[4]Although machine computability and λ-definability are equivalent, machine computation is more easily realized on computers via Turing's work than via λ-calculus. This gave rise to imperative programming. During the last decades computer aided computing via λ-calculus has become more efficient, resulting in *Functional Programming*. This may give the computer revolution another boost. Another ingredient, not related to λ-calculus, is deep learning, something that also was initiated by Turing (1948), with applications in Artificial Intelligence.

As notation for variables we use $x, y, x, \ldots$ and for terms $M, N, L, \ldots \in \Lambda$.

(ii) The equational theory of the λ-calculus is axiomatized by

$$(\lambda x.M)N = [x/N]M^5 \tag{β}$$

and the equality axiom and rules, including

$$\frac{M = N}{\lambda z.M = \lambda z.N}.$$

We write[6] $M =_\beta N$ for $\lambda \vdash M = N$.

(iii) The axiom (β) is in its intention asymmetric. This is expressed by

$$(\lambda x.M)N \geqslant [x/N]M, \tag{β-red}$$

where $\geqslant$ is axiomatized to be a reflexive, transitive, and compatible[7] relation. We write[8] $M \geqslant_\beta N$ for $\lambda \vdash M \geqslant N$.

(iv) One may add to the theory **λ** the rule of extensionality

$$Fx = Gx, \text{ for a fresh variable } x \;\Rightarrow\; F = G \tag{ext}$$

.

PROPOSITION 1.2. *Extensionality can be captured by the axiom of η-equality*

$$\lambda x.Fx =_\eta F, \textit{ for } x \textit{ fresh.} \tag{η}$$

PROOF. Indeed, working with η-conversion based on η-reduction one has

$$Fx = Gx \;\Rightarrow\; F =_\eta \lambda x.Fx = \lambda x.Gx =_\eta G.$$

And conversely, assuming extensionality one has

$$(\lambda x.Fx)x = Fx \;\Rightarrow\; \lambda x.Fx = F. \qquad \square$$

Equality including the η-rule and hence extensionality can be axiomatized by combining β-reduction with η-reduction introduced by

$$\lambda x.Mx \geqslant_\eta M, \tag{η}$$

provided x doesn't occur (freely) in M. The extensional theory can be proved consistent by an analysis of the combined βη-reduction (Church-Rosser Theorem). We will not do this, because the thesis proves that λ-calculus is consistent by the Church-Rosser Theorem for β-reduction, and moreover it is shown that adding the ω-rule, which is stronger than extensionality, preserves consistency. In Klop (1980) an extensive analysis of the interaction of β-reduction together with η-reduction is given.

[5]In later work I denoted this substitution by $M[x := N]$

[6]This notation was not yet used in the thesis.

[7]This means that $M \geqslant N$ implies $ZM \geqslant ZN$, $MZ \geqslant NZ$, and $\lambda z.M \geqslant \lambda z.N$.

[8]Also this notation was not used in the thesis.

Clash of variables

In mathematics a variable can be free or bound. In

$$\Sigma_{x=1}^{2} x^2 = 1^2 + 2^2$$

it doesn't make sense to substitute something for the variable x, it is bound. However in

$$\Sigma_{x=1}^{2} xy^2 = y^2 + 2y^2 \tag{2}$$

it does make sense to substitute for y a number like 3, or even en expression like $z + 1$.

With the distinction between a free and a bound variable[9] one can formulate another pitfall. In (2) the variable y is free. If one defines

$$f(y) = \Sigma_{x=1}^{2} xy^2,$$

then one should be careful not to substitute for y the expression $x + 1$, as $f(x + 1) = \Sigma_{x=1}^{2} x(x + 1)^2$ is not what is intended: the free variable x becomes bound. The intended meaning is obtained by first renaming the bound variable x to say z

$$f(y) = \Sigma_{z=1}^{2} zy^2,$$

and then substituting $x + 1$ for y, obtaining

$$f(x + 1) = \Sigma_{z=1}^{2} z(x + 1)^2 = (x + 1)^2 + 2(x + 1)^2.$$

Similarly, the expression $A(x) \triangleq \exists y.y + y = x$ expresses over the natural numbers that x is even. But substituting for the free variable x the variable $3y$ one obtains $A(3y) \iff \exists y.y + y = 3y$, something that never holds. Again the bound variable y better be changed in the predicate $A(x)$, which then becomes $A(x) \triangleq \exists z.z + z = x$. Now $A(3y)$ makes sense: $\exists z.z + z = 3y$ and it is in arithmetic equivalent to $A(y)$ stating again that y is even.

This confusion caused by free variables becoming bound has been made in the work of Ackermann (1925), as spotted by von Neumann (1927). Church[10] must have learned from von Neumann and formulated for the λ-calculus the α-rule that allows a change of bound variables: $\lambda x.x =_\alpha \lambda y.y$.

DEFINITION 1.3. Let $M \in \Lambda$.

(i) The set of free variables in M, in notation $FV(M)$, is defined as follows.

$$\begin{aligned} FV(x) &= \{x\}; \\ FV(MN) &= FV(M) \cup FV(N); \\ FV(\lambda x.M) &= FV(M) - \{x\}. \end{aligned}$$

[9] More precisely, a free or bound *occurrence* of a variable

[10] In the bibliography Church (1936a) the paper of von Neumann is marked with an asterisk, indicating its 'especial interest or importance from the point of view of symbolic logic'. In Church (1944) it is remarked that even in Gödel (1934) the confusion of variables had been made.

(ii) M is called *closed* if $FV(M) = \emptyset$.
(iii) $\Lambda^o = \{M \mid FV(M) = \emptyset\}$ is the set of closed terms, also called combinators.

For example $\Omega = (\lambda x.xx)(\lambda x.xx) \in \Lambda^o$, but $\mathsf{KI}x \notin \Lambda^o$, even if the latter term equals I.

Restricted λI-calculus and full K-calculus

Church usually considered a restricted kind of λ-terms, defined by the following inductive definition.

$$\begin{array}{rcl} & & x \in \Lambda^{\mathsf{I}}; \\ M \in \Lambda^{\mathsf{I}},\ N \in \Lambda^{\mathsf{I}} & \Rightarrow & (MN) \in \Lambda^{\mathsf{I}}; \\ M \in \Lambda^{\mathsf{I}},\ x \in FV(M) & \Rightarrow & (\lambda x.M) \in \Lambda^{\mathsf{I}}. \end{array}$$

For example $\mathsf{I}, \mathsf{S} \in \Lambda^{\mathsf{I}}$, but $\mathsf{K} \notin \Lambda^{\mathsf{I}}$. The λI-calculus consists of equations $M = N$, with $M, N \in \Lambda^{\mathsf{I}}$, provable from the β-rule. To emphasize that $M \in \Lambda$ belongs to the full set of λ-terms, one writes $\Lambda^{\mathsf{K}} = \Lambda$. Also one speaks about the λK-calculus, intending the full λ-calculus.

Because in the λK-calculus one can throw away an 'infinite object', e.g. $\mathsf{KI}\Omega = \mathsf{I}$, Church preferred the restricted λI-calculus. Schönfinkel and Curry were not afraid of throwing away terms like Ω, as these are not infinite themselves, but just the code for an infinite computation.

Combinatory Logic

The (type-free) theory of combinatory logic was initiated in a talk for Hilbert's seminar in 1920 by Schönfinkel (1924), written down four years later by his colleague H. Behmann. Independently Curry (1930) rediscovered the field and continued it, after adding the K combinator following Schönfinkel. Among other things Curry found the fixed point combinator by analyzing the Russell paradox, added types, and simplified very much the paradox in Kleene & Rosser (1935). The relation between CL with λ-calculus was clarified by Rosser (1935). The theory consists of applicative terms built up from constants **I, K, S** and variables; it has as axioms

$$\mathbf{I}x = x; \quad (1.1)$$

$$\mathbf{K}xy = x; \quad (1.2)$$

$$\mathbf{S}xyz = xz(yz). \quad (1.3)$$

One has for example that $\mathbf{SII}x = xx$ is derivable in CL.

Also to CL one may add the rule of extensionality as above. Then

$$\mathrm{CL} + \mathrm{ext} \vdash \mathbf{SKK} = \mathbf{I}.$$

Indeed, $\mathbf{SKK}x = \mathbf{K}x(\mathbf{K}x) = x = \mathbf{I}x$ holds in CL. Hence $\mathrm{CL} + \mathrm{ext} \vdash \mathbf{SKK} = \mathbf{I}$.

Relating λ-calculus and CL

PROPOSITION 1.4. *There are maps* $\phi\colon \mathrm{CL} \to \Lambda$ *and* $\psi\colon \Lambda \to \mathrm{CL}$. *These are defined in I1.4.5 and I1.4.9. For mnemonic reasons we will write*

$$\begin{aligned} P_\lambda &= \phi(P), && \textit{for } P \in \mathrm{CL}; \\ M_{\mathrm{CL}} &= \psi(M), && \textit{for } M \in \Lambda. \end{aligned}$$

One has for arbitrary $M, N \in \Lambda$ *and* $P, Q \in \mathrm{CL}$

$$\begin{aligned} \mathrm{CL} + \mathrm{ext} &\vdash (P_\lambda)_{\mathrm{CL}} = P; \\ \lambda + \mathrm{ext} &\vdash (M_{\mathrm{CL}})_\lambda = M; \\ \mathrm{CL} + \mathrm{ext} &\vdash P = Q \iff \lambda + \mathrm{ext} \vdash P_\lambda = Q_\lambda; \\ \lambda + \mathrm{ext} &\vdash M = N \iff \mathrm{CL} + \mathrm{ext} \vdash M_{\mathrm{CL}} = N_{\mathrm{CL}}. \end{aligned}$$

Without extensionality several of these equivalences do not hold. For example $\lambda \vdash (\mathbf{SKS})_\lambda = \mathsf{SKS} = \lambda x.\mathsf{SKS}x = \lambda x.x = \mathbf{I}_\lambda$, but $\mathrm{CL} \nvdash \mathbf{SKS} = \mathbf{I}$.

1.3 Inconsistency & consistency

Inconsistency: the Curry paradox

Now we present Curry's paradox for a simple extension of λ-calculus intended to represent part of logic (and other axiomatic theories). It turned out that already for propositional logic this leads to inconsistency, in the sense that all statements are provable.

DEFINITION 1.5. So called Illative Combinatory Logic, in notation ICL_0, is an extension of CL with the intention to derive statements.

(i) A new constant **P** is introduced, intended to capture implication: **P**AB is abbreviated as $A \to B$. Terms are built up from the constants **I**, **K**, **S**, **P** using application, forming the set ICL_0.

(ii) Statements are defined as follows. If $M, N \in \mathrm{ICL}_0$, then $M = N$ is a statement.

(iii) If $M \in \mathrm{ICL}_0$, then M is a statement.

(iv) The axioms for **I**, **K**, **S** remain valid, as well as the axioms and rules for equality.

(v) There is the rule $\Gamma \vdash M = N, \Gamma \vdash M \Rightarrow \Gamma \vdash N$.

(vi) There are the introduction and elimination rules for implication.

$$\begin{aligned} \Gamma \vdash M \to N, \Gamma \vdash M, &\Rightarrow \Gamma \vdash N, && \text{(Modus Ponens)}; \\ \Gamma, M \vdash N &\Rightarrow \Gamma \vdash M \to N. \end{aligned}$$

The system is presented in natural deduction style of Gentzen (1969), so that $\Gamma \vdash X$ for a set of statements Γ containing X.

The following is called Curry's paradox. Its proof is impressively short, notably when compared to the proof of the paradox of Kleene & Rosser (1935), and doesn't contain negation.

PROPOSITION 1.6 (CURRY (1941)). ICL_0 *is inconsistent.*

PROOF. Let $\mathsf{M} \in \mathsf{ICL}_0$ be any term considered as proposition. We will show $\vdash \mathsf{M}$. By the fixed point theorem there exists an X such that $\vdash \mathsf{X} = \mathsf{X} \to \mathsf{M}$. Now one can proceed as follows.

$$\begin{array}{rcll}
\mathsf{X} & \vdash & \mathsf{X}, & \text{as this stands for } \{\mathsf{X}\} \vdash \mathsf{X}, \\
\mathsf{X} & \vdash & \mathsf{X} \to \mathsf{M}, & \text{since} \vdash \mathsf{X} = \mathsf{X} \to \mathsf{M}, \\
\mathsf{X} & \vdash & \mathsf{M}, & \text{by Modus Ponens}, \\
& \vdash & \mathsf{X} \to \mathsf{M}, & \text{by} \to\text{-introduction}, \\
& \vdash & \mathsf{X}, & \text{since} \vdash \mathsf{X} \to \mathsf{M} = \mathsf{X}, \\
& \vdash & \mathsf{M}, & \text{by Modus Ponens.} \quad \square
\end{array}$$

In Chapter III.3 consistent versions of ICL will be mentioned.

Consistency: the Church-Rosser Theorem

After the discovery by Kleene & Rosser (1935) of the inconsistency of the original version of Church's theory, an effort was made to prove the consistency of the part dealing with computability only. The following result, using the asymmetrical version of equality, implies consistency.

THEOREM 1.7 (CHURCH-ROSSER THEOREM).

$$\mathsf{M} =_\beta \mathsf{N} \Rightarrow \exists \mathsf{Z}[\mathsf{M} \geqslant_\beta \mathsf{Z} \;\&\; \mathsf{N} \geqslant_\beta \mathsf{Z}].$$

Consistency follows: suppose towards a contradiction that $\lambda \vdash \mathsf{I} = \mathsf{S}$. Then $\mathsf{I} =_\beta \mathsf{S}$, hence by the theorem there should be a term $\mathsf{Z} \in \Lambda$ such that $\mathsf{I} \geqslant \mathsf{Z}$ and $\mathsf{S} \geqslant \mathsf{Z}$. But as both I, S are in normal form, they only reduce to themselves and therefore the required Z doesn't exist. Contradiction.

In the thesis a proof of this theorem, due to Martin-Löf, is presented in Appendix II, Theorem 10. This implies that the λ-calculus is consistent, Corollary 1.2.11 in Part I. The history of the proof in Appendix II, that I didn't know in 1971, is interesting. Martin-Löf based his proof on a similar proof of Tait for Combinatory Logic (CL). There was, however, a simpler proof of the Church-Rosser Theorem for CL, by Rosser (1935). That simpler proof doesn't carry over to the λ-calculus. Tait's proof, however, did carry over. In Barendregt (1984) therefore I attributed the proof method to Tait and Martin-Löf collectively.

The Church-Rosser Theorem for $\geqslant_\beta$ establishes the consistency of the λ-calculus. The consistency of the extensional variant follows by the consistency of the stronger ω-rule as given in the thesis. A simpler alternative is to use the Hindley-Rosen proposition, (Barendregt 1984, 3.3.5), in order to show the Church-Rosser Theorem for the combined β- and η-rules.

1.4 Some λ-calculus results

PROPOSITION 1.8 (TURING/CURRY). *There exists a* fixed point operator[11]*: a closed λ-term* Θ *such that for every* $F \in \Lambda$ *one has* ΘF *is a fixed point of* F *(here* $=$ *stands for* $=_\beta$*)*

$$\Theta F = F(\Theta F).$$

PROOF. Take $\Theta \triangleq (\lambda ab.b(aab))(\lambda ab.b(aab))$. Write $\omega_T \triangleq (\lambda ab.b(aab))$. Then

$$\begin{aligned} \Theta F &\triangleq \omega_T\omega_T F, \\ &\triangleq (\lambda ab.b(aab))\omega_T F, \\ &= F(\omega_T\omega_T F), \\ &\triangleq F(\Theta F). \quad \Box \end{aligned}$$

Note that one even has $\Theta F \geqslant_\beta F(\Theta F)$, which explains the funny feeling one gets learning for the first time about λ-calculus fixed points. By contrast $YF \not\geqslant_\beta F(YF)$.

COROLLARY 1.9. *In* CL *the fixed point combinator of Turing is mapped to*

$$\Theta_\lambda = \mathbf{SII}(\mathbf{S}(\mathbf{K}(\mathbf{SI}))(\mathbf{SII})),$$

and acts like a fixed point combinator: $\mathrm{CL} \vdash \Theta_\lambda P = P(\Theta_\lambda P)$*, for all* $P \in \mathrm{CL}$.

COROLLARY 1.10. *Let* $t = t[\vec{x}, f] \in \Lambda[\vec{x}, f]$*. Then there exists an* $F \in \Lambda^o$ *such that*

$$F\vec{x} = t[\vec{x}, F].$$

PROOF. Take $F \triangleq \Theta(\lambda f\vec{x}.t[\vec{x}, f])$. Then

$$F\vec{x} = (\lambda f\vec{x}.t[\vec{x}, f])F\vec{x} = t[\vec{x}, F]. \qquad \Box$$

[11]The term Θ is due to Turing. A different fixed point combinator is implicit in Curry (1934), see Cardone & Hindley (2009)

$$Y \triangleq \lambda f.(\lambda x.f(xx))(\lambda x.f(xx)).$$

Indeed

$$YF = (\lambda x.F(xx))(\lambda x.F(xx)) = F((\lambda x.F(xx))(\lambda x.F(xx))) = F(YF).$$

DEFINITION 1.11. (i) Define λ-terms representing Booleans as follows.

$$\begin{aligned} \text{true} &= \lambda xy.x; \\ \text{false} &= \lambda xy.y. \end{aligned}$$

(ii) Define the conditional as follows

$$\text{If B then P else Q} = \mathsf{BPQ}.$$

Then

$$\begin{aligned} \text{If B then P else Q} &= \mathsf{P}, && \text{if } \mathsf{B} = \text{true}; \\ &= \mathsf{Q}, && \text{if } \mathsf{B} = \text{false}. \end{aligned}$$

In other cases the value is not specified.

(iii) Define $\mathsf{Zero}_? = \lambda n.n(\mathsf{K}\,\text{false})\text{true}$. Then

$$\begin{aligned} \mathsf{Zero}_?\, \mathbf{c}_n &= \text{true} && \text{if } n = 0; \\ &= \text{false}, && \text{else.} \end{aligned}$$

(iv) Define $\mathsf{S}^+ \triangleq \lambda nfx.f(nfx)$. Then $\mathsf{S}^+\mathbf{c}_k = \mathbf{c}_{k+1}$, showing that the successor function is λ-definable.

THEOREM 1.12. *Let* $f\colon \mathbb{N}^p \to \mathbb{N}$. *Then* f *is* μ*-computable* $\iff$ f *is* λ*-definable.*

PROOF. (For total functions. In Part I this is also proved for partial functions.) (⇒) The μ-computable functions are obtained from the initial functions $\mathsf{S}^+x = x+1$, $\mathsf{P}^k_i(x_1,\dots,x_k) = x_i$, and $\mathsf{Z}(x) = 0$, using composition, primitive recursion and minimalization. The initial functions are clearly λ-definable, by respectively $\lambda ab.b(ab)$, $\lambda x_1 \dots x_k.x_i$, and $\lambda x.\mathbf{c}_0$. Now we show that the λ-definable functions are closed under substitution, primitive recursion and minimalization.

Substitution. Suppose wlog that $f(x) = g(h(x), x)$ and that g, h are λ-defined by respectively $G, H \in \Lambda^o$. Then f is λ-defined by $F = \lambda x.G(Hx)x$.

Primitive recursion. Wlog let f be defined as follows

$$\begin{aligned} f(0) &= k_0; \\ f(n+1) &= g(f(n), n). \end{aligned}$$

In order to λ-define f, we are going to do this for a slightly more complex function $f'\colon \mathbb{N} \to \mathbb{N}^2$ defined by $f'(n) = (f(n), n)$. For $M_1, M_2 \in \Lambda^o$ write $[M_1, M_2] = \lambda z.zM_1M_2$, with a fresh variable z. Write, as in functional programming $M \cdot i = M(\lambda x_1x_2.x_i)$. Then

$$[M_1, M_2] \cdot i = (\lambda z.zM_1M_2)(\lambda x_1x_2.x_i) = (\lambda x_1x_2.x_i)M_1M_2 = M_i.$$

We like to λ-define f' by F' such that

$$F'_{\mathbf{c}_n} = [\mathbf{c}_{f(n)}, \mathbf{c}_n],$$

in the hope to get an F that λ-defines f. Note that then

$$\begin{aligned} F'\mathbf{c}_{n+1} &= [\mathbf{c}_{f(n+1)}, \mathbf{c}_{n+1}] = [\mathbf{c}_{g(f(n),n)}, \mathbf{c}_{n+1}], \\ &= [G(\mathbf{c}_{f(n)})\mathbf{c}_n, \mathbf{c}_{n+1}], \\ &= [G(F'\mathbf{c}_n \cdot 1)(F'\mathbf{c}_n \cdot 2), S^+(F'\mathbf{c}_n \cdot 2)], \\ &= T(F'\mathbf{c}_n), \end{aligned}$$

with $T = \lambda y.[G(y \cdot 1)(y \cdot 2), S^+(y \cdot 2)]$. It follows that

$$F'\mathbf{c}_n = T^n[\mathbf{c}_{f(0)}, \mathbf{c}_0] = \mathbf{c}_n T[\mathbf{c}_{k_0}, \mathbf{c}_0]$$

and we can define $F' = \lambda n.nT[\mathbf{c}_{k_0}, \mathbf{c}_0]$. Therefore f can be λ-defined by the term $F = \lambda n.F'n \cdot 1$, since then $F\mathbf{c}_n = F'\mathbf{c}_n \cdot 1 = [\mathbf{c}_{f(n)}, \mathbf{c}_n] \cdot 1 = \mathbf{c}_{f(n)}$.

Minimalization. Wlog let the total function f be defined by $f(x) = \mu y.[g(x,y) = 0]$, with g λ-defined by G. By the fixed point theorem construct H such that

$$H = (\lambda hxy.\mathtt{If}\ \mathtt{Zero_?}\,(Gx)\ \mathtt{then}\ y\ \mathtt{else}\ hx(S^+y))H.$$

Then

$$Hxy = \mathtt{If}\ \mathtt{Zero_?}\,(Gx)\ \mathtt{then}\ y\ \mathtt{else}\ Hx(S^+y).$$

Then

$$\begin{aligned} H\mathbf{c}_n\mathbf{c}_0 &= 0, && \text{if } G\mathbf{c}_n\mathbf{c}_0 = \mathbf{c}_0, \\ &= \mathbf{c}_1, && \text{else, if } G\mathbf{c}_n\mathbf{c}_1 = \mathbf{c}_0, \\ &= \mathbf{c}_2, && \text{else, if } G\mathbf{c}_n\mathbf{c}_2 = \mathbf{c}_0, \\ &= \ldots, && \text{as f is total } \exists k.g(n,k) = 0, \\ & && \text{hence } \exists k.G\mathbf{c}_n\mathbf{c}_k = \mathbf{c}_0, \\ &= \mathbf{c}_m, && \text{where } m = \mu k.[G\mathbf{c}_n\mathbf{c}_k = \mathbf{c}_0], \\ &= \mathbf{c}_m, && \text{where } m = \mu k.g(n,k) = 0, \\ &= \mathbf{c}_{f(n)}. \end{aligned}$$

Therefore $F \triangleq \lambda x.Hx\mathbf{c}_0$ λ-defines f.

(⇐) Suppose f is λ-definable. Then for some $F \in \Lambda^o$

$$\lambda \vdash F\mathbf{c}_{n_1} \ldots \mathbf{c}_{n_p} = \mathbf{c}_m \iff f(n_1, \ldots, n_p) = m.$$

Therefore the graph of f, being $\{(\vec{n}, m) \mid f(\vec{n}) = m\}$, is computably(/recursively) enumerable. It follows that f is partial, hence total, computable. □

1.5 Imperative and functional programming

The computational model introduced by Turing readily can be implemented on digital computers. This gave rise to what is called 'Imperative programming'. Programming in this style is essentially type-free: both the program and the input are represented as data. In Böhm (1954) use of this feature is made by constructing a compiler for a programming language L in the language L, in such a way that the compiler could compile itself. As explained in Barendregt (2020) this one way leading to bootstrapping that made the high efficiency of computers possible.

The computational model of Church, the λ-calculus, became the foundation for a new style writing software: functional programming. The first functional programming language related to type free λ-calculus was Lisp[12], McCarthy et al. (1962), although the language isn't purely functional, it also has imperative features. Other work towards functional programming can be found in Landin (1966) and Böhm (1966), Böhm & Gross (1966).

[12]Also early implementations of this language made similar invalid substitutions by confusing free and bound variables, as those noted by von Neumann (1927) in the work of Ackermann. In the Lisp community this was called 'dynamic binding', a bug that was considered as a feature.

in the hope to get an F that λ-defines f. Note that then

$$\begin{aligned}
F'\mathbf{c}_{n+1} &= [\mathbf{c}_{f(n+1)}, \mathbf{c}_{n+1}] = [\mathbf{c}_{g(f(n),n)}, \mathbf{c}_{n+1}],\\
&= [G(\mathbf{c}_{f(n)})\mathbf{c}_n, \mathbf{c}_{n+1}],\\
&= [G(F'\mathbf{c}_n \cdot 1)(F'\mathbf{c}_n \cdot 2), S^+(F'\mathbf{c}_n \cdot 2)],\\
&= T(F'\mathbf{c}_n),
\end{aligned}$$

with $T = \lambda y.[G(y \cdot 1)(y \cdot 2), S^+(y \cdot 2)]$. It follows that

$$F'\mathbf{c}_n = T^n[\mathbf{c}_{f(0)}, \mathbf{c}_0] = \mathbf{c}_n T[\mathbf{c}_{k_0}, \mathbf{c}_0]$$

and we can define $F' = \lambda n.nT[\mathbf{c}_{k_0}, \mathbf{c}_0]$. Therefore f can be λ-defined by the term $F = \lambda n.F'n \cdot 1$, since then $F\mathbf{c}_n = F'\mathbf{c}_n \cdot 1 = [\mathbf{c}_{f(n)}, \mathbf{c}_n] \cdot 1 = \mathbf{c}_{f(n)}$.

Minimalization. Wlog let the total function f be defined by $f(x) = \mu y.[g(x, y) = 0]$, with g λ-defined by G. By the fixed point theorem construct H such that

$$H = (\lambda hxy.\mathsf{If}\ \mathsf{Zero}_?\,(Gx)\ \mathsf{then}\,y\ \mathsf{else}\,hx(S^+y))H.$$

Then

$$Hxy = \mathsf{If}\ \mathsf{Zero}_?\,(Gx)\ \mathsf{then}\,y\ \mathsf{else}\,Hx(S^+y).$$

Then

$$\begin{aligned}
H\mathbf{c}_n\mathbf{c}_0 &= 0, && \text{if } G\mathbf{c}_n\mathbf{c}_0 = \mathbf{c}_0,\\
&= \mathbf{c}_1, && \text{else, if } G\mathbf{c}_n\mathbf{c}_1 = \mathbf{c}_0,\\
&= \mathbf{c}_2, && \text{else, if } G\mathbf{c}_n\mathbf{c}_2 = \mathbf{c}_0,\\
&= \ldots, && \text{as f is total } \exists k.g(n, k) = 0,\\
& && \text{hence } \exists k.G\mathbf{c}_n\mathbf{c}_k = \mathbf{c}_0,\\
&= \mathbf{c}_m, && \text{where } m = \mu k.[G\mathbf{c}_n\mathbf{c}_k = \mathbf{c}_0],\\
&= \mathbf{c}_m, && \text{where } m = \mu k.g(n, k) = 0,\\
&= \mathbf{c}_{f(n)}.
\end{aligned}$$

Therefore $F \triangleq \lambda x.Hx\mathbf{c}_0$ λ-defines f.

(⇐) Suppose f is λ-definable. Then for some $F \in \Lambda^o$

$$\lambda \vdash F\mathbf{c}_{n_1} \ldots \mathbf{c}_{n_p} = \mathbf{c}_m \iff f(n_1, \ldots, n_p) = m.$$

Therefore the graph of f, being $\{(\vec{n}, m) \mid f(\vec{n}) = m\}$, is computably(/recursively) enumerable. It follows that f is partial, hence total, computable. □

1.5 Imperative and functional programming

The computational model introduced by Turing readily can be implemented on digital computers. This gave rise to what is called 'Imperative programming'. Programming in this style is essentially type-free: both the program and the input are represented as data. In Böhm (1954) use of this feature is made by constructing a compiler for a programming language L in the language L, in such a way that the compiler could compile itself. As explained in Barendregt (2020) this one way leading to bootstrapping that made the high efficiency of computers possible.

The computational model of Church, the λ-calculus, became the foundation for a new style writing software: functional programming. The first functional programming language related to type free λ-calculus was Lisp[12], McCarthy et al. (1962), although the language isn't purely functional, it also has imperative features. Other work towards functional programming can be found in Landin (1966) and Böhm (1966), Böhm & Gross (1966).

[12]Also early implementations of this language made similar invalid substitutions by confusing free and bound variables, as those noted by von Neumann (1927) in the work of Ackermann. In the Lisp community this was called 'dynamic binding', a bug that was considered as a feature.

2 The period 1969-1971

2.1 Models

By the end of 1969 Dana Scott had invented the lattice models $\mathcal{D}_\infty$ of the λ-calculus, providing a clear interpretation of the λ-abstraction operator. That was a breakthrough and became an important tool for providing semantics of programming languages. It, however, didn't satisfy the goal I had assigned to myself: to explain how Kleene had obtained result in computability theory by the intuition coming from λ-calculus. For this I wanted to literally interpret λ-calculus results into a model based on computable functions. So I continued working on this problem. Moreover, since I hoped to modify $\mathcal{K}$ into an extensional combinatory algebra, one would also obtain a model of the equivalent extensional λ-calculus.

In 1970 and 1971 all attempts to modify Kleene's partial combinatory algebra into a total one had failed, as described in Chapter II.2. But they did lead to notions and questions in the thesis that turned out to be fruitful for λ-calculus: (un)solvability and universal generators (eventually leading to the notion of Böhm-trees, Barendregt (1977)), and the ω-rule (eventually leading to ω-incompleteness Plotkin (1974)).

2.2 The ω-rule

In Section II 2.4 Kleene's pca $\mathcal{K}$ was turned into a total ca $\mathcal{K}_\infty^{\mathrm{CL}}$. All elements of this model are the denotation of a closed term in CL^o. Also the model is by construction extensional. Therefore the following ω-rule is valid in $\mathcal{K}_\infty^{\mathrm{CL}}$:

$$\frac{\mathsf{FZ} = \mathsf{GZ} \text{ for all } \mathsf{Z} \in \mathrm{CL}^o}{\mathsf{F} = \mathsf{G}},$$

more precisely

$$\mathcal{K}_\infty^{\mathrm{CL}} \models \mathsf{FZ} = \mathsf{GZ} \text{ for all } \mathsf{Z} \in \mathrm{CL}^o \;\Rightarrow\; \mathcal{K}_\infty^{\mathrm{CL}} \models \mathsf{F} = \mathsf{G}.$$

But I did not succeed to prove that $\mathcal{K}_{\infty}^{\text{CL}}$ was non-trivial. If it was non-trivial indeed, then adding the ω-rule to CL would produce a consistent theory. Therefore I studied the ω-rule. If this rule turned out to be inconsistent, then $\mathcal{K}_{\infty}^{\text{CL}}$ would be a trivial model. Then I forgot about the model and kept focussing on the ω-rule itself, notably its consistency and the stronger property of its validity[1]. This led to the following in Part I.

THEOREM I 2.2.13. The ω-rule to CL is consistent.

PROOF. In Section I 2.2 a transfinite ordinal is assigned in a natural way to proofs using the ω-rule. By transfinite induction it is shown that a contradiction cannot arise. □

Partial validity of the ω-rule

The possibility remained that the ω-rule would be valid, i.e. provable in CL + ext. On the one hand that would be a pity, because then the consistency of CL + ω-rule would be a trivial consequence of the consistency of CL + ext. But I just wanted to know whether

---

[1]Often one uses the notion of admissibility and derivability of a rule. For some reason I always get confused when thinking about the notions 'admissible' vs 'derived'. Let us recall these notions that for equational theories like CL and CL + ext obtains the following form.

DEFINITION 2.1. Let $\mathcal{A}$ range over extensional combinatory algebras.

(i) The ω-rule is *admissible* for CL + ext: for all $\mathsf{F}, \mathsf{G} \in \text{CL}^{\text{o}}$ one has

$$(\forall\mathcal{A}[\mathcal{A} \models \mathsf{FZ} = \mathsf{GZ} \text{ for all closed } \mathsf{Z}]) \Rightarrow (\forall\mathcal{A}[\mathcal{A} \models \mathsf{F} = \mathsf{G}]) \qquad (\omega\text{-rule admissible})$$

(ii) The ω-rule is *derivable* if

$$\forall\mathcal{A}\Big([\mathcal{A} \models \mathsf{FZ} = \mathsf{GZ} \text{ for all closed } \mathsf{Z}] \Rightarrow \mathcal{A} \models \mathsf{F} = \mathsf{G}.\Big) \qquad (\omega\text{-rule derivable})$$

Clearly derivability implies admissibility.

PROPOSITION 2.2. *Let $\mathcal{A}$ range over models of* CL, *i.e. over combinatory algebras. Then*

$$(\forall\mathcal{A} \models \mathsf{P} = \mathsf{Q}) \iff \text{CL} \vdash \mathsf{P} = \mathsf{Q} \qquad (\textit{completeness})$$

Now let $\mathcal{A}$ range over extensional combinatory algebras. Then

$$(\forall\mathcal{A} \textit{ extensional} .\mathcal{A} \models \mathsf{P} = \mathsf{Q}) \iff \text{CL} + \text{ext} \vdash \mathsf{P} = \mathsf{Q} \qquad (\textit{completeness for extensional models})$$

PROOF. (i) ($\Leftarrow$) If $\mathsf{P} = \mathsf{Q}$ is provable in CL, then it is valid in all models of CL. This is because by definition a combinatory algebra satisfies the axioms of CL and logical derivation (in the case of CL the equality axioms and rules) preserve validity.

($\Rightarrow$) If $\mathsf{P} = \mathsf{Q}$ is valid in all combinatory algebras, then it is valid in the term model $\mathcal{M}(\text{CL})$ (or $\mathcal{M}^{\text{o}}(\text{CL})$) consisting of the (closed) terms modulo provable equality. Therefore $\mathsf{P} = \mathsf{Q}$ is derivable.

(ii) Similarly, but now taking the open term model $\mathcal{M}(\text{CL})$ of terms containing variables. □

By completeness admissibility is equivalent with validity:

$$[\text{CL} + \text{ext} \vdash \mathsf{FZ} = \mathsf{GZ} \text{ for all closed } \mathsf{Z}] \Rightarrow \text{CL} + \text{ext} \vdash \mathsf{F} = \mathsf{G}. \qquad (\omega\text{-rule valid})$$

It will turn out that the ω-rule is neither admissible nor derivable.

the ω-rule was valid. At first I had some hope to show the general validity of the ω-rule as follows.

PROPOSAL 2.3. *Let* $F, G \in CL^o$. *Suppose* $CL \vdash F\Omega = G\Omega$. *Then*
(i) $CL \vdash Fx = Gx$, *for a fresh variable* x.
(ii) *Therefore* $CL + ext \vdash F = G$.

FAKE PROOF. (i) If $F\Omega = G\Omega$, by the Church-Rosser Theorem

$$F\Omega \twoheadrightarrow_w P \ {}_w\!\twoheadleftarrow G\Omega$$

for some $P \in CL^o$. Since Ω only reduces to itself,

$$Fx \twoheadrightarrow_w N' \ {}_w\!\twoheadleftarrow Gx.$$

(ii) By (i) and extensionality. □

But the conclusion in (i) is not correct. The error in the reasoning is that although Ω only reduces to itself, it differs from a variable, as Ω can be created in a reduction, while a fresh variable cannot. In fact there is a counterexample. Taking $F = \omega$ and $G = \Omega$ one has indeed $F\Omega =_\beta \Omega\Omega =_\beta G\Omega$, but $Fx \neq_\beta Gx$.

If there would be a term like Ω that is not generated by F or G, then taking this as argument would make a valid argument. But is this possible? Perhaps there are terms that generate all other terms. But for those terms that didn't generate all other terms the ω-rule turned out to be valid in $\lambda + ext$.

THEOREM I.2.5.29 The ω-rule is valid (in λ+Ext) if F, G are not universal generators[2].

PROOF. If F, G are not universal generators, then there is a term Ξ that will not be generated by either F or G. The classical reasoning towards this statement is as follows. If there doesn't exist a universal generator, then FG is not a universal generator, so that some term X will not appear in reducts of F and G and one can take $\Xi = \Omega X$. If there exists a universal generator U, then one can take $\Xi = \Omega U$. Now can show

$$\lambda + Ext \vdash M\Xi = N\Xi \Rightarrow \lambda + Ext \vdash M = N. \qquad \square$$

When I had proved this, it was not yet known whether universal generators exist. At first I hoped to show that universal generators didn't exist. Then as corollary the general validity of the ω-rule would follow. But I was wrong, it turned out that universal generators do exist.

THEOREM I.2.4.4 There exists a λ-term $U \in \Lambda^o$ that is a universal generator, i.e. every λ-term appears as subterm of a reduct of U.

[2]Although it is not stated, the context of this result shows that 'not $\beta\eta$-universal generator' is intended here. There is a result due to Jan Willem Klop that requiring only 'not to be β-universal generators' is not sufficient for warranting the validity of the ω-rule. See (Barendregt 1984, Exercise 17.5.13)

PROOF. Take the universal constructor E constructed by Kleene such that

$$\{\mathsf{E}c_n \mid n \in \mathbb{N}\}$$

is the set of all closed terms. Using the fixed point theorem one can construct a term G such that

$$\mathsf{G}c_n = [\mathsf{E}c_n, \mathsf{G}c_{n+1}] \triangleq \lambda z.z(\mathsf{E}c_n)(\mathsf{G}c_{n+1}).$$

Then $\mathsf{U} = \mathsf{G}c_0$ is a universal generator. □

The proof of the partial validity of the ω-rule is remarkable, as the assumption is that $\mathsf{F}Z = \mathsf{G}Z$ for all closed Z, while in the proof only one of these arguments is used. Kreisel suggested that if I would use more arguments, then perhaps the ω-rule would turn out to be valid in general. This I doubted. Two years later Gordon Plotkin showed that in general the ω-rule is not valid, by constructing two universal generators F, G as refutation, proving me right. But in some sense also Kreisel was right. In a later result of Plotkin, written up in a letter to me and recorded in Barendregt (1984) as Theorem 17.3.24, it was shown that if only one of the closed terms F, G is not a universal generator, then the ω-rule holds for these. This had to be proved via a Ξ such that in the extensional λ-calculus

$$\mathsf{M}\Xi = \mathsf{N}\Xi \;\&\; \mathsf{M}\Omega = \mathsf{N}\Omega \;\Rightarrow\; \mathsf{M} = \mathsf{N}.$$

This is the best one can get.

That in general the ω-rule is not valid in the extensional λ-calculus was proved in a spectacular way in Plotkin (1974), by constructing complex universal generators. The counterexample is also presented in (Barendregt 1984, Theorem 17.3.30). This invalidity was later expressed as the lack of enough points for certain objects D such that $[\mathsf{D} \to \mathsf{D}]$ is a retract of D in some Cartesian closed category Koymans (1982), see also (Barendregt 1984, 5.5.7(iv)).

A serious but failed attempt to prove the validity of the ω-rule in the extensional λ-calculus I learned from Jacopini in 1973 during another discussion in Rome. Before the counterexample of Plotkin was known Jacopini had the following proof strategy. Suppose that for $\mathsf{F}, \mathsf{G} \in \Lambda^o$ one has $\mathsf{F}Z = \mathsf{G}Z$ for all $Z \in \Lambda^o$. Take $\Omega_1 = \Omega\mathsf{I}$ and $\Omega_2 = \Omega\mathsf{S}$. Then

$$\left.\begin{array}{lcl} \mathsf{F}\Omega_1 & = & \mathsf{F}\Omega_1; \\ \mathsf{F}\Omega_2 & = & \mathsf{F}\Omega_2. \end{array}\right\} \qquad (1)$$

This seemed to imply that $\mathsf{F}x = \mathsf{G}x$ for a fresh variable x, hence $\mathsf{F} = \mathsf{G}$ by extensionality. We couldn't find a counterexample, i.e. a pair of terms satisfying (1) and

$$\mathsf{F}x \neq \mathsf{G}x. \qquad (2)$$

Only after Plotkin's counterexample against the validity of the ω-rule it became clear how to construct such F and G. If one has an $\mathsf{F} \in \Lambda^o$ such that $\mathsf{F}\Omega_1 = \mathsf{F}\Omega_2 \neq \mathsf{F}x$, then one can take $G = K(F\Omega_1)$. Indeed:

$$\begin{array}{rcll} F\Omega_1 & = & G\Omega_1, & \text{by definition of } G; \\ F\Omega_2 & = & F\Omega_1, & \text{by the property of } F, \\ & = & G\Omega_2, & \text{by definition of } G; \\ Fx & \neq & F\Omega_1, & \text{by the property of } F, \\ & = & Gx, & \text{by definition of } G. \end{array}$$

In order to construct such an F, try $F = AB$. By the fixed point theorem applied twice one can find A, B such that $A = \lambda xy.A(x\Omega_1)\Omega_2$ and $B = B\Omega_1$. Then indeed

$$\begin{array}{rcccl} F\Omega_1 & = & AB\Omega_1 & = & A(B\Omega_1)\Omega_2; \\ F\Omega_2 & = & AB\Omega_2 & = & A(B\Omega_1)\Omega_2; \\ Fx & = & ABx & \neq & AB\Omega_1 = F\Omega_1 \end{array}$$

The trick used here to find F, G satisfying (1) and (2), together with the idea behind a universal generator are essential steps in the construction of Plotkin's counterexample against the ω-rule..

2.3 Solvable terms

As discussed above, the work on the partial combinatory algebra $\mathcal{K}$ gave me as wrong impression the consistency of

$$CL + \{P = Q \mid P, Q \text{ have no CL-normal form}\}.$$

A counterexample is the theory extended by the equation

$$\lambda x.x\mathsf{K}\Omega = \lambda x.x\mathsf{S}\Omega,$$

with $\Omega = (\lambda x.xx)(\lambda x.xx)$, being the minimal term without a normal form. Indeed, from this equation follows that $\mathsf{K} = \mathsf{S}$, by applying both sides to K. This gave rise to the notion of solvability[3]. Sometimes one needs to apply a term P to several arguments $\vec{Q}$ in order to make $P\vec{Q}$ have a normal form. For example for the terms $L_1 = [[\Omega, \mathsf{K}], \Omega]$ and $L_2 = [[\Omega, \mathsf{S}], \Omega]$ one has $L_1\mathsf{K}(\mathsf{KI}) = \mathsf{K}$, while $L_2\mathsf{K}(\mathsf{KI}) = \mathsf{S}$.

DEFINITION 2.4. (i) A closed term $P \in CL^o$ is CL-*solvable* if

$$\exists Q_1, \ldots, Q_n \in CL.CL \vdash PQ_1 \ldots Q_n = \mathbf{K},$$

otherwise P is CL-*unsolvable*.

[3]In the thesis there is a shortcoming that I didn't require the term to be a combinator. This makes a free variable x being unsolvable. This is unnatural, as was pointed out to me by Chris Wadsworth. Terms R containing variables $\vec{x}$ should be called solvable if $\lambda\vec{x}.R$ is solvable in the sense above.

(ii) A general term $P \in CL$ is solvable if its closure $\lambda^*\vec{x}.P$ is solvable.

REMARK 2.5. Note that $P \in CL^o$ is solvable iff $\forall R \exists \vec{Q} \in CL.CL \vdash P\vec{Q} = R$.
The reason is that if $\vdash P\vec{Q} = K$, then $\vdash P\vec{Q}RI = R$.

Similarly one defines solvability in the extensional case and in the λ-calculus. It is shown in the thesis that solvability is invariant under translations between λ and CL and under adding or not extensionality (or even the ω-rule). This is recapitulated in III.1 Theorem 1.7. The unsolvable terms are playing a key role in the thesis.

THEOREM 2.6. (i) *Let* U *be an unsolvable* CL*-term. Then for any variable* x

$$CL \vdash FU = \mathbf{K} \Rightarrow CL \vdash Fx = \mathbf{K}.$$

(ii) *Let* U *be an* $\beta\eta$*-unsolvable* λ*-term. Then for any variable* x

$$\lambda + \text{Ext} \vdash FU = N \ \&\ N \textit{ has a } \beta\eta\textit{-normal form} \ \Rightarrow \lambda + \text{Ext} \vdash Fx = \mathbf{K}.$$

(iii) *The following set of equations is consistent with* CL

$$\mathcal{H}_{CL} = \{U = V \mid U, V \textit{ are unsolvable}\}.$$

PROOF. (i) See I.3 Theorem 2.3 (1).
(ii) See I.3 Theorem 2.3 (2).
(iii) See I.3 Corollary 2.15. □

In Church (1941) a partial function $\psi: \mathbb{N}^k \rightarrow \mathbb{N}$ is called λ-*definable* if for some closed term F and all $n_1, \ldots, n_k \in \mathbb{N}^k$ one has

$$\begin{array}{rcll} F\mathbf{c}_{n_1}\ldots\mathbf{c}_{n_k} & = & \mathbf{c}_m, & \text{if } \psi(\vec{n}) = m; \\ & = & \text{has no normal form,} & \text{if } \psi(\vec{n}) \text{ is undefined.} \end{array}$$

and it is proved that all partial computable functions are λ-definable. In the thesis this is strengthened by requiring that

$$\begin{array}{rcll} F\mathbf{c}_{n_1}\ldots\mathbf{c}_{n_k} & = & \mathbf{c}_m, & \text{if } \psi(\vec{n}) = m; \\ & = & \text{is unsolvable,} & \text{if } \psi(\vec{n}) \text{ is undefined.} \end{array}$$

A term P is of *order 0* if never $P = \lambda x.Q$. Closed terms of order 0 are unsolvable. In Visser (1980) it is shown that for partial computable functions one can strengthen this to

$$\begin{array}{rcll} F\mathbf{c}_{n_1}\ldots\mathbf{c}_{n_k} & = & \mathbf{c}_m, & \text{if } \psi(\vec{n}) = m; \\ & = & \text{is of order } 0, & \text{if } \psi(\vec{n}) \text{ is undefined.} \end{array}$$

This line of results culminates in the Statman Master Theorem, see Barendregt (1992), from which the three previous results follow. Let $\mathcal{D}$ be a computably enumerable set of terms that is closed under β-conversion ($P = Q \in \mathcal{U} \Rightarrow P \in \mathcal{D}$). Then one has the following. (This mention belongs more to the next section about what happened after 1971, but is reported here.) A partial function $\psi\colon \mathbb{N}^k \to \mathbb{N}$ is computable iff for some closed term F and all $n_1, \ldots, n_k \in \mathbb{N}^k$ one has

$$\begin{array}{rcll} \mathsf{F}\mathbf{c}_{n_1}\ldots\mathbf{c}_{n_k} & = & \mathbf{c}_m, & \text{if } \psi(\vec{n}) = m; \\ & \notin & \mathcal{D} & \text{if } \psi(\vec{n}) \text{ is undefined.} \end{array}$$

This result follows directly from the ADN theorem in Visser (1980).

Invariance of solvability

DEFINITION 2.7. (i) Let $P \in CL$ be a combinator (term without (free) variables). Then P is called CL-*solvable* if if for some $n \in \mathbb{N}$ and some combinators $Q_1 \ldots Q_n$ one has

$$CL \vdash PQ_1 \ldots Q_n = \mathbf{K}.$$

Similarly one defines P is CL+Ext-solvable (respectively CLω-solvable) if

$$CL + \text{Ext} \vdash PQ_1 \ldots Q_n = \mathbf{K}$$

respectively

$$CL\omega \vdash PQ_1 \ldots Q_n = \mathbf{K}.$$

(ii) Let $M \in \lambda$ be a combinator (closed λ-term). Then M is λ-solvable if if for some $n \in \mathbb{N}$ and some terms $N_1 \ldots N_n$ one has

$$\lambda \vdash MN_1 \ldots N_n = \mathsf{K}.$$

Similarly one defines M to be λ+Ext-solvable (respectively $\lambda\omega$-solvable).

Solvability is invariant under translations between CL and λ-calculus. Also it is invariant under adding extensionality and the ω-rule.

THEOREM 2.8. *Let* $M \in \lambda$ *and* $P \in CL$ *be combinators.*

(i) *The following are equivalent.*

(1) M *is* λ*-solvable;*

(2) M *is* λ*+ext-solvable;*

(3) M *is* $\lambda\omega$*-solvable.*

(ii) *The following are equivalent.*

(1) P *is* CL*-solvable;*

(2) P *is* CL*+ext-solvable;*

(3) P *is* CLω*-solvable.*

(iii) P *is CL-solvable* $\iff$ $\phi(P)$ *is* λ*-solvable.*
Similarly for the version with Ext and ω*.*

(iv) M *is* λ-*solvable* $\iff \psi(M)$ *is* CL-*solvable.*
Similarly for the version with Ext and ω.

PROOF. The proof hinges on several results.

Step 1. λ-solvable $\Rightarrow$ λ+Ext-solvable $\Rightarrow$ $\lambda\omega$-solvable,
and similarly for CL solvability. This is trivial.

Step 2. P is CL-solvable $\Rightarrow$ $\phi(P)$ is λ-solvable.
This follows easily from 1.4.5(1) in Part I of this thesis stating

$$\mathrm{CL} \vdash P = Q \Rightarrow \lambda\phi(P) = \phi(Q).$$

Step 3. $\mathrm{CL} + \mathrm{Ext} \vdash P = \psi(\phi(P))$. (One also has $\lambda \vdash \phi(\psi(M)) = M$.
This is 1.4.10(2). Therefore modulo $\mathrm{CL}\omega$ the map ψ is surjective.

Step 4. $\lambda\omega \vdash M = N \Rightarrow \mathrm{CL}\omega \vdash \psi(M) = \psi(N)$.
By induction on derivations in $\lambda\omega$. Theorem 1.4.9 in Part I states

$$\lambda + \mathrm{Ext} \vdash M = N \Rightarrow \mathrm{CL} + \mathrm{Ext} \vdash \psi(M) = \psi(N).$$

Therefore the axioms and rules in λ+Ext are covered. An application of the ω-rule in $\lambda\omega$ maps to one in $\mathrm{CL}\omega$:

$$\begin{array}{rcll} \lambda\omega \vdash MZ & = & NZ, & \text{for all combinators } Z, \\ \Rightarrow \mathrm{CL}\omega \vdash \psi(M)\psi(Z) & = & \psi(N)\psi(Z), & \text{for all combinators } Z, \\ \Rightarrow \mathrm{CL}\omega \vdash \psi(M)Q & = & \psi(N)Q, & \text{for all combinators } Q \text{ by 3}, \\ \Rightarrow \mathrm{CL}\omega \vdash \psi(M) & = & \psi(N). & \end{array}$$

Step 5. M is $\lambda\omega$-solvable $\Rightarrow$ $\psi(M)$ is $\mathrm{CL}\omega$-solvable.
Indeed, suppose M satisfies

$$\begin{array}{ll} & \lambda\omega \vdash M\vec{N} = K, \text{ for some combinators } \vec{N}, \\ \Rightarrow & \mathrm{CL}\omega \vdash \psi(M)\psi(N_1)\cdots\psi(n_n) = \psi(K) = \psi(\phi(\mathbf{K})) = \mathbf{K} \qquad \text{by 4}, \\ \Rightarrow & \psi(M) \text{ is } \mathrm{CL}\omega\text{-solvable.} \end{array}$$

Step 6. P is $\mathrm{CL}\omega$-solvable $\Rightarrow$ P is CL-solvable.
This follows directly from Corollary 2.2.12 in the thesis:

$$\mathrm{CL}\omega \vdash P = \mathbf{K} \Rightarrow \mathrm{CL} \vdash P\mathbf{K}_{2n} = \mathbf{K}.$$

Now the 16 implications in the Theorem follow by a diagram chase.

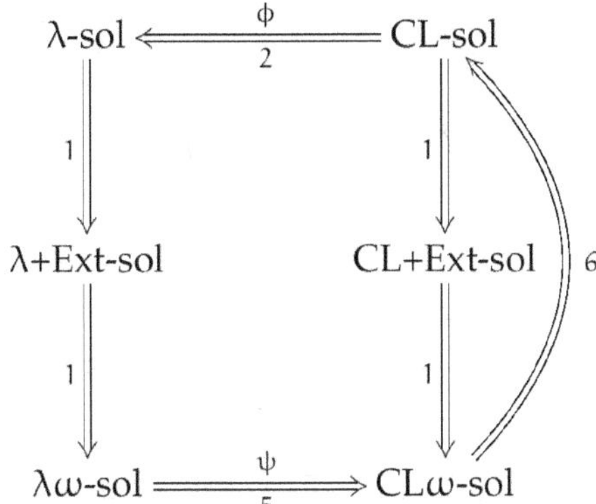

□

The thesis contains two main results about unsolvable terms.

THEOREM 2.9 (GENERICITY LEMMA). *Let* P *be a* CL*-unsolvable term* CL. *Suppose* $\vdash$ FP $=$ **K**. *Then for all* Q $\in$ CL *one has* $\vdash$ FQ $=$ **K**.

PROOF. This is Theorem 3.2.3 in Part I. □

THEOREM 2.10. *Let* $\mathcal{H}_{\mathrm{CL}} = \{P = Q \mid P, Q \in \mathrm{CL}$ *unsolvable*$\}$. *Then* $\mathrm{CL} + \mathcal{H}_{\mathrm{CL}}$ *is consistent.*

PROOF. This is Corollary 3.2.15 in Part I. □

3 The period 1971-1980

3.1 Renaming bound variables

The problem of a clash between free and bound variables, in particular that a free variable in N becomes bound after making a 'naive' substitution $[x: = N]$ into a free variable of a term M may be solved by identifying λ-terms differing in the names of bound variables, like $\lambda x.x \equiv \lambda y.y$. This solution is not fully satisfactorily treated in the thesis. In my later book "The lambda calculus, its syntax and semantics" the problem was shifted to the De Bruijn notation, in which bound variables are not named ('nameless dummies'). To check that this is 100% correct requires some effort that was fulfilled only by a thorough analysis and formal proof development found in Norrish & Westergaard (2007). This work refers to yet another approach, by Andy Pitts and his students, using instead of substitutions of variables permutations of these. The difference is that

$$P \equiv Q \Rightarrow P[x := y] \equiv Q[x := y],$$

but not conversely, while for a permutation of variables π one has

$$P \equiv Q \Leftrightarrow P^{\pi} \equiv Q^{\pi}.$$

See Gabbay & Pitts (2002), Urban et al. (2004). The latter work shows that in formal proof developments one can reason with the same ease as with using the variable convention used in Barendregt (1984).

3.2 Böhm trees

The universal generator constructed above motivated me to introduce in Barendregt (1977) the notion of *Böhm tree* BT(M) of a term M. We give some examples to get an intuitive picture.

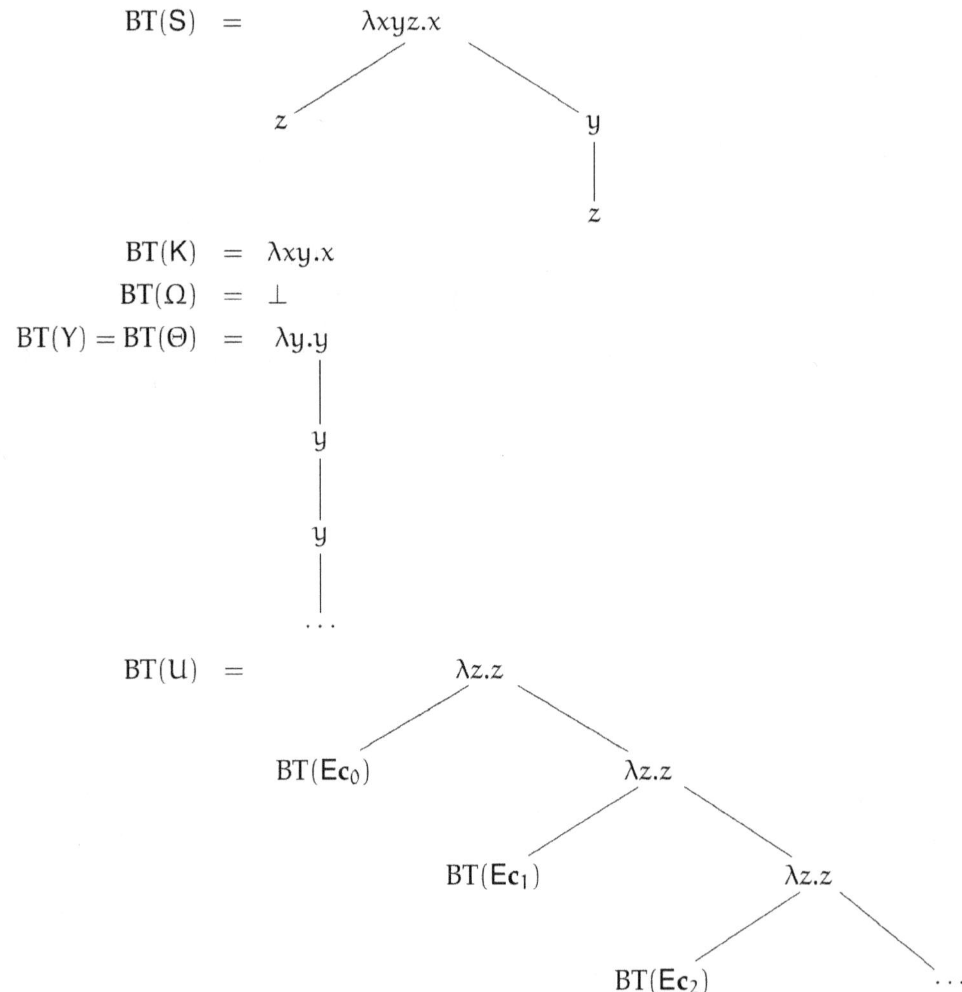

Here Y and Θ are the fixed point combinators of respectively Curry and Turing

$$\begin{aligned} \mathsf{Y} &= \lambda f.(\lambda x.f(xx))(\lambda x.f(xx)); \\ \Theta &= (\lambda ab.b(aab))(\lambda ab.b(aab)); \\ \mathsf{U} &= \mathrm{B}c_0, \text{ with } \mathrm{B}c_n = [\mathbf{E}c_n, \mathrm{B}c_{n+1}] = \lambda z.z(\mathbf{E}c_n)(\mathrm{G}c_{n+1}). \end{aligned}$$

This U is the universal generator constructed in Section I 2.4.

DEFINITION 3.1. The general intuitive co-inductive definition is as follows.

$$\mathrm{BT}(M) = \begin{array}{c} \lambda\vec{x}.y \\ \diagup \quad \diagdown \\ \mathrm{BT}(M_1) \quad \cdots \quad \mathrm{BT}(M_n) \end{array}, \quad \text{if } M = \lambda\vec{x}.yM_1 \ldots M_n$$

$$= \perp, \qquad \text{else.}$$

DEFINITION 3.2. (i) For a model $\mathcal{D}$ of the λ-calculus write

$$\mathrm{Th}(\mathcal{D}) = \{M = N \mid M, N \in \Lambda^o \ \& \ \mathcal{D} \models M = N\}.$$

(ii) $\mathcal{B} = \{M = N \mid \mathrm{BT}(M) = \mathrm{BT}(N)\}$.

The theory $\lambda\mathcal{B} = \lambda + \mathcal{B}$, equating terms with the same Böhm tree, is consistent. Let $P\omega$ be the λ-calculus model independently found by Plotkin (1972/1993) and Scott (1974), and let $\mathbb{T}^\omega$ be the model of Plotkin (1978).

THEOREM 3.3. (i) $\mathrm{Th}(P\omega) = \mathcal{B}$.
(ii) $\mathrm{Th}(\mathbb{T}^\omega) = \mathcal{B}$.

PROOF. (i) This was announced in Hyland (1976) and fully proved in Barendregt (1981) based on lectures of Hyland in Utrecht in 1977.
(ii) Proved in Barendregt & Longo (1980), similarly but slightly more complex. □

3.3 Classes of terms

DEFINITION 3.4. The following applies to any notion of reduction R, but are taken here for $R = \beta$.
(i) $\mathrm{NF} = \{M \in \Lambda \mid M \text{ is in normal form}\}$.
(ii) $\mathsf{WN} = \{M \in \Lambda \mid M \text{ has a normal form}\}$.
(iii) $\mathrm{SN} = \{M \in \Lambda \mid \text{ all reductions starting with } M \text{ terminate}\}$.
(iv) $\infty(M) \iff M \in \Lambda - \mathrm{SN}$.

EXAMPLES 3.5. (i) $\mathsf{I}, \mathsf{K}, \mathsf{S}, \omega \in \mathrm{NF}$.
(ii) $\omega\mathsf{SI} \in \mathrm{SN}$.
(iii) $\mathsf{KI}\Omega \in \mathsf{WN}$, but $\mathsf{KI}\Omega \notin \mathrm{SN}$.
(iv) $\mathsf{Y}(\mathsf{KI}) \in \mathsf{WN}$, $\mathsf{Y}(\mathsf{KI}) \notin \mathrm{SN}$, but proper subterms of this term are in SN.

In Barendregt (1973), see also (Barendregt 1984, Corollary 9.4.21), it is shown that in the λI-calculus the notions of having a normal form and solvability coincide. By the 'second Church-Rosser Theorem' that is called 'conservation theorem' in (Barendregt 1984, 11.3.4, 11.3.5) this implies the following.

PROPOSITION 3.6. *In the λI-calculus the following are equivalent.*

- M *has a normal form.*
- M *is strongly normalizing.*
- M *is solvable.*

Differentiating the following one obtains more interesting examples.

DEFINITION 3.7. Let $M \in \Lambda$.
(i) M is I-solvable if $\exists \vec{P} \in \Lambda^I . M\vec{P} =_\beta I$.
(ii) M is K-solvable if $\exists \vec{P} \in \Lambda^K . M\vec{P} =_\beta I$.

The following figure shows the different sets of terms. As can be seen, the situation is more complex in the λK-calculus than in the λI-calculus.

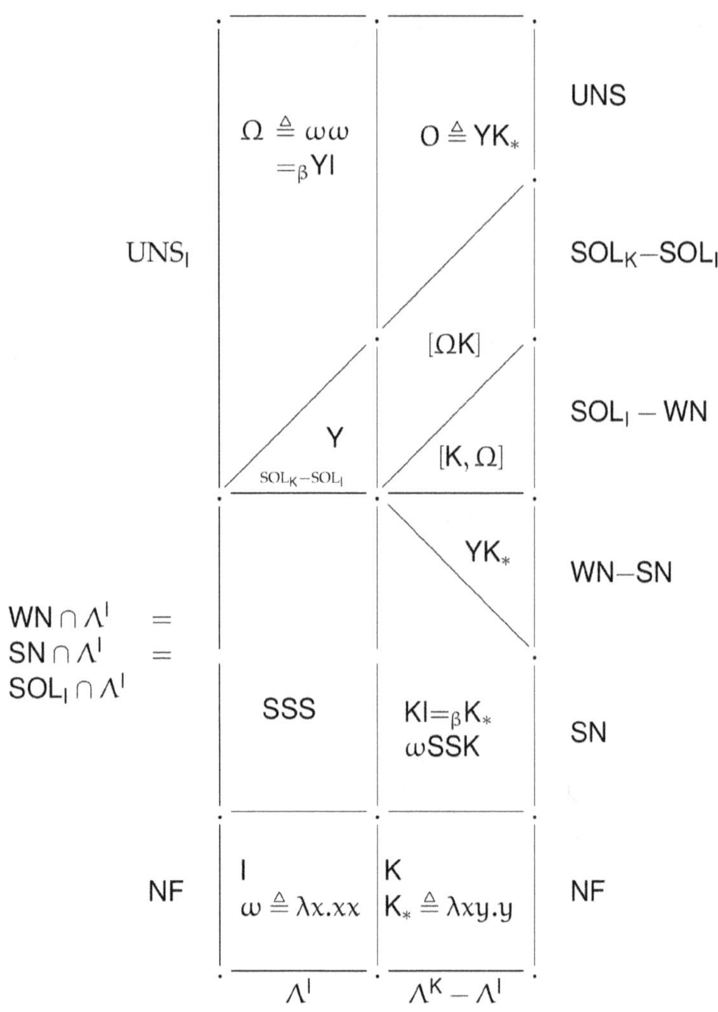

Figure 3.1: NF, SN, WN, SOL in λI versus λK.

REMARK 3.8. (i) K-solvable is the same as solvable.
(ii) $\Omega =_\beta YI$ and $O \triangleq YK$ are neither K-solvable nor I-solvable. The term O is named after the hungry Ogre: $OM =_\beta KOM =_\beta O$ for all M.
(iii) Y, $[\Omega] \in \Lambda^I$ and $[\Omega K] \in \Lambda^K$ are K-solvable, but not I-solvable: all three terms applied to the sequence K, K yield K.

(iv) $[\mathsf{K},\Omega] \in \Lambda^{\mathsf{K}}$ is I-solvable: $[\mathsf{K},\Omega]\omega =_\beta \mathsf{KK}\Omega = \mathsf{K}$.
(v) $\mathsf{Y}(\mathsf{K}_*)$ is WN but not SN. Indeed, one has $\mathsf{Y}(\mathsf{K}_*) \twoheadrightarrow \mathsf{K}_*(\mathsf{Y}(\mathsf{K}_*)) \twoheadrightarrow \mathsf{I}$, but also

$$\mathsf{Y}(\mathsf{K}_*) \twoheadrightarrow \mathsf{K}_*(\mathsf{Y}(\mathsf{K}_*)) \twoheadrightarrow \mathsf{K}_*^2(\mathsf{Y}(\mathsf{K}_*)) \twoheadrightarrow \dots .$$

THEOREM 3.9. *In the* $\lambda\mathsf{I}$*-calculus the following is a maximally consistent extension:*

$$\lambda\mathsf{I}_\perp = \lambda\mathsf{I} + \{M = N \mid M, N \notin \mathsf{WN}\}.$$

SKETCH. This is proved in (Barendregt 1984, Theorem 16.2.12). The main ingredients are

(1) Böhm's theorem for the $\lambda\mathsf{I}$-calculus: different $\beta\eta$-nf's cannot be consistently equated.

(2) For $M \in \Lambda^{\mathsf{I}}$ one has M is I-unsolvable iff $M \notin \mathsf{WN}$ (M has no $\beta(\eta)$-normal form).

(3) The consistency of $\mathcal{H}_\mathsf{I}$ in $\lambda\mathsf{I}$, equating I-unsolvables.

(4) Let $\Omega_3 = (\lambda x.xxx)(\lambda x.xxx)$. Then the equation $\mathsf{I} = \Omega_3$ is inconsistent Jacopini (1975):

$$\mathsf{I} = \Omega_3 \vdash \mathsf{I} = \Omega_3 = \Omega_3(\lambda x.xxx) = \mathsf{I}(\lambda x.xxx) = \lambda x.xxx,$$

giving a contradiction by (1).

(5) Equating a solvable and an unsolvable term is inconsistent, by (4). □

The following result is included here because of its remarkable nature, unique in its kind. There is a necessary characteristic of terms that are not SN (and thus a sufficient characteristic of SN terms.)

DEFINITION 3.10. Let $w_1, w_2 \in \Sigma^*$ be words over an alphabet Σ. Write $w_1 \prec w_2$ if w_1 can be obtained from $w_2 = a_1 \dots a_k$ by deleting some elements in the sequence $a_1 \dots a_k$. For example if $\Sigma = \{p, q, r\}$, then $prq \prec rqppqrq$.

THEOREM 3.11 (SØRENSEN (1998)). (i) *Suppose* $\infty(M)$. *Then* $\Omega \prec M$.
(ii) *Suppose* $\Omega \not\prec M$. *Then* $\mathrm{SN}(M)$.

The proof makes use of the tree embedding theorem of Kruskal (1960). Part (ii) is just the contrapositive of (i). As an example, we know that $\infty(\Theta)$. Writing out Curry's fixed point combinator $\mathsf{Y} = \lambda f.(\underline{\lambda x}.f(\underline{xx}))(\underline{\lambda x}.f(\underline{xx}))$, one can see Ω lurking inside it. The same holds for Turing's version $\Theta \triangleq (\underline{\lambda a}b.b(\underline{aa}b))(\underline{\lambda a}b.b(\underline{aa}b))$.

3.4 The kite of theories

DEFINITION 3.12. Let $\mathcal{C} \subseteq \Lambda^o$. Then the following set of equations is called *Morris' theory* over $\mathcal{C}$

$$\mathcal{T}_{\mathcal{C}} = \{M = N \mid M, N \in \Lambda^o \ \& \ \forall F \in \Lambda^o [FM \in \mathcal{C} \iff FN \in \mathcal{C}]\}.$$

PROPOSITION 3.13. *For every $\mathcal{C}$ one has $\mathcal{T}_{\mathcal{C}}$ is a (possibly inconsistent) λ-theory.*

Every λ-theory can be represented as a Morris' theory.

DEFINITION 3.14. Let $\mathcal{T}$ be a λ-theory. For $X \in \Lambda$ (notably for pairs $[M, N] \triangleq \lambda z.zMN$) we write $X \cdot i = X(\lambda x_1 x_2.x_i)$. Then $[M_1, M_2] \cdot i =_\beta M_i$. Now define

$$\mathcal{C}_{\mathcal{T}} = \{X \in \Lambda^o \mid X \cdot 1 =_{\mathcal{T}} X \cdot 2\}$$

PROPOSITION 3.15 (SCOTT). *Let $\mathcal{T}$ be a λ-theory. Then for all $M, N \in \Lambda^o$*

$$M =_{\mathcal{T}} N \iff (M = N) \in \mathcal{T}_{\mathcal{C}_{\mathcal{T}}}.$$

Therefore $\mathcal{T} = \mathcal{T}_{\mathcal{C}_{\mathcal{T}}}$.

PROOF. ($\Rightarrow$) Assume $M =_{\mathcal{T}} N$ and let $F \in \Lambda^o$. If $FM \in \mathcal{C}_{\mathcal{T}}$, then $FM \cdot 1 =_{\mathcal{T}} FM \cdot 2$, hence $FN \cdot 1 =_{\mathcal{T}} FM \cdot 1 =_{\mathcal{T}} FM \cdot 2 =_{\mathcal{T}} FN \cdot 2$, so that $FN \in \mathcal{C}_{\mathcal{T}}$. Similarly $FN \in \mathcal{C}_{\mathcal{T}} \Rightarrow FM \in \mathcal{C}_{\mathcal{T}}$. Therefore one has $(M = N) \in \mathcal{C}_{\mathcal{T}}$.

($\Leftarrow$) Conversely assume $(M = N) \in \mathcal{C}_{\mathcal{T}}$. Define $F = \lambda x.[M, x]$. Then $FM =_\beta [M, M] \in \mathcal{C}_{\mathcal{T}}$. Hence $[M, N] =_\beta FN \in \mathcal{C}_{\mathcal{T}}$, by assumption. It follows that $M =_\beta FN \cdot 1 =_{\mathcal{T}} FN \cdot 2 =_\beta N$. Therefore $M =_{\mathcal{T}} N$. □

DEFINITION 3.16. (i) NF $= \{M \mid M$ has a β-normal form$\}$.
(ii) UNS $= \{M \mid M$ is unsolvable$\}$.

The following diagram extends one in (Barendregt 1984, Theorem 17.4.16): the ten λ-theories $\lambda, \lambda, \lambda\omega, \mathcal{H}, \mathcal{H}, \mathcal{H}\omega, \mathcal{B}, \mathcal{B}, \mathcal{B}\omega$, and $\mathcal{H}^*$ were depicted in a kite-shaped picture, such that if $\mathcal{T}_1$ is above $\mathcal{T}_2$, then $\mathcal{T}_1 \subsetneq \mathcal{T}_2$. The λ-theory $\boldsymbol{\lambda}$ is the usual λ-calculus, axiomatized by β-conversion. If $\mathcal{T}$ is a λ-theory, then $\mathcal{T}$ is axiomatized by $\mathcal{T}$ + ext, and $\mathcal{T}\omega$ is axiomatized by $\mathcal{T}$ plus the ω-rule. The λ-theory $\mathcal{H}$ is axiomatized by (equating all unsolvables)

$$\mathcal{H}_0 = \{M = N \mid M, N \in \text{UNS}\}.$$

The λ-theory $\mathcal{B}$ is axiomatized by $\{M = N \mid \text{BT}(M) = \text{BT}(N)\}$. That Th(P$\omega$ = $\mathcal{B}$ holds is Theorem 3.3. Finally the theory $\mathcal{H}^*$ is by definition Morris' theory $\mathcal{T}_{\text{SOL}}$ and equals Th($\mathcal{D}_\infty$), Hyland (1976) and Wadsworth (1976).

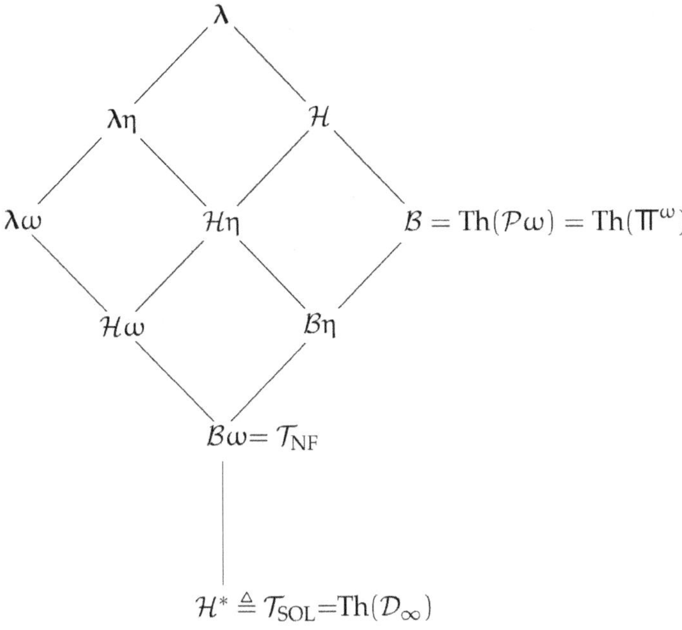

Kite revisited

In the original kite the place of $\mathcal{T}_{\text{NF}}$ was conjectured[1] to be properly in the tail between its two ends: $\mathcal{B}\omega \subsetneq \mathcal{T}_{\text{NF}} \subsetneq \mathcal{H}^*$. This turned out to be not the case. Using breathtaking arguments it has been shown recently by Intrigila et al. (2019) that

$$\mathcal{B}\omega = \mathcal{T}_{\text{NF}},$$

as indicated above, building on the result that $\mathcal{B}\omega \subseteq \mathcal{T}_{\text{NF}}$ in Breuvart et al. (2016). See also Barendregt & Manzonetto (2022) for the full story.

3.5 Completing and collapsing partial combinatory algebras

$\mathcal{A}^{\odot}$ changing application

In a talk at Amsterdam University around 1970 Dana Scott lectured about his recently found $\mathcal{D}_\infty$ models of the λ-calculus. At the end of the lecture I got up and mentioned that I had tried to complete Kleene's pca $\mathcal{K}$, but that all attempts failed, sketching some details reported in Part II on the board. Scott mentioned to be happy about that, as it showed that it was not so easy to find a model of the λ-calculus. Thereafter, in a letter to

[1]This conjecture was attributed to P. Sallé. In recent correspondence he didn't remember to have stated this conjecture.

Anne Troelstra, the following was proposed by Scott, with a mention "Henk Barendregt may know this".

DEFINITION 3.17. (i) Given a pca $\mathcal{A} = \langle A, \cdot, i, k, s \rangle$, define for $a, b \in \mathcal{A}$

$$\begin{aligned} a \odot b &= sab; \\ c' &= kc, \qquad \text{for } c \in \{i, k, s\}. \end{aligned}$$

(ii) Set as before $a \sim b$ if $\forall x \in \mathcal{A}. ax \simeq bx$.

PROPOSITION 3.18. *The relation $\sim$ on $\mathcal{A}$ is a congruence with respect to $\odot$. Therefore one can define* $[a]_\sim \odot [b]_\sim = [a \odot b]_\sim$.

PROOF. Suppose $a \sim a', b \sim b'$ towards $a \odot b \sim a' \odot b'$. Then for all $x \in \mathcal{A}$ one has $ax \simeq a'x$, and $bx \simeq b'x$. Then one has $a \odot b \cdot x = sabx \simeq ax(bx) \simeq a'x(b'x) \simeq sa'b'x = a' \odot b'x$ and the conclusion follows. □

PROPOSAL 3.19. $\mathcal{A}^\odot = \langle \mathcal{A}/{\sim}, \odot, i', k', s' \rangle$ *is a total combinatory algebra.*

PROOF. In order to show $s' \odot a \odot b \odot c \sim a \odot c \odot (b \odot c)$, we compute

$$\begin{aligned} (s' \odot a \odot b \odot c)x &\simeq (ks \odot a \odot b \odot c)x, \\ &= s(s(s(ks)a)b)cx, \\ &\simeq s(ax)(bx)(cx), \\ &\simeq (ax)(cx)((bx)(cx)), \\ &\simeq (a \odot c)(b \odot c)x. \end{aligned}$$

Therefore the conclusion holds. In a more easy way it follows similarly that $i' \odot a \sim a$ and $k' \odot a \odot b \sim a$. □

At first I did believe the reasoning, and was a bit disappointed that I didn't find this result myself. The proposal was stated as Theorem 1.14 in Barendregt (1971a). Later I found a gap in the proof of the proposal. The culprit is again the combinator k, one doesn't have $k' \odot a \odot b \sim a$:

$$\begin{aligned} k' \odot a \odot b \cdot x &= s(s(sk)a)bx, \\ &\simeq k(ax)(bx), \\ &\not\simeq ax, \end{aligned}$$

because bx may be undefined. Liking to travel I went to Oxford to tell Scott about this. His reaction was: "Happy that I didn't publish this!"

Interestingly the construction $\mathcal{A}^\odot$ was also introduced in Jacopini (1974), but for a total combinatory algebra $\mathcal{A}$. In that case the construction works.

DEFINITION 3.20. Let $\mathcal{A}$ be a ca.

(i) The *interior* of $\mathcal{A}$, in notation $\mathcal{A}^o$ is the sub-algebra

$$\mathcal{A}^o = \{a \in \mathcal{A} \mid a = [\![P]\!] \text{ for some } P \in \mathrm{CL}^o\}.$$

(ii) $\mathcal{A}$ is *hard* or *minimal* if $\mathcal{A} = \mathcal{A}^o$.

(iii) $\mathcal{A}$ is called an ω-*model* if for all $f, g \in \mathcal{A}$ one has

$$[\forall z \in \mathcal{A}^o. fz = gz] \Rightarrow f = g.$$

If $\mathcal{A}$ is an ω-model, then $\mathcal{A}$ is extensional.

DEFINITION 3.21. Let $\mathcal{T}$ be a set of equations between CL-terms.

(i) $\mathcal{T}$ is called *consistent* if

$$\mathrm{CL} + \mathcal{T} \nvdash \mathbf{K} = \mathbf{S}.$$

(ii) Let $\mathcal{T}$ be a consistent set of equations between CL-terms. Then the CL-*term-model* of $\mathcal{T}$, in notation $\mathcal{M}_{\mathrm{CL}}(\mathcal{T})$ is $\mathrm{CL}/{=_\mathcal{T}}$.

Applying $\odot$ to $\mathcal{M}^o_{\mathrm{CL}}(\mathrm{CL} + \mathrm{ext})$ one obtains $\mathcal{M}(\mathrm{CL} + \mathrm{ext})^{\odot}$. Using this Jacopini got the false impression that $\mathcal{M}(\mathrm{CL} + \mathrm{ext})$ was an ω-model, so that the ω-rule does hold. But we will see this is not the case.

THEOREM 3.22. (i) [Jacopini] *Not every extensional model is an* ω-*model.*

(ii) $\mathcal{M}(\mathrm{CL} + \mathrm{ext})$ *is an extensional model that is not an* ω-*model.*

(iii) $\mathcal{M}^o(\mathrm{CL} + \mathrm{Ext})$ *is not extensional.*

(iv) [Plotkin] *The* ω-*rule is not valid in* $\mathrm{CL} + \mathrm{ext}$.

SKETCH. (i) In the addendum in Part I on p. 139 it is shown that one can take the open term model of $\mathrm{CL} + \mathrm{ext} + \{\Omega\mathbf{K}Z = \Omega\mathbf{S}Z \mid Z \in \mathrm{CL}^o\}$. This result follows also from (ii).

(ii) Follows from (iii).

(iii) Follows from (iv).

(iv) This is the classical result of Plotkin (1974), also presented in (Barendregt 1984, Theorem 17.3.30). Actually Plotkin proved this for the $\lambda\eta$-calculus. But this theory is fully equivalent with $\mathrm{CL} + \mathrm{ext}$. □

Embedding and collapsing pca's

In Section II 2.2 we have described how we failed to find another model of the λ-calculus by collapsing Kleene's first pca $\mathcal{K}$ to a total one. We still do not know whether this is possible.

It is, however, possible to embed some pca's into a total combinatory algebra, a so called completion. In Klop (1982), and Bethke et al. (1996) sufficient criteria are formulated[2] for a pca to be completable. Kleene's pca $\mathcal{K}$ does satisfy these. This completed

[2]One of these was first formulated in Chapter II.3: $sab = sa'b' \Rightarrow a = a' \;\&\; b = b'$.

pca would not have satisfied me in 1971, because the proof that the completion exists is rather syntactic and I wanted to construct a non-syntactic model.

In Bethke et al. (1999) a pca is constructed that is incompletable. Going in the other direction, in Bethke & Klop (1995) a pca is considered, that is extensional collapsable but still yielding a pca, of which the collapse is hard (built up from the set $\{k, s\}$, the authors called it 'minimal'), irreducible (aka final or simple), and incompletable.

4 After 1980

4.1 Types

In physics constants have a dimension, e.g. speed is measured in km/h. When we bike at $v = 12\text{km/h}$ and we do this for $t = 3\text{h}$, we have gone $vt = 12\text{km/h} \cdot 3\text{h} = 36\text{km}$. Dimensions prevent that we want to consider e.g. vt^2 to compute the distance. Similarly programming languages come with a type system helping to ensure correctness. A program expecting a number (: Int) should not receive a judgment (: Bool). Assigning to a module F a type A is denoted by F:A (read F in A). One starts typing the data, e.g. 3:Int, True:Bool.

Simple types for λ-calculus are built up from basic type variables $\alpha_0, \alpha_1, \cdots$, and/or type constants, like Int and Bool, and are closed under the operation $\rightarrow$ forming *function types*. There are two different styles of adding types to type-free terms.

Curry type assignment

The style of Curry, in which to each type-free $M \in \Lambda$ a class of types, possibly empty, is assigned. For example $I = \lambda x.x$ gets all types of the form $A \rightarrow A$. One denotes this by $\vdash \lambda x.x : (A \rightarrow A)$.

Simply typed λ-calculus

Now we present the official definition.

DEFINITION 4.1 (TYPES). Let $\mathbb{A}$ be a set (of atomic type symbols). The simple types generated by $\mathbb{A}$, in notation $\mathbb{T}_{\mathbb{A}}$ is the least set containing $\mathbb{A}$ that is closed under $\rightarrow$. That is $A, B \in \mathbb{T}_{\mathbb{A}} \Rightarrow (A \rightarrow B) \in \mathbb{T}_{\mathbb{A}}$.

For example if $\mathbb{A} = \{0\}$, then expressions like $0 \rightarrow 0$, $0 \rightarrow (0 \rightarrow 0)$ belong to $\mathbb{T}^{\mathbb{A}}$. The latter type will be denoted by $0 \to 0 \to 0$, association to the right[1]. If $\mathbb{A} = \{\mathsf{nat}, \mathsf{bool}\}$, then $\mathsf{nat} \to \mathsf{nat} \to \mathsf{bool}$ can represent the type of binary Boolean valued functions on nat, to be seen as binary predicates on nat.

DEFINITION 4.2. The assignment system $\lambda_\to$ over the set of type symbols $\mathbb{A}$, in notation $\lambda_\to^\mathbb{A}$, assigns to each λ-term a set of types, that is a subset of $\mathbb{T}^\mathbb{A}$ that is possibly empty, possibly consisting of one or more elements. The assignment depends on what types are assigned to the free variables in M.

NOTATION. *If* $\Gamma = \{x_1{:}A_1, \ldots, x_n{:}A_n\}$, *then* $\Gamma \vdash_{\lambda_\to} M : A$ *denotes that* $A \in \mathbb{T}^\mathbb{A}$ *is assigned to* M *in context* Γ. *The easy intuition is given by* $\Gamma \vdash_{\lambda_\to^\mathbb{A}} (xy) : B$ *if* $\Gamma = \{x : (A \to B), y : A\}$. *This is also written as (the dependency of* $\lambda_\to^\mathbb{A}$ *is taken for granted)*

$$x{:}(A \to B), y{:}A \vdash (xy) : B$$

DEFINITION 4.3. The type assignment system $\lambda_\to^\mathbb{A}$ is defined by the following rules.

$$\Gamma \vdash x : A, \text{ if } (x : A) \in \Gamma$$

$$\frac{\Gamma \vdash M : (A \to B) \quad \Gamma \vdash N : A}{\Gamma \vdash (MN) : B} \qquad \frac{\Gamma, x : A \vdash M : B}{\Gamma \vdash (\lambda x.M) : (A \to B)}$$

The following are easy examples of type assignments.

EXAMPLES 4.4.

$$\begin{aligned} &\vdash_{\lambda_\to^\mathbb{A}} \mathsf{I} &&: A \to A. \\ &\vdash_{\lambda_\to^\mathbb{A}} \mathsf{K} &&: A \to B \to A. \\ &\vdash_{\lambda_\to^\mathbb{A}} \mathsf{S} &&: (A \to B \to C) \to (A \to B) \to A \to C. \end{aligned}$$

This holds for all types A, B, C. A proof of the type assignments for S runs through

$$\begin{aligned} x{:}A \to B \to C, y{:}A \to B, z{:}A &\vdash xz : B \to C \\ x{:}A \to B \to C, y{:}A \to B, z{:}A &\vdash yz : B \\ x{:}A \to B \to C, y{:}A \to B, z{:}A &\vdash xz(yz) : C \\ x{:}A \to B \to C, y{:}A \to B &\vdash \lambda z.xz(yz) : A \to C \\ x{:}A \to B \to C &\vdash \lambda yz.xz(yz) : (A \to B) \to A \to C \\ &\vdash \lambda xyz.xz(yz) : (A \to B \to C) \to (A \to B) \to A \to C. \end{aligned}$$

When Curry, who invented $\lambda_\to^\mathbb{A}$, saw this example he remarked, see Curry & Feys (1958), "There is a striking resemblance between the types of the basic combinators I, K, S and some of the axioms of proposition calculus." This was one of the places where the Curry-Howard-De_Bruijn correspondence was born, see Wadler (2015) for its history.

[1]Conor McBride says as *pons asinorum* "The λ-terms like PQR are the workers and associate to the left: $PQR = (PQ)R$. The types are the ruling classes that do not work but manage the workers and they associate to the right: $A \to B \to C = A \to (B \to C)$."

EXAMPLES 4.5. Let $A = (((0 \to 0) \to 0) \to 0) \to 0 \to 0 \in \mathbb{T}^{\mathbb{A}}$ with $\mathbb{A} = \{0\}$. Then $\vdash \lambda\Phi x.\Phi(\lambda f.f(\Phi(\lambda g.g(fx)))) : A$. Type A is called the *monster type* in Barendregt et al. (2013), where all possible $\lambda_{\to}^{\mathbb{A}}$ inhabitants are listed and given a specific role.

If a term has a type, then self application like $\lambda x.xx$ is no longer possible. In fact all terms having a type are (strongly) normalizable.

THEOREM 4.6. *Suppose* $\Gamma \vdash_{\lambda_{\to}^{\mathbb{A}}} M : A$.

(i) *Then* $M \in \mathsf{SN} \subseteq \mathsf{WN}$ *i.e. every* β*-reduction sequence starting with* M *terminates. In particular* M *has a* β*-nf.*

(ii) *Suppose moreover* $M \twoheadrightarrow_\beta N$. *Then* $\Gamma \vdash_{\lambda_{\to}^{\mathbb{A}}} N : A$.

That every $M \in Ł$ typable in $\lambda_{\to}^{\mathbb{A}}$ is WN was proved by Turing (unpublished), see Gandy (1980) and Barendregt & Manzonetto (2013). Property (ii) above is called *'subject reduction'* in Curry & Feys (1958). It implies that if a functional program is correct at compile time, then it remains correct during computation (reduction).

Recursive types

The types in $\mathbb{T}^{\mathbb{A}}$ are freely generated from the atomic types: there are no identifications like $a \to b = a$. With recursive types there do exist such identifications. The best way to do this, suggested in Scott, is to consider type algebras: a collection of types $\mathcal{A}$ endowed with a binary operation $\to$ in which one may have $a \to b = a$ or $a \to b = b \to a$ etcetera. In this way one obtains a type assignment system $\lambda_{=}^{\mathcal{A}}$ defined by the same rules as in 4.11. The innocent looking change taking types from a type algebra is dramatic. No longer typable terms have a normal form.

EXAMPLES 4.7. Suppose $\mathcal{A}$ is a type structure such that $a = a \to b$ for some $a, b \in \mathcal{A}$. Then both self-application $\omega = \lambda x.xx$ and the unsolvable term $\Omega = \omega\omega$ have a type.

(i) $\vdash_{\lambda_{=}^{\mathcal{A}}} \omega : a$.

(ii) $\vdash_{\lambda_{=}^{\mathcal{A}}} \Omega : b$.

(iii) $\vdash_{\lambda_{=}^{\mathcal{A}}} \lambda x.\Omega : a$.

PROOF. We show (i)-(iii).

$$
\begin{array}{rll}
x{:}a \vdash & x : a, & \\
x{:}a \vdash & x : (a \to b), & \text{as } a = a \to b, \\
x{:}a \vdash & xx : b, & \\
\vdash & \lambda x.xx : (a \to b), & \\
\vdash & \omega : a, & \text{as } a = a \to b; \\
\vdash & \Omega = \omega\omega : b; & \\
\vdash & \lambda x.\Omega : a \to b = a. & \square
\end{array}
$$

There are sufficient conditions for a term $M \in \Lambda$ to be strongly normalizable in terms of typability in some $\lambda_{=}^{\mathcal{A}}$, see (Barendregt et al. 2013, Theorem 9.3.16).

Intersection types

Now the type algebras $\mathcal{A} = \langle \mathsf{A}, \to \rangle$ get extended to a meet semi-lattice, i.e. a partial order having greatest lower bounds.

DEFINITION 4.8. A *type structure* $\mathcal{S} = \langle \mathsf{A}, \to, \leq, \cap \rangle$. Given such an $\mathcal{S}$ one can define *intersection type assignment* as follows.

$$\Gamma \vdash x : A, \text{ if } (x : A) \in \Gamma$$

$$\frac{\Gamma \vdash M : (A \to B) \quad \Gamma \vdash N : A}{\Gamma \vdash (MN) : B} \qquad \frac{\Gamma, x : A \vdash M : B}{\Gamma \vdash (\lambda x.M) : (A \to B)}$$

$$\frac{\Gamma \vdash M : A \quad \Gamma \vdash M : B}{\Gamma \vdash M \in (A \cap B)} \qquad \frac{\Gamma \vdash M : A, \ A \leq B}{\Gamma \vdash M : B}$$

The resulting type assignment system is denoted by $\lambda_\cap^{\mathcal{S}}$.

In particular, since $A \cap B \leq A$ and $A \cap B \leq B$ one has

$$\frac{\Gamma \vdash M \in (A \cap B)}{\Gamma \vdash M \in A} \qquad \frac{\Gamma \vdash M \in (A \cap B)}{\Gamma \vdash M \in B}$$

DEFINITION 4.9. A *type structure with top* is of the form $\mathcal{S} = \langle \mathsf{A}, \to, \leq, \cap, \mathsf{U} \rangle$, with $a \leq \mathsf{U}$ for all $a \in \mathcal{S}$. Such structures may be denoted by $\mathcal{S}^{\mathsf{U}}$. Given such an $\mathcal{S}$ one can extend the intersection type assignment by adding

$$\frac{}{\Gamma \vdash M : \mathsf{U}}$$

This type assignment system is denoted by $\lambda_\cap^{\mathcal{S}^{\mathsf{U}}}$.

EXAMPLES 4.10. (i) $\vdash_{\lambda_\cap^{\mathcal{S}}} \omega : (A \cap (A \to B)) \to B$.
(ii) $\vdash_{\lambda_\cap^{\mathcal{S}^{\mathsf{U}}}} \lambda x.x\Omega : (\mathsf{U} \to A) \to A$.

For an $M \in \Lambda^o$ and appropriate type structures $\mathcal{S}$ the set

$$[\![M]\!] = \{A \in \mathcal{S} \mid \vdash M : A\}$$

is a filter. These filters can be applied to each other in a natural way, obtaining a *filter* λ*-model*. By choosing the right $\mathcal{S}$ one obtains λ-models that describe the various versions of e.g. Scott's $\mathcal{D}_\infty$ models and the equations valid in these, see (Barendregt et al. 2013, Section 16.3). Also terms that are SN (strongly normalizable), WN (having a normal form) and solvable can be characterized by intersection term assignment.

Church typed terms

In the style of Church the λ-terms get embellished before they can obtain types. In that case one has

$$\vdash \lambda x{:}A.x : (A \to A).$$

Church version of $\lambda_{\to}$

DEFINITION 4.11. The type assignment system $\lambda_{\to}^{\mathbb{A}}$ is defined by the following rules.

$$\Gamma \vdash x : A, \text{ if } (x : A) \in \Gamma$$

$$\frac{\Gamma \vdash M : (A \to B) \quad \Gamma \vdash N : A}{\Gamma \vdash (MN) : B} \qquad \frac{\Gamma, x : A \vdash M : B}{\Gamma \vdash (\lambda x{:}A.M) : (A \to B)}$$

As we see the difference is minimal. In the Church style each term has a unique type, whereas in the Curry style there are possibly more types for one term. Below we will encounter essential uses of the Church style of typing as a way to formalize proofs.

4.2 IT applications

Functional programming

Turing computability via machines forms a very simple model, akin shifting beads on an abacus, that is easy to mechanize. Lambda calculus computability, on the other hand, is *a priori* more powerful: algorithmic statements of arbitrary complexity can be made in a compact fashion. Therefore it is not obvious that λ-calculus can be executed by a machine. As Turing showed the equivalence of both models, also λ-calculus computations can be performed by a machine and also Turing Machine computations are powerful. Computability via Turing machines gave rise to Imperative Programming. Computability described via λ-calculus gave rise to Functional Programming. As imperative programs are more easy to run on hardware, this style of software became predominant.

Versions of λ-calculus using types improve applicability for functional programming. Early languages like Lisp McCarthy et al. (1962) are untyped a typed version (also unpure) is ML, see Milner et al. (1990). Using types an application Fa is only allowed if the types match, i.e. $F{:}A \to B$ and $a{:}A$. The functional programmer indicates the types of the data structures and basic functions and the machine performs type-inferencing at compile-time. This is a major help for combining software modules in a correct way: many bugs are caught as the result will be an untypable program.

Early implementations of λ-calculus started in the 1960s, see Lisp McCarthy et al. (1962) (although not a pure language, i.e. having also imperative features), Landin (1966), and Böhm (1966), and came of age in the 1980s, see Turner (1986) for language development and Peyton Jones & Salkild (1989) for implementation[2]. See Hughes (1989)

[2] At first graphs with sharing were used to represent λ-terms, Wadsworth (1971), in order to prevent duplication of work when in a β-reduction a term is duplicated. However, sometimes graph representation is making things more complex, e.g. when dealing with purely arithmetic expressions. A hybrid proposal was made in the so called G-machine, see Johnsson (1984, 1995), in which graphs are built depending on the type of a term and its subterms.

for an explanation of the pragmatic power of functional programming languages and Barendregt et al. (2013) for a short comparison of the two styles of programming, with a short indication of a rich new world of types.

Some functional programming languages, like Lisp, have an implementation that is called 'eager'. In order to evaluate FA, first A is evaluated to normal form. This works for languages corresponding to the λI-calculus. Other such languages are implemented in a 'lazy' way. In these an argument that may run forever can be discarded. This corresponds to the λK-calculus. One advantage of lazy languages is that there are a terms for infinite lists, like that of the primes

$$[2, 3, 5, 7, 11, \ldots] = [2, [3, [5, [7, [11, \mathrm{rest}]]]]],$$

similar to the construction of the universal generator in Section I 3.2, from which one can project (using K) to get the n-th element. This often provides a comfortable level of abstraction for programming.

Hardware description

Synchronous digital hardware components can mathematically be seen as functions of type

$$s \to i \to (s, o)$$

where s is the type of the values in the internal state, i the type of its input, and o the type of its output. The types s, i, o can be of arbitrary complexity, be it, that they have to be of first order. That is, values inhabiting these types must be representable by sequences of binary values, since values are sent over wires by electric pulses (high, low). This interpretation of hardware architectures makes functional languages well suitable to specify such architectures, as already observed around 1980, Sheeran (1984) and Arvind & Shen (1999). Besides, functional languages offer strong abstraction mechanisms to express parameterized architectures, such as higher order functions and polymorphic types. Because of the fast development of Von Neumann style processors the usage of functional languages remained limited to academic research. But that development came to a rather abrupt halt around 2005 Sutter (2005). From that moment computations were more frequently performed performed directly in parallel digital hardware, in particular on FPGAs. Consequently, hardware description became more common in practical developments and also compilers for hardware design are being developed that have a functional language as source language, see Baaij (2015) for an overview.

4.3 Proofs, formalization, and certification

A second important use of λ-calculus is in the field of certification of mathematics and its applications.

Informal proofs

The power of mathematics is described well by the Austrian writer Musil.

The force, precision, and certainty of this [mathematical] *thinking, unequalled in life, almost made him melancholic.*

Robert Musil: The man without qualities, Rohwolt 1930-1944.

Mathematics describes objects (notions) and properties that these objects may or may not have. One starts with primitive notions from which one defines more complex objects. The primitive notions come with axioms that state what properties the primitive notions enjoy. By means of definitions new concepts are introduced and by means of proofs new results are derived. This is the *axiomatic method*, as described by Aristotle.

The following is a stylized presentation of a mathematical result. In context Γ, consisting of primitive notions, axioms, and definitions, one has $A(\vec{x})$ for all $\vec{x}$. In symbols

$$\Gamma \vdash \forall\vec{x}.A(\vec{x}).$$

This means that in context Γ one can prove $\forall\vec{x}.A(\vec{x})$. In such a case there is an informal proof p of $\forall\vec{x}.A(\vec{x})$ from Γ. We indicate the role of p as follows

$$\Gamma \vdash_p \forall\vec{x}.A(\vec{x}). \tag{1}$$

Let us first see what Musil meant with the above quote.

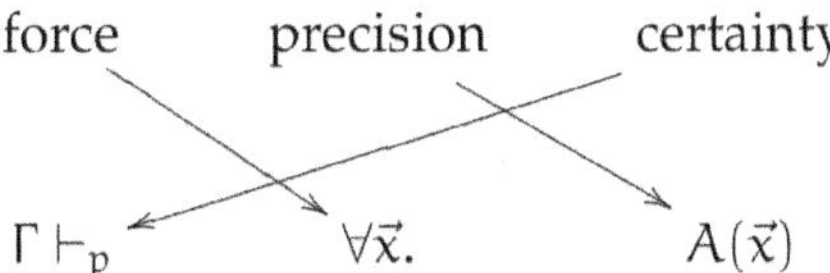

There is force: indeed, the statement holds for all (possibly infinitely many) $\vec{x}$. (Often the simplest way to prove something for a complex instance, like $A(\vec{a})$, is to show first the universal closure.) There is precision: $A(\vec{x})$ can be a quite intricate qualitative statement. There is certainty: this is because there is a proof p. This proof is an informal but precise and convincing reasoning (one speaks about 'informal rigor'), written in a paper or textbook.

Formal proofs

It is important to realize that not all mathematician can understand every informal proof. One could say that a proof p is *private evidence*, existing in the mind of some mathematicians. For most mathematicians there will exist proofs that cannot be followed by them. This is also the case for Fields medalists: they even may no longer understand their own proofs. Or worse, their own proofs may contain errors, as sometimes has happened. Therefore there is a need to formalize and certify proofs, see Voevodsky (2014).

Aristotle already remarked that it is possible to check whether a putative proof of $\Gamma \vdash A$ indeed is a proof[3]. Basically one just needs to follow whether each claim (step in the proof) is made according to logic or is one of the axioms.

The remark of Aristotle is expressed in the following result of Gödel's that (provided that the set of axioms Γ is finite or computably enumerable) there is a predicate $B_\Gamma(p, a)$ over $\mathbb{N}$ such that

$$\left.\begin{array}{l} B_\Gamma(p, 'A') \text{ for some } p \iff \Gamma \vdash A; \\ B_\Gamma \text{ is primitive recursive.} \end{array}\right\} \qquad \text{(C1)}$$

Here $'A'$ is a suitable coding of A and p is a coding of an informal proof, both as elements of $\mathbb{N}$. As B is primitive recursive (computable) it can be checked by machine whether A is provable from Γ. This is certification.

Another way to formalize and certify proofs is to design a formal system $\vdash'$, with formal expressions Γ' and A' representing Γ and A, and proofs p such that $p : A'$ is a well-formed formula in this language and moreover is such that

$$\left.\begin{array}{l} 1.\ \Gamma' \vdash' p : A' \text{ for some } p \iff \Gamma \vdash A; \\ 2.\ \Gamma \vdash' p : A \text{ is decidable.} \end{array}\right\} \qquad \text{(C2)}$$

Both C_1 and C_2 imply that it is possible to to certify in an automatized way provability. The informal proof of $\Gamma \vdash A$ should be given in enough detail. Then if p is encoded in the right way, a computer can check its validity. The p involved in C1 and C2 are called *proof-objects* of claim A. As there are just, say, a dozen rules of logic, a relatively simple program can verify whether $B(p, a)$ or $\Gamma \vdash' p : A$ holds. This is called the *De Bruijn* criterion for proof checking and the reason why there is a gain in certainty. We prefer method C2 over that of C1. For C1 one has to code proofs and statements, define B, prove the adequacy of B for the coding used, and show that B is (primitive) computable. For C2 one needs to define $\vdash'$, prove its adequacy with respect to $\vdash$, and show that it is decidable. Therefore C2 seems to entail less work than C1; also the task for C2 is more structured.

Formal proofs as annotated λ-terms

One possible way to construct formal proofs in the style C2 is by using forms of typed λ-calculus (with dependent and possibly higher-order types). We give an example how an

[3]Aristotle also remarked that if no proof is given of a putative theorem, then it is not always easily possible to verify whether it is valid indeed. This is made precise by Church and Turing who showed that it is undecidable in predicate logic whether $\Gamma \vdash A$. Church concluded this by showing that the undecidable question of having a normal form for $M \in \Lambda$ can be translated into a question of provability in predicate logic. Turing did the same using the undecidable halting problem. Grzegorczyk improved this by showing the undecidability of equational consequences within the theory CL not even containing logical operators. Therefore automated deduction (undecidable) and automated proof checking (decidable) are different, though related, endeavors.

easy result is being formalized in a what is essentially the pioneering system Automath for proof formalization and certification, de Bruijn (1970), Barendregt (1992). Automath was designed by De Bruijn inspired by the intuitionistic interpretation of implication: $A \to B$ is valid when one has a means to transform a proof of A into one of B. The proof rules of Automath contain the following.

$$\frac{\Gamma \vdash A : \mathrm{Set} \quad \Gamma \vdash B : \mathrm{Set}}{\Gamma \vdash (A \to B) : \mathrm{Set}} \qquad \frac{\Gamma \vdash A : \mathrm{Set} \quad \Gamma, x{:}A \vdash P : \mathrm{Prop}}{\Gamma \vdash (\forall x{:}A.P) : \mathrm{Prop}}$$

$$\frac{\Gamma, x{:}A \vdash M : P}{\Gamma \vdash (\lambda x{:}A.M) : (\forall x{:}A.P)} \qquad \frac{\Gamma \vdash M : (\forall x{:}A.P) \quad \Gamma \vdash a : A}{\Gamma \vdash Ma : P[x := a]}$$

PROPOSITION 4.12. *Let* A *be a set and let* R *be a binary predicate on* A. *If* R *is anti symmetric, then* R *is irreflexive.*

PROOF. 1. Informal. Assume that R is anti symmetric. That is $Rab \to Rba$ for all $a, b \in A$. We need to show $\neg Raa$ for all $a \in A$. Let $a \in A$. Suppose Raa towards a contradiction. By assumption one obtains $\neg Raa$. With Raa this yields a contradiction. Therefore $\neg Raa$. Since $a \in A$ was arbitrary one has $\neg Raa$ for all $a \in A$. Therefore R is irreflexive. □

PROOF. 2. Natural deduction. Write $\neg P \triangleq P \to \bot$, where $\bot$ is falsehood. We want to show the formal statement:

$$\big(\forall a, b \in A.(Rab \to \neg Rba)\big) \to \forall a \in A.\neg Raa.$$

The natural deduction proof is in between the informal and formal proof:

$$\cfrac{\cfrac{\cfrac{\cfrac{\cfrac{\cfrac{[\forall a, b \in A.(Rab \to \neg Rba)]^1}{Raa \to \neg Raa} \qquad [Raa]^2}{\neg Raa} \qquad [Raa]^2}{\bot}}{\neg Raa}\,[2]}{\forall a : A.\neg Raa}}{\big(\forall a, b \in A.(Rab \to \neg Rba)\big) \to \big(\forall a \in A.\neg Raa\big)}\,[1]$$

□

PROOF. 3. Automath.
Let $\Gamma = A : \mathrm{Set}, R : A \to A \to \mathrm{Prop}$. Then

$$\Gamma \vdash p : \big(\forall a, b \in A.(Rab \to \neg Rba)\big) \to \big(\forall a \in A.\neg Raa\big),$$

with (the reader is encouraged to check this proof using the Automath rules above) $p = \lambda q : \big(\forall a, b \in A.(Rab \to \neg Rba)\big)\lambda a : A\lambda r : (Raa).qaarr.$ □

This proof is a clear example of the formulas-as-types and proofs-as-terms correspondence, first remarked in Curry & Feys (1958) as a coincidence and later independently rediscovered by de Bruijn (1970) (written in 1968) and Howard (1980) (written in 1969). De Bruijn also emphasized that it is not sufficient to formalize results like this in the way that predicate logic captures proofs. An important part of mathematics consists of definitions that form a tower of abstraction upon abstraction. (This happens also in common language, where a common notion as 'Thursday' consists of layered abstractions.) There should be also a way to handle definitions. This is made possible by a reduction relation on expressions. For more on the Propositions-as-Types correspondence see also Nordström et al. (1990), de Groote (1995), Sørensen & Urzyczyn (2006), Nederpelt & Geuvers (2014), and Wadler (2015).

Certification

Constructing a formal p is complex in both cases. Therefore interactive *proof assistants* have been constructed that help the user formulate a context Γ and a 'goal' A in order to construct a formal proof p for A from Γ. The proof assistant also includes a proof checker that immediately checks whether the constructed p is a proof indeed.

Using proof objects the evidence for a mathematical result is no longer private, but *public*: the putative proof can be verified reliably by the proof-checking algorithm, that usually runs efficiently by the *De Bruijn criterion*.

4.4 Computations, programs, and certification

Computations versus proofs

It is important to certify not only propositions, but also computations. The reason will be given below. Before that, let us see what this means. If f is a function from e.g. $\mathbb{N}$ to itself, then we want to prove and certify statements of the kind

$$f(n) = m.$$

This can be done only if there is a notation F, a program, for this function in the language of the proof assistant and we can certify $F\underline{n} = \underline{f(n)}$, for numerals $\underline{k}$ corresponding to $k \in \mathbb{N}$ (like in λ-definability). But this is only half the story. The result m of this computation usually is needed to prove something and for this one must show that F satisfies a certain (partial) specification $S(F)$. Therefore we want to construct a term F satisfying

$$S(F) \;\&\; F\underline{n} = \underline{f(n)}.$$

This states that (1) F acts sufficiently like f (for our goals), and (2) the computation $f(n) = m$ is correctly performed.

Let us discuss now the reasons why we want to certify computations. We give examples.

1. Numerical results. For practical reasons one would like to know approximate values of the number π, and for philosophical reasons one would like to deduce these, rather than to measure them. Archimedes established in antiquity that

$$\frac{223}{71} < \pi < \frac{22}{7}.$$

2. Computations with algebraic entities like polynomials are needed for establishing results not referring to these. Consider for examples the theorem of Lagrange about natural numbers that every number is the sum of four squares:

$$\forall n \exists pqrs. n = p^2 + q^2 + r^2 + s^2.$$

This was reduced to the same property for the prime numbers, by realizing that

$$\begin{aligned}(a^2 + b^2 + c^2 + d^2)(A^2 + B^2 + C^2 + D^2) \quad = \quad & (aA + bB + cC + dD)^2 + \\ & (aB - bA + cD - dC)^2 + \\ & (aC - cA + dB - bD)^2 + \\ & (aD - dA + bC - cB)^2.\end{aligned}$$

In order to certify Lagrange's theorem, one needs to certify such polynomial equations as holding for all variables involved. This will be done in the next subsection.

3. The Four color Theorem (4CT) has been proved, formalized and certified by Gonthier, based on a proof by Robertson et al. (1996), by certifying

$$(\forall c.(H_{633}(c) \to Rc = 1)) \to S(R) \to 4CT.$$

This says that if all configurations (in a large collection of 633 elements with characteristic function H_{633}) are reducible, and if the characteristic function R that checks reducibility meets its specification S, then 4CT holds. In the original proof Robertson et al. (1996) of the 4CT it was checked that $\forall c.(H_{633}(c) \to Rc = 1)$, but not certified. In the fully certified proof Gonthier (2008) also the specification of R and implication towards 4CT was certified.

Certified programs are important, because they yield certified values (provided that the computational process is also certified) and moreover, they can help certify statements. On the other hand certified statements can help certify programs. Therefore the library of certified objects needs both statements and programs.

Certifying computations

Now that we have seen that it is useful to have certified computations, we will look for possibilities how to do this. Wlog let us assume that for a function $f\colon \mathbb{N} \to \mathbb{N}$ we want to certify $f(n) = m$. For this one needs to represent numbers $n \in \mathbb{N}$ as expressions $\underline{n}$ that can be handled by the proof-assistant. Moreover f needs to be represented as an expression F, for which a certain specification needs to be proved (as in example 4 above) in order to assure that something may be done with the result. Now we focus on the problem of certifying

$$F\underline{n} = \underline{m}.$$

In order to prove propositions beyond the generality of logic computations become essential.

Method 1. The Poincaré principle. One needs to express F in terms of a functional programming language that contains for example a recursor constant R for primitive recursion over $\mathbb{N}$ for which one postulates

$$\left.\begin{array}{rcl} Rab\underline{0} & = & a; \\ Rab\underline{n+1} & = & b(Rabn)n \end{array}\right\} \qquad (R)$$

The equality in R is interpreted as a conversion generated by a reduction. For this reduction no need for a formal verification is required, because of the simplicity of rule R. This is called the *Poincaré Principle* for R. In Poincaré (1909) it is stated that $2 + 2 = 4$ doesn't require a proof, but just a verification. This is because making the reduction steps of R is of similar complexity as applying logical steps like modus ponens. The PP puts some strain on the de Bruijn principle of having a simple proof-checker: now one needs to check that the conversions in R are performed well, and not only for the recursor but also for other forms of recursion over inductively defined types (of which R and $\mathbb{N}$ are a prime example), see Paulin-Mohring (1993). Ways to use this method are described in Barendregt & Barendsen (2002) and Barendregt (2013). The method often applies 'reflection', first described for certified statements in Howe (1992). For example a polynomial equation $p_1(\vec{x}) = p_2(\vec{x})$, and its validity for all $\vec{x}$ in the relevant domain, can be proved by distinguishing between a polynomial function p and its notation 'p', showing that $\forall\vec{x}.\text{eval}_{\vec{x}}\text{'}p\text{'} = p$ because $\text{eval}_{\vec{x}}\text{'}p\text{'}$ reduces to p, and constructing a term `simplify` such that `simplify'p1'=simplify'p2'`. In a similar way one can prove formally in an automated way that functions defined by expressions like

$$f(x) = e^{\sin^2 x + \cos 3x}$$

are continuous because of the way they are represented.

Method 2. Ephemeral proof-objects. This method doesn't put a burden on the de Bruijn principle, by in principle producing extremely long proof-objects, involving an annotated computation chain. These annotations provide the official justification and in fact certification that the made steps are provably correct. In order to keep the proof-object manageable the part of them securing the validity of the computation will not be stored. One can imagine that this part is written in sand and immediately verified, after which the sea comes and erases such a long proof. As an example we can imagine that a proof of an algebraic equality like $(x+1)(x-1) = x^2 - 1$ is treated as follows.

$$
\begin{array}{rcll}
(x+1)(x-1) & = & x(x-1) + 1(x-1), & \text{by the distributive law,} \\
& = & (x \cdot x + x \cdot -1) + (1 \cdot x + 1 \cdot (-1)), & \text{by the distributive law,} \\
& = & (x^2 - x) + (x - 1), & \text{as } \forall x.[1 \cdot x = x \ \&\ x \cdot -1 = -x] \\
& = & x^2 + ((-x) + (x - 1)), & \text{by the associative law,} \\
& = & x^2 + ((-x + x) - 1), & \text{by the distributive law,} \\
& = & x^2 + (0 - 1), & \text{since } -x + x = 0, \\
& = & x^2 - 1, & \text{since } \forall y.0 + y = y.
\end{array}
$$

We have not even bothered stating that $=$ is a congruence with respect to $+$ and $\cdot$. For the proof-checker Hol and derivates one generates proofs like these, that are however not stored. Hence the name *ephemeral proof-objects*.

4.5 Applications of certification

One can apply proof-checking to verify claims in both mathematics and computer science. This gives rise to a new style of working in these two subjects, reaching a novel style of precision and level of certification.

Applications in Computer Science and Technology

In computer science and Information and Communication Technology there is a strong need to produce reliable components. Intel had sold a faulty chip in the 1990-s and had to set aside 480M$ for claims. One of the reasons that the construction of hardware and software is complex, is that there are many cases to be considered that are not always remembered easily. Already about forty years ago the methodology of 'Formal Methods' was proposed. It consists of specifying what a product (hardware or software) should do, making a design, and proving that the design satisfies the specification. One may wonder how a concrete products can be proved to satisfy desired behavior. This seems outside the reach of mathematics. Although this is the case, quality control can be essentially increased by a method in which mathematical proofs play an essential role. One develops a language for designs and one for specifications. These should be such that the path from design to realization is short and reliable and similarly from (desired) behavior to (formal) specification. That a formal design meets a formal specification now becomes subject to mathematical proof. This enables the manufacturer to issue a warranty for the product. This is explained in the rationality square in figure 4.1, Wupper (2000), a way to clarify the method.

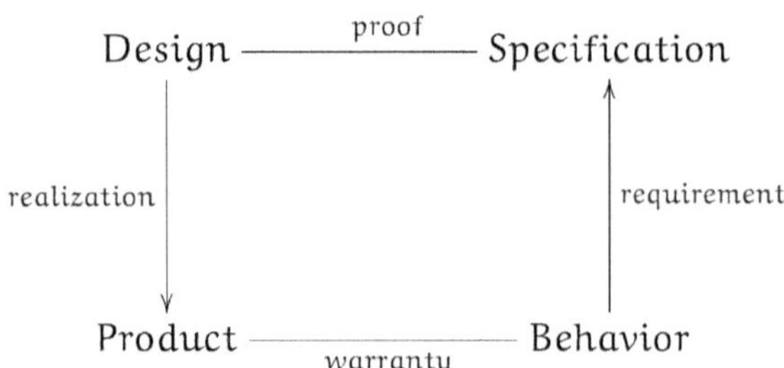

Figure 4.1: Rationality square

At first formal methods had only a modest impact, because the necessary proofs are of the same or even higher complexity than that of the components themselves. But the situation changed dramatically after certification using proof assistants came of age. Even then the method is often restricted to partial specifications, as a full one is difficult, expensive, and not always necessary.

The method of certification has been used in computer science and technology in different areas: theory and the construction of hardware and software. Theoretical results and their proofs can be certified as in mathematics. Hardware, operating systems, compilers, and other software can be specified and certified.

We mention a few impressive cases.

- The ARM6 processor—predecessor of the ARM7 embedded in the large majority of mobile phones, personal organizers and MP3 players—was certified by mentioned method, Fox (2003).
- The seL4 operating system has been fully specified and certified, Klein et al. (2009).
- The same holds for a realistic kernel of an optimizing compiler for the C programming language, Leroy (2009).
- In Dutle et al. (2020) the Compact Position Reporting algorithm, that enables an aircraft to share its position and velocity with other aircraft in its vicinity, has been secured, after correcting some errors in an earlier version.

The last two items show that rather than writing a program and developing a proof of correctness afterwards, it is possible to write proofs from which secured programs can be obtained.

Applications in mathematics

In the 1970s, when the principal pioneer of proof-checking[4], the established mathematician N. G. de Bruijn, proposed certification of proofs, mathematicians reacted in a luke-

[4]To our knowledge the first mention of formalizing proofs in order to verify these by computer is in McCarthy (1962). In that same paper it is proposed to include software for symbolic computation. Proofs

warm to cold manner: "We know how to construct correct proofs," was their reaction. Besides this there must have been another reason for their reaction: a proof verified by a machine doesn't feel as real[5] as one that is in the mind of a human. Another reason for the reaction to proof-checking is that formalizing proofs, even with state-of-the-art proof-assistants has a steep learning curve.

Only after the boost of proof assistants for the certification of results in Computer Science and ICT some mathematicians became interested in the method. These have produced by a tour-de-force some impressive formalizations. We mention the following impressive examples of what has been certified within mathematics.

- The four color theorem, Gonthier (2008), in the proof assistant Coq for the calculus of inductive constructions, which is essentially an extension of the Automath system with higher order types Coquand & Huet (1985), and inductive types Coquand & Paulin (1990).
- The prime number theorem, with elementary proof by Selberg in the proof assistant Isabelle based on higher order logic, Avigad et al. (2007), and with an analytical proof in the style of of Hadamard and de la Vallée Poussin in HOL-light also based on higher order logic, Harrison (2009).
- The Odd Order Theorem stating that every finite group of odd order is solvable, Gonthier et al. (2013), in the proof assistant Coq.
- Proof of the Kepler conjecture in a combination of the HOL-light and Isabelle proof assistants, Hales et al. (2017).
- Essentially complete certification in Isabelle/HOL, Immler (2018), of the computations in Tucker (2002), using a solver for ordinary differential equations, to show that the attractor described in Lorenz (1963) indeed describes deterministic chaos.

QED

As we have seen there are impressive case studies applying the art of formal proof-development and certification. By the possibility of formalization followed by machine certification using a simple, reliable, and efficient program, the founders of the subject had and inspired to have a dream that is very probably realistic. This dream is

were formalized in the style of Hilbert, as sequences of statements that are either an axiom or follow by a logical rule from one or more previous sentences. It was mentioned that one could have formalized proofs following natural deduction proofs, but McCarthy didn't follow this up.

[5] A proof in the mind of a human may be called a 'romantic proof', a notion taken from Barendregt & Wiedijk (2005), one that is verified by computer as a 'cool' proof (even if the proof-checking algorithm has been verified in the romantic way). The situation is comparable with biology: there is the romantic biologist that goes out to catch butterflies in a net and identifies plants and flowers; then there is the cool biologist that looks at cells, or even at the molecular codes of genetic information. Of course, both types of doing biology are valid and they can reinforce each other. The same is true for romantic and cool proofs.

sometimes called "The QED project" with as result "Computer Mathematics" (CM). The name 'QED' has been coined in a manifesto to go for the certification of mathematics, with as aim to help users study, develop, and apply the subject. See for example the QED Manifesto Gödel (1994), and modern versions Ringer et al. (2019) and project Xena (2020). CM is based on the idea to represent arbitrary mathematical objects, operations, and theorems on a computer. Not just natural numbers, with their arithmetical operations like on an abacus. Not just rational numbers, in decimal approximations, with their arithmetical operations like on a simple calculator. Not just real numbers, in decimal approximations, with their algebraic and transcendental operations like on a scientific calculator. Not just 'computable' objects with their numerical and symbolic operations, like in Computer Algebra systems like Mathematica (for real and complex analysis and much more) or Magma (for number theory, abstract algebra, and much more). Computer Mathematics aims to represent arbitrary mathematical objects, finite or infinite, their operations, computable or not, and their properties, decidable or not. These notions, operations, and properties are simply represented by mathematical symbols, just like in a book, and only if something is known about these, they can be manipulated.

In order to have a mature system for CM one needs the following.

1. A formalism for statements and proofs. It is preferably close to what is used by the working mathematician.

2. A proof-assistant, including a proof-checker. This helps the user to formulate results and develop a certified proof. Flexible automation: not just present in the proof-assistant, but extendable by the user.

3. A library of certified theorems and algorithms, including a searchable catalog.

Computer Mathematics is an interesting research topic. On all these items there is active research and development.

As to 1. Although substantial results have been certified in the systems Hol and Coq, there are parts of mathematics in need for new formal systems. In Voevodsky (2014) a plea is made for a new system for formalizations: Homotopy Type Theory, that enjoys active research, see The Univalent Foundations Program (2013).

As to 2. The feasible dream of CM went through the mind of many pioneers of proof-checking. Essentially the first one was formulated in the Automath project, see de Bruijn (1970) and the Automath Archive (2012) for a documentation, with a formulation of a language designed for proofs and an accompanying mathematical assistant, consisting of a proof checker but not yet a proof development system.

Before Automath there was the proposal in McCarthy (1962) to have the human sketch the creative part of a proof and have a machine fill in the more standard details and check the result. In this paper also the importance of symbolic computing was emphasized. This idea went into the direction of Automated Theorem Proving (ATP), see the webpage ACL2 (2020), whereas Automath has led to Interactive Theorem Proving (ITP). A mature system for CM will have both aspects. ATP is only possible if the human gives hints to the machine what are intermediate steps, and ITP only becomes feasible if some automated procedures are available to assist the user. The ease to use ITP, is enhanced by Automated Deduction including Machine Learning techniques, see Blanchette, J. C. and Kaliszyk, C. and Paulson, L. C. and Urban, J. (2016) and Kaliszyk, C. and Urban, J. (2014). A milestone that has not been reached yet is that formalizing a known proof into a proof assistant takes a comparable effort as writing down an informal version in LaTeX. This will help the development of CM and its use by the working mathematician.

As to 3. Grown up systems for computer mathematics have not yet been developed, in spite of the fact that the idea is around for about half a century.

At this moment in time, 2020, there are several formal systems with corresponding proof assistants able to help users to formalize and certify non-trivial industrial products and mathematical theorems. We have not mentioned these systematically[6]. To get a feel how some of the systems can be used see Wiedijk (2006); for recent surveys see Ringer et al. (2019), focusing on ICT applications, and Blanchette & Mahboubi (2021), focusing on mathematics and computer science. An interesting project is Logipedia (n.d.), which among other things aims at translating results from one proof assistant into another one, logical power permitting.

It is not clear which mathematical assistants will develop into a full grown system for CM with an extensive library, such that the working mathematician can use it to develop ideas.

Conclusion

For surveys of CM see Blanchette & Mahboubi (2021), focusing on mathematics and computer science, and Ringer et al. (2019), focusing on ICT applications. When formalizing becomes standard practice, as is expected by the believers of CM, it will become a good way of storing (Barendregt & Cohen (2001)), teaching, studying, developing, and applying mathematics. A referee only needs to verify whether the notions are properly formalized, and whether the result is interesting. Even if CM will not become standard practice, certification will remain to be an interesting enterprise for safety critical applications. Because of the substantial applications of CM in ICT, the side remark of Musil, *"unequalled in life"* in the citation at the beginning of Section 4.3 doesn't hold any longer, but the main part of his description of mathematics is as valid as ever.

[6]We should mention at least the following systems. Mizar based on set theory, Isar like Isabelle with some features of Mizar, MetaPRL based on extensional type theory, Agda based on intuitionistic type theory of Martin-Löf, Per (1998), Lean based on the calculus of inductive constructions. The theoretical basis for several of these systems reflects closely the possible views one may have on the foundations of mathematics, Barendregt (2013).

4.6 Illative Combinatory Logic

As stated in Section 1.1 λ-calculus and Combinatory Logic were conceived with the intention to provide a basis for reasoning and computing. The first attempts didn't work out as shown in Section 1.3. In Curry (1941) it is stated and proved neatly that combinatory completeness and deductive completeness (the deduction theorem) are incompatible.

After this Curry and his students started a program to carefully develop theories named *illative*[7] *systems* towards a consistent foundation for mathematics based on combinatory logic, in which one can derive both logic and computability results. Full comprehension in naive set theory, claiming the existence of a set $X = \{x \mid P(x)\}$, leads to the Russell paradox. It was restricted in Zermelo Fraenkel set theory by requiring only the existence of

$$X = \{x \in A \mid P(x)\},$$

where A is an already given set. In a similar way deductive completeness was restricted in various attempts, Curry et al. (1972). In a collaboration with Curry's former PhD student Bunder consistent forms of ICL have been formulated in which predicate logic can be interpreted into some extended λ-calculus, parameterized by a combinator, Barendregt et al. (1993), Dekkers et al. (1998,a). This combinator can be chosen in such a way that the Curry-Howard-De_Bruijn interpretation is obtained, while another choice yields an interpretation in which proofs do not constitute a first class citizen. Although this work is a step in the direction of the original aim of Church and Curry to provide a foundation for mathematics based on a theory with functions as first class citizens, it is not clear whether these forms of Illative Combinatory Logic can be used in an efficient and scalable way to formalize mathematics. An open problem is for example whether higher order logic can be captured consistently by the systems in above references.

[7] From 'inferre' Latin for 'to infer'.

Part III

The making of a PhD

1

Preparation

The Netherlands

After obtaining a Master's in mathematics at Utrecht University under supervision of Dirk van Dalen in December 1968, I started working towards a PhD. That was beginning 1969, and I joined a working group consisting of van Dalen and his Amsterdam colleagues Dick de Jongh and Anne Troelstra. We studied the PhD thesis of Goodman (1968). In this work λ-terms and combinators were used and they quickly raised my interest.

During my undergraduate studies in 1966 Dirk van Dalen returned from a sabbatical year spent at MIT and brought back dittoed[1] chapters of the still unpublished book Rogers Jr (1967) on computability theory. His lectures on this topic I loved. A principal operator in this theory is the essentially partial function of two variables $\varphi_x(y)$ denoting the result of the unary partial computable function with code $x \in \mathbb{N}$ applied to $y \in \mathbb{N}$. (Kleene's notation for this function is $\{x\}(y)$.)

As remarked in Chapter II 1 my motivation was to clarify how results in λ-calculus could be interpreted in the theory of computable functions, as was done by Kleene, obtaining e.g. the S^m_n-theorem and the recursion theorem. Above, in Part II the approach was sketched: adding, like Wagner (1969) and Strong (1968) a $*$ for undefined and finding numbers $i, k, s \in \mathbb{N}$ behaving as the basic combinators. I could prove that under a natural coding (that takes into account the notion length of computation) the interpretation of a CL term without a normal form becomes $*$. Therefore I announced in our working group the consistency of the combinatory theory

$$\mathrm{CL}_\perp = \mathrm{CL} + \{P = Q \mid P, Q \text{ have no normal form}\}.$$

As explained in Section II 2.3 this turned out to be false. The next week I had to report

[1]A Ditto machine is a commercial version of a *spirit duplicator* used from its invention in 1923 until the 1970's (when photocopying became widely available).

in the working group that $CL_\perp$ was not consistent after all. Then Troelstra said with a flash: "But then your model is incorrect." Touché.

In the meantime Dana Scott had discovered in November 1969 the lattice theoretic models $\mathcal{D}_\infty$. Some notes, in his beautiful handwriting, were circulating with the non-trivial construction. It explained the semantics of the binding λx operation in a way similar to the interpretation of a quantifier $\forall x$ This, however, didn't settle my quest of finding an interpretation of combinators to obtain Kleene's basic results in computability theory. In Scott's notes there was also a reference to work of Corrado Böhm who seemed to have proved that if $M, N \in \Lambda^o$ have different $\beta\eta$-normal forms, then the equation $M = N$ is inconsistent. In that case there exists an $F \in \Lambda^o$ separating M and N, i.e.

$$\begin{aligned} FM &= \text{true} &= \lambda xy.x; \\ FN &= \text{false} &= \lambda xy, y. \end{aligned}$$

This did interest me. Trying to find Böhm's paper, it turned out that it was only available from the library of the Mathematical Center in Amsterdam[2]. Finally, after getting access to the paper, it turned out a disappointment: the paper was written in Italian and in a style that made it impossible for me to understand it. I decided to drive to Rome, where Böhm was working, to look him up and ask some explanations.

In Section II 2.6 it is explained how I came to consider the ω-rule. Having met Curry, who was a professor at Amsterdam University, and Hindley who was visiting there, I learned that the ω-rule was uncharted territory.

Italy

The following summer of 1970 I drove in my Renault 4 to Italy, in order to meet Böhm and ask him the following two questions. 1. How is his separability theorem proved? 2. Does the ω-rule hold, or is it at least consistent?

Arrived in Rome, finding Böhm was not so easy. First I went to the Istituto Nazionale per le Applicazioni del Calcolo, where his paper had appeared. There they understood I was interested in a proof and were so kind to provide me with Böhm's private address. I couldn't find it on a detailed map of Rome that I had bought, in spite of the fact that at the INAC one had indicated in which part of town it was located. At a police station in the right neighborhood the officer could explain why I couldn't find the address: it was located in a private street. Such phenomena were non-existent in the Netherlands. Finally arrived at the right address Böhm wasn't at home. The concierge told me he was on holidays in the Dolomites in northern Italy. He was so kind to call Böhm and handed the phone to me. Böhm was pleased someone took an interest in his theorem. As we couldn't meet, he suggested that I would call his colleague Wolf Gross.

The next day Gross invited me for a cappuccino to the stylish[3] Antico Caffè Greco, near the Spanish stairs. He suggested to try proving the consistency of equating any

[2]Although the internet was created in 1969, it only had four nodes, all in the USA.

[3]"Be careful not to break your cup, they will charge you 10.000 Lire for it," Gross warned.

two ogres[4]. From this it would follow that there are non-trivial models outside the class of Scott's lattice theoretic models $\mathcal{D}_\infty$, since two different elements in the original $\mathcal{D}$ are mapped onto different ogres in $\mathcal{D}_\infty$. (If there are no different elements in $\mathcal{D}$, then also $\mathcal{D}_\infty$ is trivial.) As mentioned in Remark I 3.2.17 this motivated me to prove that unsolvables could be equated consistently, Theorem I 3.2.15.

Gross also had invited Giuseppe Jacopini to come a bit later to Caffè Greco. When he arrived we discussed that the rule of extensionality in Rosenbloom (1950) was misstated as the ω-rule. From claims in this work it would follow that the ω-rule is equivalent with the rule of extensionality. The proof in that book must however be defective (because of Plotkin's counterexample found in 1973). Later Jacopini (1974) (written before Plotkin (1974)) would also make an incorrect claim that the ω-rule follows from extensionality. In the meantime I was motivated to continue work on the ω-rule and managed to prove its consistency by a transfinite induction over ordinals assigned to prooftrees, and partial validity for terms that are not universal generators. Together with the work on (un)solvable terms this did earn me a PhD.

USA

After having obtained a PhD in June 1971, I got a grant for a Postdoc position at Stanford university and went to California. The first city to visit in the USA was Pittsburgh in order to meet Haskell Curry on September 12, that happened to be his seventy first birthday. As a present I offered him a combinator X, found during the previous summer, such that from this term both K and S could be defined. I believe it was $\mathsf{X} = \lambda z.z\mathsf{SK}$; then $\mathsf{X}(\mathsf{X}(\mathsf{XX})) = \mathsf{K}$ and $\mathsf{XK} = \mathsf{S}$. It follows that $\{\mathsf{X}\}$ is a singleton basis[5] for the combinators. After Pittsburgh I visited Buffalo, invited by Dick de Jongh. There I gave a talk on my thesis, with as title 'News in Combinatory Logic'. In the audience there was Nicholas Goodman. Before the talk had started a Catholic nun came up to me saying "I do not come for the logical part, but for the combinatorial part," a remark that triggered my curiosity. Later I learned it was Sister Celine Fasenmeyer, who, next to her religious engagement, succeeded to prove interesting results in combinatorial[6] mathematics. Later in September, settled at Stanford, I met for the first time Corrado Böhm, who was visiting Donald Knuth[7]. Then he did explain to me the proof of his separability theorem. For the intuition of that result see (Barendregt 2020, Section 4).

[4]A term P is an *ogre* if for all Q one has $\mathsf{PQ} = \mathsf{P}$. An ogre is called a 'fixed point' in Part I and 'special fixed point' in Chapter II 2, names that are a bit confusing.

[5]Later Rosser simplified this construction into $\mathsf{R} = \lambda z.z\mathsf{KSK}$. Then $\mathsf{RRR} = \mathsf{K}$ and $\mathsf{RK} = \mathsf{S}$.

[6]Unfortunately for Sister Céline combinatorial mathematics is very different from combinatory logic, so she may have been disappointed; Nicholas Goodman, though, did appreciate the talk.

[7]Böhm showed to Knuth the evidence that in his published PhD thesis Böhm (1954) he constructed the first programming language L with a compiler for L to machine language *in the language* L *itself*. See Barendregt (2020).

2

The Teacher & the student

The story that follows speaks for itself, but I make some additions.

1. Back in 1971 the λ-calculus was not yet an established theory. My official supervisor Georg Kreisel often had made a point to be interested in neglected areas in logic and mathematics and asked me why I was intrigued by the λ-calculus. Me: "Well, the theory can be described in a simple way. All partial computable functions can be represented in it. Then there is the fixed point theorem." Kreisel objected: "There may be many more 'interesting' results, but a century ago one studied a particular kind of groups, the hemi-demi-semi groups. One found some results about these. Then more and more followed. Finally there was a result implying all the previous ones: there is only one hemi-demi-semi group, namely the trivial one $\{e\}$!" I suspected that the story was made up by Kreisel. But anyhow it made me pay particular attention to consistency questions.

2. Just after having arrived in Stanford in September 1971, Corrado Böhm, called me and proposed to meet. The next day I invited him and Kreisel—both born in 1923—for dinner. The mood was pleasant, notably when Böhm told Kreisel that at the ETH in Zürich one of the supervisors of his PhD (1951) had been Paul Bernays, one of the few persons who Kreisel admired.

Kreisel: "Ah, when was that?"

Böhm: "O, that was a long time ago."

Kreisel, with a flash of elegance: "Yes I know, we are old."

3. After the main text had gone to the printer I thought to be done with my thesis. But Kreisel kept me busy by requiring me to work on an extra Part II to be given as handout to the exam committee for the PhD. Its contents have been published later as Barendregt (1975) and are included in this republication as Chapter II.3. The handout also contained the addenda on pages 139-144 in Part I containing: (i) a result of Jacopini about the ω-rule (not affecting my results on this rule); (ii) a sketch of the proof of Rosser of the confluence of (the I-version of) CL; and (iii) a correction.

The following text Barendregt (1996) appeared in the book "Kreiseliana, about and around Georg Kreisel," edited by Piergiorgio Odifreddi, and published by A. K. Peters, dedicated to the seventieth birthday of Georg Kreisel. A request to obtain the rights to republish it here has been made.

Kreisel, lambda calculus, a windmill and a castle

Henk Barendregt

Faculty of Mathematics and Computer Science
Catholic University Nijmegen
and
Department of Software Technology
CWI, Amsterdam

To GK

This paper gives some idea of the role that Kreisel played at the start of my scientific career. The facts are taken mainly from the period starting spring 1971 (when I worked on my Ph.D. thesis) until summer 1972 (when I ended a stay at Stanford as a postdoc).

1. The setting

At Utrecht University in the late sixties I studied logic under reader Dirk van Dalen. In those days readers in the Netherlands did not have the *ius promovendi*, i.e. were not allowed to be official Ph.D. supervisors. Kreisel had accepted to spend a spring semester at Utrecht and van Dalen asked whether he was willing to be my Ph.D. supervisor. For this I had to send a description of my work to Kreisel and in a few days the answer was there. The 'master' found my work "congenial" and it could be the basis for discussions leading towards a thesis. Kreisel was supposed to be difficult, so I had heard. Actually this inspired me, while I prepared the manuscript before his coming to Utrecht in 1971.

When Kreisel arrived in the Netherlands, I had borrowed my fathers car (a Renault 16), because mine (a Renault 4) was total-loss due to an accident, and I picked him up from the airport. Kreisel was pleased by this reception 'in style' and for a moment he forgot to be difficult. When we stopped for gas, however, he started to ask sharp questions that were meant to frighten me. Since I did not have a high opinion about myself (I did not have a low one either), it did not matter to me that I could not answer all of his questions. The fact that I was unconditioned by his interrogation mellowed him down and in high spirits we arrived at Utrecht University.

It was well-known that Kreisel always requests a quiet place to sleep. After some effort Mrs. Dook van Dalen had found a candidate place in Bilthoven, a fancy village near Utrecht. But one never knows if it is really adequate. Therefore I showed Kreisel a picture of my home—a windmill in the countryside along the Waal river, the main branch of the Rhine—and offered him to stay there in case he wanted.

After the obligatory inspection of the house in Bilthoven, Kreisel decided to stay in the windmill. This brought Mrs. van Dalen in an awkward situation. The owner of the house had been asked to provide a quiet room for Kreisel. Being sensitive to who was to come into her house, the landlady had emptied her own bedroom on the garden side for the use of the famous professor. From the cool reaction of Mrs. van Dalen about Kreisels decision to stay in the windmill one could deduce the fury of the old lady when her kind offer was declined.

The windmill was situated 45 minutes by car from the University, a relatively long distance in the Netherlands. Arrived there, Kreisel told me that the next day he was invited by a baroness for tea at her castle and asked me to join him. "Of course one of the reasons to ask you is that you can help to drive me there," was his frank admission. By a remarkable coincidence the castle was only 2 kilometer upstream from the windmill. I knew the place, but had no idea who lived there.

Against my expectations the baroness was a young woman, good-looking with two small children. After being introduced to her I felt a bit uneasy about the angle in which she shook hands. Was I supposed to give a handkiss?[1] The baroness was British and lived with her husband in London. Often during weekends the baroness and her children would come to their Dutch castle, while the lord remained in London. In the 15th century ancestors of the baron had been victors of a small battle in the Netherlands. Because of this historical fact his lineage was proclaimed to be 'Baron van Ophemert en Zennewijnen' since that time.

During tea Kreisel invited the lady to come to his first lecture in Utrecht, the following week. She accepted. "It is better for you to leave the lecture-hall after twenty minutes, because then I will start to be rather technical," was Kreisels advice.

On the morning of the day of the first lecture I dropped Kreisel at the castle. He and the baroness were going to have lunch in Utrecht and would come together to the University. At 2:00 p.m. the logicians in the Netherlands were eagerly waiting. At 2:15 Kreisel was still not there. I gave them some details. Nobody yet at 2:30. Finally at 2:40 a taxi entered the parking place of the department,

[1] The next day I borrowed a book on etiquette from a girl-friend in Utrecht. My question was not answered, though.

directly followed by a car with a British license plate. Kreisel came out of the British car and paid the taxi and the baroness parked her car. This scene could be followed by all Dutch logicians from the lecture-hall on the sixth floor of the building. Troelstra remarked that Kreisel was still wearing the same trousers as in Stanford.[2] When at last the lecture started at 2:50, it went as follows. "Logic is the science of deduction. How we can derive from a statement A another statement B. ... " This went on for twenty minutes. When the baroness left—as foreseen—she had to pass a door next to the blackboard in front of the audience. Shyly she opened the door. Kreisel, however, was fully at ease. With an elegant bow he paid his respects to the lady. At 3:10 the real lecture started. It was on Rosser sentences, brilliant and full of firework. I could not follow it.[3]

A few days later Kreisel and I were invited by the baroness for dinner at her castle. Impressive stairs went down to a cellar with burning torches on the walls. Some of the dishes were exotic. During the dessert Kreisel showed a side of his, that was new to me. One of the children started to whine about the pudding. "Ma, I do not want the raisins in it; ma, I want you to take them out. ..." It went on and on. Then Kreisel spoke very slowly to the little one, a boy about six years old: "Listen. What do you think is worse: your mother does not want to take the raisins out; or, your mother is not able to take them out." The little boy had to think for a while. "It is worse, if she does not want to take them out," was the answer. "Well," Kreisel continued, "it is simply the case that she is not able to take them out!" The boy could do nothing else but eat his pudding.

Kreisel and I often visited the castle. Since then the baron also came more frequently to the Netherlands. I was impressed by Kreisels explanations to the lord and his wife on the research I was doing in combinatory logic: "When we reason, we make steps, deductive steps. These can be smaller or larger steps. Barendregt studies the smallest possible such steps—the so-called atomic steps—and the way they can be combined to form larger ones." The high-born couple understood this, and at the same time I learned to be more flexible when expressing myself.

Also in other places of the world Kreisel introduced me to his 'upper-class' friends. The definition of this predicate varied from country to country. Sometimes they were aristocratic refugees from pre-war Europe, sometimes highly successful leaders of industry; but also there were high party members of some—then—powerful political party.

---

[2] Troelstra had been a visitor at Stanford a few years before.

[3] Later I mentioned this to Kreisel, telling him at the same time that in private conversations I could understand perfectly well his technical remarks. Also I said that I could not understand many of his writings. "Oh, but Gödel can, and Bernays can," was his reaction.

2. The work

In the early 1970s the λ-calculus was considered to be a fringe area of logic. This in spite of the breakthrough by Dana Scott, who constructed in November 1969 the first set-theoretic model D_∞ of the λ-calculus. Kreisel, who makes a point of being interested in neglected areas of research, showed some genuine interest in the subject. This was very encouraging to me. I will discuss two main themes of my thesis (the ω-rule and (un)solvability) and their later developments.

The ω-rule

For my thesis, Barendregt [1971, 1971a], I wanted to construct a recursion theoretic model of the type-free λK-calculus.[4] Even today I have never been able to complete the construction. But the attempts proved fruitful. One of the candidate models was extensional and a hard one, i.e. generated by the closed terms. This implied the consistency of the following ω-rule.

$$FZ = GZ, \text{ for all closed terms } Z \quad \Rightarrow \quad F = G. \tag{1}$$

Since the model was resisting, I wanted to settle the consistency of this rule by other means. This was done using a proof-theoretic ordinal analysis. Then I wanted to know whether the proof was relevant. Perhaps rule (1) was simply derivable; in that case the consistency is trivial. It turned out that rule (1) was derivable (for $\beta\eta$-reduction), except possibly for some pathological terms F, G, the so-called *universal generators*. This almost proved the validity of the ω-rule. In Plotkin [1974], however, some impressive universal generators were constructed for which rule (1) in fact does not hold.

This ω-incompleteness had some repercussions on the notion of model of the λ-calculus. There are λ-models and λ-algebras. The λ-models are well-behaved and include Scott's set-theoretic models and the open term models. The λ-algebras are less well behaved and include closed term models. Nevertheless, the latter models have interesting properties, notably as pre-complete numerations in the sense of Ershov [1973/75/77]; see also Visser [1980]. In Barendregt [1977] and [1981] the notions of λ-model and λ-algebra are described in a correct but rather ad hoc syntactical manner. A nice description in first order logic of the notion of λ-model was given independently in Scott [1980] and Meyer [1982]. Koymans [1982] completed the story of finding the description of λ-calculus models. Based on work of Scott he gave a description of λ-algebras in terms of cartesian closed

[4] The construction was related to Kreisels HRO (hereditarily recursive operations), which forms a model of the typed λ-calculus, see Troelstra [1973].

categories (CCC's)[5], in which λ-models form a special case.[6] The details of all this can be found in Barendregt [1984].

Finally, based on the work of Koymans [1982], in Curien [1986] so-called categorical combinators are developed for the use of implementations of functional programming languages. A successful application of this is CAM (categorical abstract machine) and the compiler CAML, used for implementing the proof-checker/developer COQ (based on the calculus of constructions, Coquand and Huet [1988]).

It also should be mentioned that in the proof of the partial validity of rule (1) the hypothesis ($FZ = GZ$, for all closed terms Z) was used in an extremely weak form: only one special closed term Z was used. Kreisel insisted that I should try to make use of more arguments in order to prove the full rule (1). I did not succeed and by Plotkins construction we know why. Nevertheless Kreisel turned out to be right that one can make use of more arguments. In Plotkin [1974a] it is proved that rule (1) is valid, provided that only one of F, G is not a universal generator, see Barendregt [1984], §17.3, for the details. In this proof the hypothesis of (1) is used for two different Z. In this line the best result is due to Nakajima [1975] and Wadsworth [1976]. They showed, using infinitely many Z, that the (axiom corresponding to the) rule (1) is valid in Scott's models D_∞; see also Barendregt [1984], §19.2.

So history proved that the interest of Kreisel in a neglected area of logic was fully justified.

Unsolvability

Another topic discussed with Kreisel for my thesis was the interpretation of the term $\Omega = (\lambda x.xx)(\lambda x.xx)$ in the recursion theoretic model. (This Ω is a λI-term and for these the candidate model is correct.) In the notation of Rogers [1967] this interpretation is

$$[\![\Omega]\!] = \varphi_e(e),$$

where e is such that $\varphi_e(x) = \varphi_x(x)$ for all $x \in \mathbb{N}$. The question was whether $[\![\Omega]\!]$ is defined or not.[7] It turned out that the answer depends on the choice of coding used to construct the universal function $\varphi_x(y)$. If a natural condition concerning lengths of computation is assumed for φ, then $[\![\Omega]\!]$ will be undefined; on the other

---

[5] A λ-algebra is a *reflexive* object in a CCC, i.e. an object D such that for some arrows $F : D \to [D \to D], G : [D \to D] \to D$ one has $F \circ G = id_{[D\to D]}$.

[6] A λ-model is a reflexive object D *having enough points*, i.e.

$$\forall f, g : D \to D[[\forall z : 1 \to D \; f \circ z = g \circ z] \;\Rightarrow\; f = g],$$

where 1 is the terminal object. Notice the relation with rule (1).

[7] This is related to a problem of Henkin, asking in arithmetic the provability of a statement H such that $\vdash H \leftrightarrow \Box H$, where $\Box H$ denotes formalized provability of H. As shown by Löb [1955] this is always the case.

hand for some 'non-standard' choices of φ this assumption is not valid and $[\![\Omega]\!]$ can be an arbitrary natural number[8]. See Barendregt [1975] for details.

Based on this result it follows that the interpretation of all λ-terms without normal form in the recursion theoretic structure with natural φ is undefined. As a consequence it seems to follow that terms without a normal form can be equated consistently.[9] This, however, is not the case. For example the equation between terms without a normal form

$$\lambda x.x\Omega\mathsf{true} = \lambda x.x\Omega\mathsf{false}$$

immediately gives $\mathsf{true} = \mathsf{false}$.[10] Analyzing the situation one sees that the two terms are *solvable*: $(\lambda x.x\Omega\mathsf{true})\vec{P}$ has a normal form for some $\vec{P}$ (and similarly for the other one). This notion turned out to be fruitful. All unsolvable terms can be identified consistently.[11] The consistency of the identification of unsolvable terms was proved later in Hyland [1976] and in Wadsworth [1976] by semantic methods (because $[\![M]\!]^{D_\infty} = \bot$, for M unsolvable). Moreover in these two papers it is proved that for closed terms M, N one has

$$\begin{aligned} D_\infty \models M = N \quad &\Leftrightarrow \quad \forall F[FM \text{ is solvable} \Leftrightarrow FN \text{ is solvable}] \\ &\Leftrightarrow \quad M = N \text{ belongs to the unique maximally consistent} \\ &\qquad \text{extension of the } \lambda\text{-calculus equating the unsolvables.} \end{aligned}$$

In this way solvability is a natural organizing principle for semantics of the λ-calculus. Along similar lines in Abramsky and Ong [1993] an alternative semantics is introduced that reflects features of implementations of lazy functional programming languages (one does not reduce 'under' a λ).

3. GK: person and influence

The person

Who is Georg Kreisel? Although the answer should be given by professional biographers, let me make some personal remarks.

Surely Kreisel is one of the most remarkable and enigmatic figures among logicians (and non-logicians). His behavior is non-conventional. Take for example

---

[8]This non-standard φ is nevertheless an acceptable enumeration of the partial recursive functions of one argument in the sense of Rogers [1967].

[9]This presupposes that the recursion theoretic interpretation is a model for the λK-calculus.

[10]One needs an application to the combinator $\mathsf{K}_* \equiv \lambda xy.y$, which is a λK-term. In fact the recursion theoretic model does work for the λI-calculus. Hence we have the consistency of the λI-calculus $+ \{M = N \mid M, N$ have no normal form$\}$.

[11]In order to prove this one needs the so-called 'genericity lemma': if M is unsolvable and N a normal form, then $FM = N \Rightarrow Fx = N$. In the λI-calculus the unsolvable terms are exactly the terms without normal forms, see Barendregt [1973]. This gives an alternative proof of the consistency of the theory mentioned in footnote 10.

his daily sleeping time: Kreisel goes to bed at 9:00 p.m. Sometimes I suspect that for him this is a convenient way to avoid social obligations and to get some extra work done.[12] In any case it is a fact, that Kreisel receives daily more than a dozen letters and/or articles. All this correspondence is usually answered by return mail.[13] This requires a discipline and concentration that I have experienced otherwise only among zen monks.

Another characteristic is that Kreisel seems to like to create a certain distance between himself and persons that he does meet. In many cases this is indeed the case. At the same time this creation of distance is applied to his own emotions as well. This quality I have experienced otherwise only in theravadin monks, albeit that the latter use a somewhat different method for doing so. Kreisels method to successfully keep a proper distance from his emotions is by a logical analysis. If this is skillfully done, then it is possible to disintegrate one's emotions into smithereens. And the resulting parts and pieces are harmless.[14]

Let me give some examples. Being in a certain country, Kreisel was asked by the late professor X—locally a well-known logician—the following. "Perhaps it is a stupid question, but can you tell me why this and this." Kreisels reaction: "Ah, this question is not stupid at all, not stupid at all. The matter is so and so." The questioner continued eagerly: "Hence one also has that and that?" At this point Kreisel remarked in a flash: "Now *that* is a stupid question!"

This is what I would call creating a distance. And in this case Kreisel did so justifiedly: one does not want to be close to someone that either asks stupid questions while he knows it or wants to show off how smart he is. Kreisel gave this professor X both what he had hoped to hear and what he had feared to hear.

An example of Kreisels way to decompose his own emotions is more difficult to give. Let me make it clear that his mastery of argumentation is of a high standard.[15] Given this skill, he can accomplish a lot.[16] A good example of an analysis of emotions into nothingness is the way Kreisel made the son of the baroness eat his pudding. But remember, the boy was only six. Given the sophistication of Kreisels arguments one can imagine what is needed for a convincing transcending analysis of his own emotions. It is beyond my capacities to reproduce any of the cases in which I have witnessed this remarkable auto-analysis of Kreisel.[17]

---

[12]This hypothesis, however, I have not been able to verify.

[13]In these answers Kreisel often asks questions about a paper that are difficult for the author to answer.

[14]The theravadin monks also analyze emotions into components, not by ratio but by *insight* based on *mindfulness*. As opposed to Kreisels analysis based on logic, this requires less energy but a longer practice.

[15]Kreisel obtained some of his education from Jesuits.

[16]Due to an academic disagreement a collegue of Kreisel almost challenged him to court. It would have been interesting to compare the arguing skills of professional lawyers with that of Kreisel.

[17]In order to get an approximate idea of this phenomenon, one should read *Der Mann ohne*

Influence

One of the main pieces of advice that Kreisel gave me, was to use *reflection.* He claimed that logicians are often too busy with technical details in order to take some distance from their work. This way they lose a chance of obtaining better results.

An example of this is the following. In Barendregt [1973] I proved[18] that in the λI-calculus a term M has a normal form iff M is solvable. As title of the paper I chose: *'A characterization of terms in the λI-calculus having a normal form'.* Kreisel thought this was a particularly bad title. With a little more thought I could have given a much more significant and memorable one. Indeed, from the well-known result of Böhm [1967] and my own result that unsolvable terms can be consistently equated it follows that the λI-calculus plus η-conversion plus the equation of terms without a normal form constitute a Hilbert-Post complete theory.[19] So the title should have been something like: *'A natural Hilbert-Post complete extension of the λI-calculus'.*

Kreisel often made me aware of my academic career. "Take for example Heyting", he once said, "with results not more technical than yours he became well-known." Also Kreisel emphasized that one should publish one's results as soon as possible. With the present 'publish or perish' insanity,[20] this may sound obvious, but in 1971 it was not.

Each time I would see Kreisel again, after a few days, a few months or a few years, he would ask me "What is new?", cutting through our natural tendency to remain with our attachments. In fact, both scientifically and personally he always emphasizes *change.*

Claiming that all the advice that Kreisel had given me would fall under the heading 'Influence' is too much to be said. I wish it were true. But enough of his remarks are there in my memory, that occasionally things go along lines of his advice. Enough to have considerably profited from them.

Coda

Let me end with describing two sides of Kreisel that are apparently contradictory.

When I did drive with Kreisel in his car, I noticed that he would arrange things in a certain way, in order to have a better view. Remembering this a few years later when Kreisel came to Europe, I arranged things the same way in my car. His reaction: "Thank you very much. My cleaning girls never do this. Does one really need a Ph.D. in logic in order to do so?" This event, trivial as it may be, shows him as a pleasant companion.

Eigenschaften by R. Musil (Rowolt Verlag, 1952).

[18] Using induction over a Σ^0_4-predicate.

[19] I.e. a maximally consistent theory.

[20] Presently one publishes too much in proceedings; this is notably the case in computer science. Good ideas deserve to be published in journals.

One of the things that made him most angry, was my use of the sentence: "People will believe your opinion on this, because of your authority." At the time his strong reaction was not clear to me. This seems to show that he is a 'difficult' person and *not* a pleasant companion.[21]

The explanation of the apparent contradiction is easy. His negative feelings are caused by a general dislike of his. Kreisel abhors insincerity.[22] Since by and large most things in this world are done with insincere intentions, Kreisel is often 'difficult'. On the other hand Kreisel behaves well with the upper class, if they are sincerely upper class, and with the middle and lower classes, if they are sincerely so.[23]

The author Iris Murdoch wrote a novel in which a figure 'Julius' is said to be inspired by Kreisel. She wrote about this person: 'He is one of the people that opens your mail in your absence. But he tells you later that he did'.[24] If one has a taste for his style of sincerity and irony, then Kreisel is a very stimulating person to have around, both scientifically and personally. My friends that I had introduced to Kreisel all were charmed by him.[25]

Reflecting on what I just wrote, I search for a counterexample. Is it really true that his being difficult is always caused by insincerity of others? It almost sounds too good to be true for an ordinary mortal. In the case of Kreisel I could find no counterexample. So at least it is consistent.

References

ABRAMSKY, S. and C.-H. ONG

[1993] Full abstraction in the lazy lambda calculus, *Information and Computation* 105 (2), 159-267.

[21]Once he said: "Because they do this, I will be difficult. And I can be difficult *as a woman.*"

[22]Indeed, his anger was justified: one should not believe in someone because of authority, but because of that person's arguments.

[23]Kreisel gave genuine attention and protection to a secretary, that had problems with a boyfriend, and to a terminally ill student.

[24]*A fairly honorable defeat*, Penguin Books, 1972. Another of her books (*An accidental man*, Penguin Books, 1973) has as simple dedication 'To Kreisel'.

[25]E.g. (in this order) my father, the musician Nol Prager, my mother, the computer scientist Corrado Böhm, the conceptual artist Hans Koetsier. Buffee Nelson, then a three year old girl that later became my adopted daughter, once picked up the phone when Kreisel called. Before she passed the call to, me she happened to listen attentively. Later she asked: "Who was that?" When I had told her, she said: "I like Kreisel!"

BARENDREGT, H.P.

[1971] *Some extensional term models for combinatory logics and λ-calculi*, Ph.D. thesis, University of Utrecht.

[1971a] *On the interpretation of terms in the lambda calculus without a normal form*, Ph.D. thesis, Part II, University of Utrecht.

[1973] A characterization of terms in the λI-calculus having a normal form, *J. Symbolic Logic* 38, 441-445.

[1975] Normed uniformly reflexive structures, in: Böhm [1975], 272-286.

[1977] The type-free lambda calculus, in: *Handbook of Mathematical Logic*, ed. J. Barwise, Studies in Logic, North-Holland, 1092-1132.

[1981] *The Lambda Calculus, its Syntax and Semantics*, Studies in Logic 103, North-Holland, Amsterdam.

[1984] *The Lambda Calculus, its Syntax and Semantics*, revised edition, Studies in Logic 103, North-Holland, Amsterdam.

BÖHM, C.

[1968] Alcune proprietà delle forme β-η-normali nel λ-K-calcolo, Pubblicazioni dell'Istituto per le Applicazioni del Calcolo, Via del Policlinico 127, Roma, no. 696.

BÖHM, C. (ED.)

[1975] *λ-calculus and Computer Science Theory*, Lecture Notes in Computer Science 37, Springer, Berlin.

COQUAND, TH. and G. HUET

[1988] The calculus of constructions, *Information and Computation* 76, 95-120.

CURIEN, P.-L.

[1986] *Categorical combinators, sequential algorithms and functional programming*, Research Notes in Theoretical Computer Science, Pitman/Wiley, London.

ERSHOV, Y.

[1973/1975/1977] Theorie der Numerierungen, *Zeitschrift Math. Logik u. Grundlagen d. Math.*, vol. 19 (1973), 289-388; vol. 21 (1975), 473-584; vol. 23 (1977), 289-371.

HYLAND, J.M.E.

[1976] A syntactic characterization of the equality of some models of the λ-calculus, *J. London Math. Society* (2), 12, 361-370.

KOYMANS, C.P.J.

[1982] Models of the lambda calculus, *Information and Control* 52, 306-332.

LÖB, M.H.

[1955] A solution of a problem of Henkin, *J. Symbolic Logic* 20, 115-118.

MEYER, A.

[1982] What is a model of the lambda calculus?, *Information and Control* 52, 87-122.

NAKAJIMA, R.

[1975] Infinite normal forms for the λ-calculus, in: Böhm [1975], 62-82.

PLOTKIN, G.

[1974] The λ-calculus is ω-incomplete, *J. Symbolic Logic* 39, 313-317.

[1974a] Personal communication.

ROGERS, H.

[1967] *Theory of recursive functions and effective computability*, McGraw-Hill, New York.

SCOTT, D.S.

[1980] Lambda calculus: some models, some philosophy, in: *The Kleene Symposium*, eds. Barwise et al., Studies in Logic 101, North-Holland, Amsterdam, 223-266.

TROELSTRA, A.S.

[1973] *Metamathematical Investigations of Intuitionistic Arithmetic and Analysis*, Lecture Notes in Mathematics 344, Springer, Berlin.

VISSER, A.

[1980] Numerations, λ-calculus and arithmetic, in: *To H.B. Curry: Essays on Combinatory Logic, Lambda-Calculus and Formalism*, eds. J.R. Hindley and J.P. Seldin, Academic Press, 259-284.

WADSWORTH, C.P.

[1976] The relation between computational and denotational properties for Scott's D_∞ models of the lambda calculus, *SIAM J. Comput.* 5, 488-521.

Appendix[1]: failure of the quest

In Chapter II2 the story is told how in 1971 I tried to construct a non-trivial extensional combinatory algebra and hence a model of the λ-calculus. The attempts did not work but brought fruitful ideas that could be explored: (un)solvability and the ω-rule. It was left open whether the approach did not work at all or whether I simply wasn't able to solve some technical problems. Now we will show that for $\mathcal{K}_\infty$ the approach fails in principle. We repeat some items from Part II, Definitions II1.9 and II2.1.

DEFINITION 2.1. (i) Kleene's (first) partial combinatory algebra (pca) is the structure

$$\mathcal{K} = \langle \mathbb{N}, \cdot, \mathsf{i}, \mathsf{k}, \mathsf{s} \rangle,$$

where $\mathsf{i}, \mathsf{k}, \mathsf{s} \in \mathbb{N}$ and for all $\mathsf{p}, \mathsf{q}, \mathsf{r} \in \mathbb{N}$

$$\begin{array}{rcll} \mathsf{p} \cdot \mathsf{q} & = & \{\mathsf{p}\}(\mathsf{q}), & \text{the result of applying the partial recursive function} \\ & & & \text{with code p to q (there isn't always such a result);} \\ \mathsf{i} \cdot \mathsf{p} & = & \mathsf{p}; & \\ \mathsf{k} \cdot \mathsf{p} \cdot \mathsf{q} & = & \mathsf{p}; & \\ \mathsf{s} \cdot \mathsf{p} \cdot \mathsf{q} \cdot \mathsf{r} & \simeq & \mathsf{p} \cdot \mathsf{r} \cdot (\mathsf{q} \cdot \mathsf{r}), & \text{where as usual association of } \cdot \text{ is to the left, and} \\ E_1 & \simeq & E_2 & \text{if one of the expressions } E_1, E_2 \text{ is defined} \\ & & & \text{then so is the other and then } E_1 = E_2. \end{array}$$

(ii) This structure was reformulated by Wagner (1969) as follows. Define $\mathbb{N}_* = \mathbb{N} \cup \{*\}$, for some $* \notin \mathbb{N}$. Consider the structure

$$\mathcal{K}^* = \langle \mathbb{N}_*, |, \mathsf{i}, \mathsf{k}, \mathsf{s} \rangle,$$

where for $\mathsf{p}, \mathsf{q} \in \mathbb{N}$

$$\begin{array}{rcll} \mathsf{p} \mid \mathsf{q} & = & \mathsf{p} \cdot \mathsf{q}, & \text{if defined,} \\ & = & *, & \text{otherwise,} \\ \mathsf{p} \mid * & = & *, & \\ * \mid \mathsf{q} & = & *, & \\ * \mid * & = & *. & \end{array}$$

The elements $\mathsf{i}, \mathsf{k}, \mathsf{s}$ from the structure $\mathcal{K}^*$ satisfy for all $\mathsf{p}, \mathsf{q}, \mathsf{r} \in \mathbb{N}$

$$\begin{array}{rcl} \mathsf{i} \mid \mathsf{p} & = & \mathsf{p}; \\ \mathsf{k} \mid \mathsf{p} \mid \mathsf{q} & = & \mathsf{p}; \\ \mathsf{s} \mid \mathsf{p} \mid \mathsf{q} \mid \mathsf{r} & = & \mathsf{p} \mid \mathsf{r} \mid (\mathsf{q} \mid \mathsf{r}). \end{array}$$

[1] Added March 31, 2021

REMARK 2.2. (i) The structure $\mathcal{K}$ is not a ca, because application is partial.
(ii) The structure $\mathcal{K}^*$ is not a ca because $\mathsf{k} \mid \mathsf{k} \mid * = * \neq \mathsf{k}$.

DEFINITION 2.3. In this context define by induction on $\mathsf{P} \in \mathrm{CL}^{\mathrm{o}}$ the element $(\!|\mathsf{P}|\!)^* \in \mathbb{N}_*$ as follows

$$\begin{array}{rcl} (\!|\mathbf{I}|\!)^* &=& \mathsf{i}, \\ (\!|\mathbf{K}|\!)^* &=& \mathsf{k}, \\ (\!|\mathbf{S}|\!)^* &=& \mathsf{s}, \\ (\!|\mathsf{P}_1\mathsf{P}_2|\!)^* &=& (\!|\mathsf{P}_1|\!)^* \mid (\!|\mathsf{P}_2|\!)^*. \end{array}$$

In the following the notion w-nf refers to weak reduction in CL axiomatized by

$$\begin{array}{rcl} \mathbf{I}\mathsf{P} &\twoheadrightarrow_w& \mathsf{P}, \\ \mathbf{K}\mathsf{P}\mathsf{Q} &\twoheadrightarrow_w& \mathsf{P}, \\ \mathbf{S}\mathsf{P}\mathsf{Q}\mathsf{R} &\twoheadrightarrow_w& \mathsf{PR}(\mathsf{QR}). \end{array}$$

In Chapter II3 it is shown that there are several possibilities for choosing $\cdot : \mathbb{N}^2 \to \mathbb{N}$ and $\mathsf{i}, \mathsf{k}, \mathsf{s} \in \mathbb{N}$. The following is Theorem II3.3, stated in a more explicit way.

THEOREM 2.4 (=II3.3). *For a natural choice of* $\cdot, \mathsf{i}, \mathsf{k}, \mathsf{s}$ *one has the following.*

$$\forall \mathsf{P} \in \mathrm{CL}^{\mathrm{o}}[\ (\!|\mathsf{P}|\!)^* = * \iff \mathsf{P} \textit{ has no } w\textit{-nf}\ ].$$

The main attempts to modify $\mathcal{K}$ (and $\mathcal{K}^*$) into a total ca have been $\mathcal{K}_\infty$ and $\mathcal{K}_\infty^{\mathrm{CL}}$. The first was proved to be an non-trivial extensional applicative structure (but possibly not combinatory complete) and the second an extensional total combinatory algebra (but possibly trivial). In Conjecture II2.17 it was stated without evidence that $\mathcal{K}_\infty$ is a non-trivial combinatory algebra. In Proposition II2.22(iii) it is proved that $\mathcal{K}_\infty^{\mathrm{CL}}$ is an extensional combinatory algebra, but it was left open whether this ca is trivial or not. Both questions I could not settle.

The this appendix will be shown that both questions have to be answered negatively: $\mathcal{K}_\infty$ is not a combinatory algebra and $\mathcal{K}_\infty^{\mathrm{CL}}$ is trivial. Although the main step in the proof for both results is easy, one has to think of the interpretation of terms in two different models simultaneously.

Both $\mathcal{K}_\infty$ and $\mathcal{K}_\infty^{\mathrm{CL}}$ fall under the following denominator.

DEFINITION 2.5. A *$\mathcal{K}$-structure* is of the form $\mathcal{A} = \langle \mathsf{A}/\triangleq, \diamond, [\mathsf{i}]_\triangleq, [\mathsf{k}]_\triangleq, [\mathsf{s}]_\triangleq \rangle$, with

1. $\mathsf{A} \subseteq \mathbb{N}$ with $\mathsf{i}, \mathsf{k}, \mathsf{s} \in \mathsf{A}$ as in the choice mentioned in Theorem 2.4;

2. $\diamond : \mathsf{A}^2 \to \mathsf{A}$ is a binary operator on A;

3. $\triangleq \subseteq \mathsf{A}^2$ is a congruence relation with respect to $\diamond$;

4. for all $n, m \in A$ one has $n \diamond m \simeq n \mid m$.

DEFINITION 2.6. Let $\mathcal{A}$ be a $\mathcal{K}$-structure. Define $(\!|P|\!)^{\mathcal{A}} \in A$ by

$$\begin{array}{rcl}(\!|\mathbf{I}|\!)^{\mathcal{A}} & = & i, \\ (\!|\mathbf{K}|\!)^{\mathcal{A}} & = & k, \\ (\!|\mathbf{S}|\!)^{\mathcal{A}} & = & s, \\ (\!|P_1P_2|\!)^{\mathcal{A}} & = & (\!|P_1|\!)^{\mathcal{A}} \diamond (\!|P_2|\!)^{\mathcal{A}}.\end{array}$$

LEMMA 2.7. *Let* $P \in CL$. *Then* $(\!|P|\!)^* \simeq (\!|P|\!)^{\mathcal{A}}$.

PROOF. By induction on the structure of P. For $P \in \{\mathbf{I}, \mathbf{K}, \mathbf{S}\}$ this is immediate, since e.g. one has $(\!|\mathbf{S}|\!)^* = s = (\!|\mathbf{S}|\!)^{\mathcal{A}}$. Let $P = P_1P_2$ and suppose the statement holds for P_1, P_2. Then

$$\begin{array}{rcll}(\!|P|\!)^* & = & (\!|P_1|\!)^* \mid (\!|P_2|\!)^*, & \\ & \simeq & (\!|P_1|\!)^* \diamond (\!|P_2|\!)^*, & \text{by Definition 2.5.4,} \\ & \simeq & (\!|P_1|\!)^{\mathcal{A}} \diamond (\!|P_2|\!)^{\mathcal{A}}, & \text{as } (\!|P_i|\!)^* \simeq (\!|P_i|\!)^{\mathcal{A}}, \text{ by the IH, and since } \simeq \\ & & & \text{is a congruence w.r.t. } \diamond, \\ & = & (\!|P_1P_2|\!)^{\mathcal{A}}, & \\ & = & (\!|P|\!)^{\mathcal{A}}. & \end{array}$$

□

PROPOSITION 2.8. *Suppose that is a* $\mathcal{K}$*-structure. Then we have*

$$\mathcal{A} \textit{ is a combinatory algebra} \Rightarrow \mathcal{A} \textit{ is trivial}.$$

PROOF. Let $X, Y \in CL^o$ be arbitrary elements. We will show that $(\!|X|\!)^{\mathcal{A}} = (\!|Y|\!)^{\mathcal{A}}$. Note that for every $Z \in CL^o$ there exists a $P_Z \in CL^o$ such that

1. $CL \vdash P_Z\mathbf{K} = Z$;

2. P_Z has no w-nf for all $Z \in CL^o$.

Indeed, take $P_Z \triangleq \lambda^*x.xZ\Omega = \mathbf{S}(\mathbf{SI}(\mathbf{K}Z))(\mathbf{K}\Omega)$, with $\Omega = \mathbf{SII}(\mathbf{SII})$. Then

$$\begin{array}{rcll}(\!|X|\!)^{\mathcal{A}} & \simeq & (\!|P_X\mathbf{K}|\!)^{\mathcal{A}}, & \text{by Definition 2.5.4,} \\ & \simeq & (\!|P_X\mathbf{K}|\!)^*, & \text{by Lemma 2.7,} \\ & = & (\!|P_X|\!)^* \mid (\!|\mathbf{K}|\!)^*, & \\ & = & * \mid (\!|\mathbf{K}|\!)^*, & \text{by Theorem 2.4 (only } (\!|\Omega|\!)^* = *, \text{ II3.2, is needed),} \\ & = & *, & \\ & = & (\!|P_Y|\!)^* \mid (\!|\mathbf{K}|\!)^*, & \text{by Theorem 2.4 (only } (\!|\Omega|\!)^* = *, \text{ II 3.2, is needed),} \\ & \simeq & (\!|P_Y\mathbf{K}|\!)^*, & \\ & \simeq & (\!|Y|\!)^*, & \text{by Definition 2.5.4 and Lemma 2.7.}\end{array}$$

It follows that $\mathcal{A} \models \lambda^*xy.x = \lambda^*xy.y$. Therefore $\mathcal{A}$ is trivial

$$\mathcal{A} \models \forall xy.x = y.$$

□

Now it will be shown that $\mathcal{K}_\infty$ definitely fails to be a combinaory algebra. Based on the second imprint of this republication Sebastiaan Terwijn showed by direct calculations that $\mathcal{K}_\infty$ is not a right model: $\mathsf{s} \notin \mathbb{N}_3 \supseteq \mathbb{N}_\infty$. After that I showed this by using the notion of $\mathcal{K}$-structure (and hoped to show that also $\mathcal{K}_\infty^{\text{CL}}$ is trivial, fully refuting the quest in Part II).

PROPOSITION 2.9. (i) *The structure* $\mathcal{K}_\infty = \langle \mathbb{N}_\infty / \sim_\infty, [\mathsf{i}]_{\sim_\infty}, [\mathsf{k}]_{\sim_\infty}, [\mathsf{s}]_{\sim_\infty}, \boxdot \rangle$, *see Definition 2.13, is not well defined:* $\mathsf{s} \notin \mathbb{N}_\infty$, *so that* $[\mathsf{s}]_{\sim_\infty} \notin \mathbb{N}_\infty / \sim_\infty$.

(ii) *Therefore the attempt in Chapter II2 to construct a non-trivial extensional combinatory algebra* $\mathcal{K}_\infty$ *essentially fails.*

PROOF. (i) Suppose $\mathsf{s} \in \mathbb{N}_\infty$ towards a contradiction. Then $\mathcal{K}_\infty$ is a $\mathcal{K}$-structure.

As to 1. By assumption $\mathsf{s} \in \mathbb{N}_\infty$, hence $[\mathsf{s}]_{\sim_\infty} \in \mathbb{N}_\infty / \sim_\infty$. That $\mathsf{i}, \mathsf{k} \in \mathbb{N}_\infty$ was already remarked after Conjecture II2.17 and is easy.

As to 2, 3. By Proposition II2.12 (i), (ii).

As to 4, $\mathsf{n} \diamond \mathsf{m} = \mathsf{n} \boxdot \mathsf{m} \sim \mathsf{n} \mid \mathsf{m}$, by Corollary II2.4 and Notation II2.5. By Definition II2.9 and Proposition II2.11(i) one has $\sim = \sim_0 \subseteq \sim_\infty$, hence $\mathsf{n} \diamond \mathsf{m} \sim_\infty \mathsf{n} \mid \mathsf{m}$.

By Proposition 2.8 it follows that $\mathcal{K}_\infty$ is trivial, contradicting Corollary II2.16.

(ii) By (i). □

The reason behind the failure is easy. In terms of Functional Programming, the 'eager' nature of computability theory, in which $(\varphi_e(*) = \{e\}(*) =)\ e \cdot * = *$, and the 'lazy' nature of CL and λ-calculus, in which $\mathsf{KI}\Omega = \mathsf{I}$, are essentially incompatible. This could have been done in 1971. But for the final refutation of the attempts to construct a computational model for CL and the λ-calculus it was essential to have this structures spelled out explicitly, and I did this only in this republication. Before that, thinking[2] always started 'from memory' and stranded, while thinking instead about unsolvables and the ω-rule was rewarding.

What remains to figure out is whether or not $\mathcal{K}_\infty^{\text{CL}}$ is a non-trivial combinatory algebra. Proposition 2.8 cannot be used, because the s of $\mathcal{K}^*$ is not the s of $\mathcal{K}_\sim$ and $\mathcal{K}_\infty^{\text{CL}}$ and therefore it is not clear that $\mathcal{K}_\infty^{\text{CL}}$ is a $\mathcal{K}$-structure.

[2]The hope was that replacing the partial operation $\mid$ by the total one $\boxdot$ would do the job.

Bibliography

Ackermann, W. (1925), 'Begründung des "tertium non datur" mittels der Hilbertschen Theorie der Widerspruchsfreiheit', *Mathematische annalen* **93**(1), 1–36.

ACL2 (2020), 'A Computational Logic for Applicative Common Lisp', `www.cs.utexas.edu/users/moore/acl2/`. V 8.3.

Arvind & Shen, X. (1999), 'Using term rewriting systems to design and verify processors', *IEEE Micro* **19**(3), 36–36.

Automath Archive (2012), `www.win.tue.nl/automath/`.

Avigad, J., Donnelly, K., Gray, D. & Raff, P. (2007), 'A formally verified proof of the prime number theorem', *ACM Transactions on Computational Logic (TOCL)* **9**(1), 2–es.

Baaij, C. P. R. (2015), Digital Circuits in Clash Functional Specifications and Type-Directed Synthesis, PhD thesis, University of Twente.

Baeten, J. & Boerboom, B. (1979), 'Ω can be anything it should not be', *Indagationes Mathematicae (Proceedings)* **82**(2), 111–120.

Barendregt, H. P. (1970), A universal generator for the λ-calculus, Technical Report 109, Electronisch rekencentrum, Rijksuniversiteit Utrecht.

Barendregt, H. P. (1971), Some extensional term models for combinatory logics and λ-calculi, PhD thesis, Rijksuniversiteit Utrecht.

Barendregt, H. P. (1971a), On the interpretation of terms without normal form (preliminary version), Technical Report 111, Electronisch rekencentrum, Rijksuniversiteit Utrecht. Original Part II of Barendregt (1971).

Barendregt, H. P. (1973), 'A characterization of terms of the λI-calculus having a normal form', *Journal of Symbolic Logic* **38**(3), 441–445.

Barendregt, H. P. (1975), Normed uniformly reflective structures, *in* 'International Symposium on Lambda-Calculus and Computer Science Theory', number 37 *in* 'Lecture Notes in Computer Science', Springer, pp. 272–286.

Barendregt, H. P. (1977), The Type Free Lambda Calculus, *in* J. Barwise, ed., 'Handbook of mathematical logic', Vol. 90 of *Studies in Logic and the Foundations of Mathematics*, Elsevier, pp. 1091–1132.

Barendregt, H. P. & Longo, G. (1980), Equality of lambda terms in the model $\mathbb{T}^{\omega}$, *in* J. R. Hindley & J. P. Seldin, eds, 'To HB Curry: Essays on Combinatory Logic, Lambda Calculus and Formalism', Academic Press, pp. 303–337.

Barendregt, H. P. (1981), *The Lambda Calculus, its Syntax and Semantics*, number 103 *in* 'Studies in Logic and the Foundations of Mathematics', first edn, North-Holland.

Barendregt, H. P. (1984), *The Lambda Calculus, its Syntax and Semantics*, number 103 *in* 'Studies in Logic and the Foundations of Mathematics', revised edn, North-Holland.

Barendregt, H. P. (1992), Lambda calculi with types, *in* S. Abramsky, D. Gabbay & T. Maibaum, eds, 'Handbook of logic in computer science', Vol. 2, Oxford University Press, pp. 118–310.

Barendregt, H. P., Bunder, M. & Dekkers, W. (1993), 'Systems of Illative Combinatory Logic complete for first-order propositional and predicate calculus', *Journal of Symbolic Logic* **58**(3), 769–788.

Barendregt, H. P. (1996), Kreisel, Lambda Calculus, a Windmill, and a Castle, *in* P. Odifreddi, ed., 'Kreiseliana, about and around Georg Kreisel', A. K. Peters, pp. 3–14.

Barendregt, H. P. & Cohen, A. M. (2001), 'Electronic communication of mathematics and the interaction of computer algebra systems and proof assistants', *Journal of Symbolic Computation* **32**(1-2), 3–22.

Barendregt, H. P. & Barendsen, E. (2002), 'Autarkic computations in formal proofs', *Journal of Automated Reasoning* **28**(3), 321–336.

Barendregt, H. P. & Wiedijk, F. (2005), 'The challenge of computer mathematics', *Philosophical Transactions of the Royal Society A: Mathematical, Physical and Engineering Sciences* **363**(1835), 2351–2375.

Barendregt, H. P., Dekkers, W. & Statman, R. (2013), *Lambda Calculus with Types*, Perspectives in logic, Cambridge University Press.

Barendregt, H. P. (2013), Foundations of Mathematics from the perspective of Computer Verification, *in* 'Mathematics, Computer Science and Logic—A Never Ending Story', Springer, pp. 1–49.

Barendregt, H. P. & Manzonetto, G. (2013), Turings contributions to lambda calculus, *in* S. B. Cooper & J. Van Leeuwen, eds, 'Alan Turing–His Work and Impact', Elsevier, pp. 139–143.

Barendregt, H. P., Manzonetto, G. & Plasmeijer, R. (2013), The imperative and functional programming paradigm, *in* S. B. Cooper & J. Van Leeuwen, eds, 'Alan Turing: His work and impact', Elsevier, pp. 121–126.

Barendregt, H. P. (2020), 'The gems of Corrado Böhm', *Logical Methods in Computer Science* **16**(3), 15:1–15:28.

Barendregt, H. P. & Manzonetto, G. (2022), *Satellite to 'Lambda Calculus, its Syntax and Semantics'*, College Publications.

Berline, Chantal (2000), 'From computation to foundations via functions and application: The λ-calculus and its webbed models', *Theoretical Computer Science* **249**(1), 81–161.

Bethke, I. & Klop, J. W. (1995), Collapsing partial combinatory algebras, *in* 'International Workshop on Higher-Order Algebra, Logic, and Term Rewriting', Springer, pp. 57–73.

Bethke, I., Klop, J. W. & de Vrijer, R. (1996), Completing partial combinatory algebras with unique head-normal forms, *in* 'Proceedings 11th Annual IEEE Symposium on Logic in Computer Science', IEEE, pp. 448–454.

Bethke, I., Klop, J. W. & Vrijer, R. d. (1999), 'Extending partial combinatory algebras', *Math. Struct. in Comp. Science* **9**, 483–505.

Bezem, M. (1985), 'Isomorphisms between HEO and $\mathrm{HRO}^{\mathrm{E}}$, ECF and $\mathrm{ICF}^{\mathrm{E}}$', *Journal of Symbolic Logic* **50**, 359–371.

Blanchette, J. C. and Kaliszyk, C. and Paulson, L. C. and Urban, J. (2016), 'Hammering towards QED', *Journal of Formalized Reasoning* **9**(1), 101–148.

Blanchette, J. & Mahboubi, A., eds (2021), *Handbook of Proof Assistants and Their Applications in Mathematics and Computer Science*, Springer.

Böhm, C. (1954), Calculatrices digitales du déchiffrage de formules logico-mathématiques par la machine même dans la conception du programme, PhD thesis, ETH, Zürich. Thesis written under supervision of E. Stiefel and P. Bernays and defended in 1951. Published in Ann. Math. PuraAppl. 37 (1954), 5–47. DOI: `doi.org/10.3929/ethz-a-000090226`.

Böhm, C. (1966), The CUCH as a Formal and Description Language, *in* 'Formal Languages Description Languages for Computer Programming', North-Holland, pp. 179–197.

Böhm, C. & Gross, W. (1966), Introduction to the CUCH, *in* E. R. Caianiello, ed., 'Automata Theory', Academic Press, New York, pp. 35–65.

Böhm, C. (1968), Alcune proprietà delle forme normali nel λK-calcolo, Technical Report 696, INAC.

Boolos, G. (1995), *The logic of provability*, Cambridge University Press.

Breuvart, F., Manzonetto, G., Polonsky, A. & Ruoppolo, D. (2016), New Results on Morris's Observational Theory: The Benefits of Separating the Inseparable, *in* '1st International Conference on Formal Structures for Computation and Deduction, FSCD 2016, June 22-26, 2016, Porto, Portugal', pp. 15:1–15:18.

Broda, S. & Damas, L. (1997), 'Compact bracket abstraction in combinatory logic', *Journal of Symbolic Logic* pp. 729–740.

de Bruijn, N. G. (1970), The mathematical language AUTOMATH, its usage, and some of its extensions, *in* 'Symposium on automatic demonstration', Vol. 125 of *Lecture Notes in Mathematics*, Springer, pp. 29–61.

Cardone, F. & Hindley, J. R. (2009), Lambda-calculus and combinators in the 20th century, *in* D. Gabbay, ed., 'Handbook of the History of Logic', Vol. 5, Elsevier, pp. 723–817.

Christopher, R. E. & Robertson, A. D. J., eds (1968), *Cybernetics: key papers*, University Park Press, Baltimore, MD, USA.

Church, A. (1932), 'A set of postulates for the foundation of logic', *Annals of mathematics* pp. 346–366.

Church, A. (1933), 'A set of postulates for the foundation of logic', *Annals of mathematics* pp. 839–864.

Church, A. (1936a), 'A bibliography of symbolic logic', *The Journal of Symbolic Logic* **1**(4), 121–216.

Church, A. & Rosser, J. B. (1936b), 'Some properties of conversion', *Transactions of the American Mathematical Society* **39**(3), 472–482.

Church, A. (1936), 'An unsolvable problem of elementary number theory', *American Journal of Mathematics* **58**(2), 345–363.

Church, A. (1941), *The Calculi of Lambda-Conversion*, Princeton University Press.

Church, A. (1944), *Introduction to mathematical logic, Part I*, Vol. 13, Princeton University Press.

Coquand, T. & Huet, G. (1985), Constructions: A higher order proof system for mechanizing mathematics, *in* 'European Conference on Computer Algebra', Vol. 205 of *Lecture Notes in Computer Science*, Springer, pp. 151–184.

Coquand, T. & Paulin, C. (1990), 'Inductively defined types'.

Crossley, J. N. (1975), Reminiscences of logicians, *in* 'Algebra and Logic', Vol. 450 of *Lecture Notes in Mathematics*, Springer, pp. 1–62.

Curry, H. B. (1930), 'Grundlagen der kombinatorischen Logik', *American Journal of Mathematics* **52**(4), 789–834.

Curry, H. B. (1934), 'Functionality in combinatory logic', *Proceedings of the National Academy of Sciences of the United States of America* **20**(11), 584.

Curry, H. B. (1941), 'The paradox of Kleene and Rosser', *Transactions of the American Mathematical Society* **50**(3), 454–516.

Curry, H. B. & Feys, R. (1958), *Combinatory Logic. Volume I*, number 1 *in* 'Studies in Logic and the Foundations of Mathematics', North-Holland, Amsterdam.

Curry, H. B., Hindley, J. R. & Seldin, J. P. (1972), *Combinatory Logic. Volume II*, North-Holland.

Davis, M. (1965), *The Undecidable*, Raven Press.

Davis, M. (1982), 'Why Gödel didn't have Church's thesis', *Information and control* **54**(1-2), 3–24.

Dekkers, W., Bunder, M. & Barendregt, H. P. (1998), 'Completeness of the propositions-as-types interpretation of intuitionistic logic into Illative Combinatory Logic', *Journal of Symbolic Logic* **63**(3), 869–890.

Dekkers, W., Bunder, M. & Barendregt, H. P. (1998a), 'Completeness of two systems of Illative Combinatory Logic for first-order propositional and predicate calculus', *Archive for Mathematical Logic* **37**(5-6), 327–341.

Dutle, A., Moscato, M., Titolo, L., Muñoz, C., Anderson, G. & Bobot, F. (2020), 'Formal analysis of the Compact Position Reporting algorithm', *Formal Aspects of Computing* .

Engeler, E. (1981), 'Algebras and combinators', *Algebra universalis* **13**(1), 389–392.

Fox, A. (2003), Formal Specification and Verification of ARM6, *in* D. A. Basin & B. Wolff, eds, 'Theorem Proving in Higher Order Logics 2003', Vol. 2758 of *Lecture Notes in Computer Science*, Springer.

Gabbay, M. J. & Pitts, A. M. (2002), 'A new approach to abstract syntax with variable binding', *Formal Aspects of Comput.* **13**, 341–363.

Gandy, R. O. (1980), 'Proofs of strong normalization', *To HB Curry: essays on combinatory logic, lambda calculus and formalism* pp. 457–477.

Gentzen, G. (1969), *The collected papers of Gerhard Gentzen*, Vol. 74 of *Studies in Logic*, North-Holland. Ed. Szabo, M. E. et al.

Girard, J.-Y., Taylor, P. & Lafont, Y. (1989), *Proofs and types*, Vol. 7, Cambridge University Press.

Gödel, K. (1931), 'Über Formal Unentscheidbare Sätze der Principia Mathematica Und Verwandter Systeme I', *Monatshefte für Mathematik* **38**(1), 173–198.

Gödel, K. (1934), 'On Undecidable Propositions of Formal Mathematical Systems', Institute for Advanced Study, mimeographed lecture notes by S. C. Kleene and J. B. Rosser. corrected and amplified in (Davis 1965, pp. 41–74).

Gödel, K. (1994), 'The QED Manifesto', *Lecture Notes in Artificial Intelligence* **814**, 238–251.

Gonthier, G. (2008), 'Formal proof-the four-color theorem', *Notices of the AMS* **55**(11), 1382–1393.

Gonthier, G., Asperti, A., Avigad, J., Bertot, Y., Cohen, C., Garillot, F., Le Roux, S., Mahboubi, A., O'Connor, R., Biha, S. O. et al. (2013), A machine-checked proof of the odd order theorem, *in* 'International Conference on Interactive Theorem Proving', Springer, pp. 163–179.

Goodman, N. (1968), Intuitionistic arithmetic as theory of constructions, PhD thesis, Stanford University. Published as Goodman (1976).

Goodman, N. (1976), 'Theory of Gödel functionals', *Journal of Symbolic Logic* **41**, 574–583.

de Groote, P., ed. (1995), *The Curry-Howard Isomorphism*, Vol. 8 of *Cahiers du centre de logique*, Academia, Louvain la Neuve.

Hales, T., Adams, M., Bauer, G., Dang, T. D., Harrison, J., Le Truong, H., Kaliszyk, C., Magron, V., McLaughlin, S., Nguyen, T. T. et al. (2017), 'A formal proof of the Kepler conjecture', *Forum of mathematics, Pi* **5**.

Harrison, J. (2009), 'Formalizing an analytic proof of the prime number theorem', *Journal of Automated Reasoning* **43**(3), 243–261.

Henkin, L. (1952), 'A problem concerning provability', *Journal of Symbolic Logic* **17**(2), 160.

Howard, W. A. (1980), The formulae-as-types notion of construction, *in* J. R. Hindley & J. P. Seldin, eds, 'To HB Curry: Essays on Combinatory Logic, Lambda Calculus and Formalism', Academic Press, pp. 479–490.

Howe, D. (1992), Reflecting the semantics of reflected proof, *in* 'Proof Theory, ed. P. Aczel', Cambridge University Press, pp. 229–250.

Hughes, J. (1989), 'Why functional programming matters', *The Computer Journal* **32**(2), 98–107.

Hyland, J. M. E. (1976), 'A syntactic characterization of the equality in some models for the λ-calculus', *Journal London Mathematical Society (2)* **12(3)**, 361–370.

Immler, F. (2018), 'A verified ODE solver and the Lorenz attractor', *Journal of Automated Reasoning* **61**(1-4), 73–111.

Intrigila, B., Manzonetto, G. & Polonsky, A. (2019), 'Degrees of extensionality in the theory of Böhm trees and Sallé's conjecture', *Logical Methods in Computer Science* **15**(1).

Jacopini, G. (1974), 'Principio di estensionalità nel calcolo dei combinatori', *CALCOLO* **11**, 465–471.

Jacopini, G. (1975), A condition for identifying two elements of whatever model of combinatory logic, *in* 'International Symposium on Lambda-Calculus and Computer Science Theory', Vol. 37 of *Lecture Notes in Computer Science*, Springer, pp. 213–219.

Johnsson, T. (1984), Efficient compilation of lazy evaluation, *in* 'Proceedings of the 1984 SIGPLAN symposium on Compiler construction', pp. 58–69.

Johnsson, T. (1995), 'Graph reduction, and how to avoid it.', *Electron. Notes Theor. Comput. Sci.* **2**, 139–152.

Kaliszyk, C. and Urban, J. (2014), 'Learning-assisted automated reasoning with Flyspeck', *Journal of Automated Reasoning* **53**(2), 173–213.

Kleene, S. C. (1936a), 'General recursive functions of natural numbers', *Mathematische Annalen* **112**(1), 727–742.

Kleene, S. C. (1936b), 'λ-definability and recursiveness', *Duke mathematical journal* **2**(2), 340–353.

Kleene, S. C. (1938), 'On notation for ordinal numbers', *The Journal of Symbolic Logic* **3**(4), 150–155.

Kleene, S. C. (1952), *Introduction to metamathematics*, Vol. 483, van Nostrand New York.

Kleene, S. C. (1981), 'Origins of recursive function theory', *Annals of the History of Computing* **3**(1), 52–67.

Kleene, S. C. & Rosser, J. B. (1935), 'The inconsistency of certain formal logics', *Annals of Mathematics* pp. 630–636.

Klein, G., Elphinstone, K., Heiser, G., Andronick, J., Cock, D., Derrin, P., Elkaduwe, D., Engelhardt, K., Kolanski, R., Norrish, M., Sewell, T., Tuch, H. & Winwood, S. (2009), seL4: formal verification of an OS kernel, *in* J. Matthews & T. Anderson, eds, 'ACM Symposium on Principles of Operating Systems', Big Sky, pp. 207–220.

Klop, J. W. (1980), 'Combinatory Reduction Systems'. PhD at Utrecht University.

Klop, J. W. (1982), 'Extending partial combinatory algebras', *Bulletin of the European Association for Theoretical Computer Science* **16**, 472–482.

Koymans, C. P. J. (1982), 'Models of the lambda calculus', *Information and Control* **52**(3), 306–332.

Kreisel, G. (1958), Constructive Mathematics. Notes of a course given at Stanford University.

Kruskal, J. B. (1960), 'Well-quasi-ordering, the tree theorem, and Vazsonyi's conjecture', *Transactions of the American Mathematical Society* **95**(2), 210–225.

Landin, P. J. (1966), A λ-calculus approach, *in* 'Advances in Programming and Non-Numerical Computation', Elsevier, pp. 97–141.

Leroy, X. (2009), 'A Formally Verified Compiler Back-end', *Journal of Automated Reasoning* **43**(4), 363–446.

Löb, M. H. (1955), 'Solution of a Problem of Leon Henkin', *Journal of Symbolic Logic* **20**(2), 115–118.

Logipedia (n.d.). {<http://logipedia.inria.fr/about/about.php>}, developed by W. Moustaoui, F. Thiré, G. Dowek, and others.

Lorenz, E. N. (1963), 'Deterministic nonperiodic flow', *Journal of the atmospheric sciences* **20**(2), 130–141.

Martin-Löf, Per (1998), An intuitionistic theory of types, *in* G. Sambin and J. M. Smith, ed., 'Twenty-five years of constructive type theory', Vol. 36 of *Oxford Logic Guides*, Oxford University Press, pp. 127–172.

McCarthy, J. (1962), Computer programs for checking mathematical proofs, *in* 'Recursive Function Theory, Proceedings of a Symposium in Pure Mathematics', Vol. 5, pp. 219–227.

McCarthy, J., Abrahams, P., Edwards, D. J., Hart, T. P. & Levin, M. I. (1962), *LISP 1.5 Programmer's Manual*, MIT Press.

Milner, R., Tofte, M., Harper, R. & McQueen, D. (1990), *The Definition of Standard ML*, The MIT Press.

Moschovakis, Y. N. (1971), Axioms for computation theories-first draft, *in* 'Studies in Logic and the Foundations of Mathematics', Vol. 61, Elsevier, pp. 199–255.

Nederpelt, R. & Geuvers, H. (2014), *Type theory and formal proof: an introduction*, Cambridge University Press.

von Neumann, J. (1927), 'Zur Hilbertschen Beweistheorie', *Mathematische Zeitschrift* **26**, 1–46.

Nordström, B., Petersson, K. & Smith, J. M. (1990), *Programming in Martin-Löf's type theory*, Vol. 200, Oxford University Press Oxford.

Norrish, M. & Westergaard, R. (2007), De Bruijn Terms Really Do Work, *in* K. Schneider & J. Brandt, eds, 'Proceedings of 'Theorem Proving in Higher Order Logics'', number 4732 *in* 'LNCS', Springer, pp. 207–222.

Paulin-Mohring, C. (1993), Inductive definitions in the system Coq rules and properties, *in* 'International Conference on Typed Lambda Calculi and Applications', Springer, pp. 328–345.

Peyton Jones, S. L. & Salkild, J. (1989), The spineless tagless G-machine, *in* 'Proceedings of the fourth international conference on Functional programming languages and computer architecture', pp. 184–201.

Plotkin, G. D. (1972/1993), 'Set-theoretical and other elementary models of the λ-calculus', *Theoretical Computer Science* **121**(1-2), 351–409.

Plotkin, G. D. (1974), 'The λ-calculus is ω-incomplete', *The Journal of Symbolic Logic* **39**(2), 313–317.

Plotkin, G. D. (1978), '$\mathbb{T}^{\omega}$ as a universal domain', *Journal of Computer and System Sciences* **17**(2), 209–236.

Poincaré, H. (1909), *Science et méthode*, E. Flammarion.

Ringer, T., Palmskog, K., Sergey, I., Gligoric, M. & Tatlock, Z. (2019), *QED at large: A survey of engineering of formally verified software*, Now Publishers Inc. arXiv:2003.06458.

Robertson, N., Sanders, D., Seymour, P. & Thomas, R. (1996), 'A new proof of the four-colour theorem', *Electronic Research Announcements of the American Mathematical Society* **2**(1), 17–25.

Rogers Jr, H. (1967), *Theory of Recursive Functions and Effective Computability*, McGraw-Hill, New York.

Rosenbloom, P. (1950), *The Elements of Mathematical Logic*, Dover.

Rosser, J. B. (1935), 'A mathematical logic without variables. I', *Annals of Mathematics* pp. 127–150.

Schönfinkel, M. (1924), 'Über die Bausteine der mathematischen Logik', *Mathematische Annalen* **92**, 305–316.

Scott, D. (1972), Continuous lattices, *in* 'Toposes, Algebraic Geometry and Logic', Springer, pp. 97–136.

Scott, D. (1974), 'The language LAMBDA', *Journal of Symbolic Logic* **39**(2), 425–427.

Sheeran, M. (1984), μFP, a language for VLSI design, *in* 'Proceedings of the 1984 ACM Symposium on LISP and functional programming', pp. 104–112.

Solovay, R. (1965), $2^{\aleph_0}$ can be anything it ought to be, *in* J. Addison, L. Henkin & A. Tarski, eds, 'The Theory of Models: Proceedings of the 1963 International Symposium at Berkeley', Studies in logic and the foundations of mathematics, North-Holland, p. 435.

Sørensen, M. H. (1998), Properties of infinite reduction paths in untyped lambda-calculus, *in* 'Tblisi Symposium on Logic, Language and Computation: Selected Papers', CSLI Publications/Center for the Study of Language & Information, pp. 353–367.

Sørensen, M. H. & Urzyczyn, P. (2006), *Lectures on the Curry-Howard isomorphism*, Elsevier.

Statman, R. (1986), On translating Lambda terms into combinators; the basis problem, *in* 'LICS, 1986', pp. 378–382.

Strong, H. R. (1968), 'Algebraically generalized recursive function theory', *IBM journal of Research and Development* **12**(6), 465–475.

Strong, H. R. (1970), 'Construction of models for algebraically generalized recursive function theory', *Journal of Symbolic Logic* **35**(3), 401409.

Sutter, H. (2005), 'The free lunch is over: A fundamental turn toward concurrency in software', *Dr. Dobbs journal* **30**(3), 202–210.

The Univalent Foundations Program (2013), *Homotopy Type Theory: Univalent Foundations of Mathematics*, {https://homotopytypetheory.org/book}, Institute for Advanced Study.

Troelstra, A. S. (1973), *Metamathematical investigation of intuitionistic arithmetic and analysis*, Vol. 344 of *Lecture Notes in Mathematics*, Springer.

Tucker, W. (2002), 'A rigorous ODE solver and Smales 14th problem', *Foundations of Computational Mathematics* **2**(1), 53–117.

Turing, A. M. (1937a), 'On Computable Numbers, with an Application to the Entscheidungsproblem', *Proceedings of the London Mathematical Society* 2 **1**(42), 230–65.

Turing, A. M. (1937b), 'Computability and λ-definability', *The Journal of Symbolic Logic* **2**(4), 153–163.

Turing, A. M. (1948), Intelligent machinery, Technical report, National Physical Laboratory. Mathematics Division. Reprinted in Christopher & Robertson (1968) and (Turing 1969, pp. 3–23).

Turing, A. M. (1969), 'Intelligent machinery', *Machine Intelligence* **5**, 3–23.

Turner, D. (1986), 'An overview of Miranda', *ACM Sigplan Notices* **21**(12), 158–166.

Urban, C., Pitts, A. M. & Gabbay, M. J. (2004), 'Nominal unification', *Theoretical Computer Science* **323**, 473–497.

Visser, A. (1980), Numerations, λ-Calculus, and Arithmetic, *in* J. R. Hindley & J. P. Seldin, eds, 'To H. B. Curry: Essays on Combinatory Logic, Lambda-Calculus, and Formalism', Academic Press, San Diego, pp. 259–284.

Voevodsky, V. (2014), 'The Origins and Motivations of Univalent Foundations', `https://www.ias.edu/ideas/2014/voevodsky-origins`.

Wadler, P. (2015), 'Propositions as types', *Communications of the ACM* **58**(12), 75–84.

Wadsworth, C. P. (1971), Semantics and Pragmatics of the λ-calculus, PhD thesis, Oxford.

Wadsworth, C. P. (1976), 'The Relation between Computational and Denotational Properties for Scotts $\mathcal{D}_\infty$-Models of the Lambda-Calculus', *SIAM Journal on Computing* **5**(3), 488–521.

Wagner, E. G. (1969), 'Uniformly Reflexive Structures: on the nature of Gödelizations and relative computability', *Transactions of the American Mathematical Society* **144**, 1–41.

Wiedijk, F. (2006), *The seventeen provers of the world*, Vol. 3600 of *Lecture Notes in Computer Science*, Springer. Foreword by Dana S. Scott.

Wupper, H. (2000), 'Design As The Discovery Of A Mathematical Theorem, What Designers Should Know About The Art Of Mathematics', *Journal of Integrated Design and Process Science* **4**(2), 1–13.

Xena (2020), 'Xena project', `xenaproject.wordpress.com/what-is-the-xena-project/`.

www.ingramcontent.com/pod-product-compliance
Lightning Source LLC
LaVergne TN
LVHW081335050326
832903LV00024B/1161

* 9 7 9 8 5 8 5 2 8 4 1 2 0 *